Religion in America

1950 to the Present

Religion in America

1950 to the Present

JACKSON W. CARROLL

DOUGLAS W. JOHNSON

MARTIN E. MARTY

Afterword by GEORGE GALLUP, Jr.

1817

Published in San Francisco by HARPER & ROW, PUBLISHERS

New York   Hagerstown   San Francisco   London

Acknowledgment is made to the Russell Sage Foundation for permission to use data from *Social Change in a Metropolitan Community,* by Otis Dudley Duncan, Howard Schuman, and Beverly Duncan, © 1973 by Russell Sage Foundation, New York.

FIRST EDITION

Designed by Jim Mennick

Library of Congress Cataloging in Publication Data

Carroll, Jackson W.
   RELIGION IN AMERICA, 1950 TO THE PRESENT.
   Includes index.
   1. United States—Religion—Addresses, essays, lectures. I. Johnson, Douglas W., joint author. II. Marty, Martin E., joint author. III. Title.
BL2530.U6C37   200′.973   77-20451
ISBN 0-06-065433-3

79 80 81 82 83 10 9 8 7 6 5 4 3 2 1

Contents

List of Maps, Figures, and Tables vii

Preface ix

I. **Continuity and Change: The Shape of Religious Life in the United States, 1950 to the Present** *by Jackson W. Carroll with the assistance of David A. Roozen* 1

    1. Introduction and Setting 3

    2. Religious Identification 8

    3. Trends in Religious Practice 18

    4. Trends in Religious Beliefs 28

    5. Interpreting the Trends 36

II. **Patterns of Religious Pluralism** 47

    6. The Maps of Religious Groups: Introduction *by Douglas W. Johnson* 49

    7. The Career of Pluralism in America *by Martin E. Marty* . . . 51

    8. Interpreting American Pluralism *by Martin E. Marty* . . 78

III. **Trends and Issues Shaping the Religious Future** *by Douglas W. Johnson* 91

    9. Searching for Meaning and Purpose 93

    10. Issues in the Religious Future 101

IV. **Afterword: A Coming Religious Revival?** *by George Gallup, Jr.* . . 111

    Index 119

List of Maps, Figures, and Tables

Maps

1. Members of Baptist Churches (by county)   55
2. Members of the Christian Church (Disciples of Christ) and the Christian
    Churches and Churches of Christ (by county)   56
3. Members of The Episcopal Church (by county)   57
4. Members of Lutheran Churches (by county)   58
5. Members of Methodist Churches (by county)   59
6. Members of Presbyterian Churches (by county)   60
7. Members of The Roman Catholic Church (by county)   61
8. Members of the United Church of Christ (by county)   62
9. Members of Adventist Churches (by county)   63
10. Members of Mennonite Churches (by county)   64
11. Members of Moravian Churches (by county)   65
12. Members of Pentecostal Churches (by county)   66
13. Members of Reformed Churches (by county)   67

Figures

1. Protestant, Roman Catholic, and Jewish Membership Trends in the
    United States, 1947–1973   12
2. Membership of Twelve Protestant Denominations and the Roman Catho-
    lic Church, 1950–1975   14
3. Percentage Change in Membership for 1955–1965 and 1965–1975 for
    Selected U.S. Churches   15
4. Percentage of Adherents Attending Religious Services in an Average
    Week, 1955–1976   20

Tables

1. Trends in Religious Preference, 1947–1975   9
2. Political Leadership by Denominations, 1967–1977   10
3. Church Attendance for Selected Groups and Years   21

4. Per-Capita Giving by Full, or Confirmed, Membership to Selected Protestant Churches and Per-Capita Disposable Income, 1950–1975 . 23
5. Trends in Belief in God, 1947–1975 29
6. Trends in Belief in Life After Death 31
7. Belief in Life After Death, by Age 32
8. Trends in Belief About the Influence of Religion on American Life 33
9. Percentage Change in United States Population by Age Groups, 1950–1974 by Decade 38
10. Attended Church or Synagogue During Average Week . . 116
11. Church/Synagogue Membership 116
12. Importance of Religious Beliefs 116
13. Influence of Religion 116
14. Involvement in Experiential Religion 116
15. Have Had a "Born Again" Experience 117
16. Belief in God 117
17. Immortality 117
18. Confidence in Organized Religion 118
19. Confidence in Key Institutions in the United States . . . 118
20. Religious Preferences in the United States 118
21. Interpretation of the Bible 118
22. Have "Witnessed" 118

Preface

In recent years there has emerged a widespread interest in developing indicators of social well-being or health in a variety of sectors of American society. Perhaps the extension of medical terminology to the assessment of social phenomena is inevitable in a health conscious society such as ours. Whatever the reason behind the concern for social well-being, we believe it to be an important one. Both concerned citizens and policy makers have a need for information that enables them to make assessments of the institutions in which they have a stake. In this book, we attempt to make a contribution to the assessment of the well-being of one important social institution: religion.

A part of our concern is to describe what has happened to religion in America, especially traditional institutions of faith, from approximately 1950 to the present. How have they fared during this time? What is their condition? Are they sick or healthy? Clearly these have been years of dramatic changes that have left no institutions untouched, and quite a few diagnosticians in recent years have judged the churches to be in bad shape, even terminally ill. In Part I, Jackson W. Carroll, with the assistance of David A. Roozen, undertakes a diagnosis from a sociological perspective, using a variety of statistics to consider trends in various dimensions of religion: religious identification and membership, church attendance and other forms of religious practice, and religious beliefs. Why the changes observed in the data have occurred is the subject of the final chapter of Part I.

To be sure, the available data used in the analysis provide only a partial diagnostic indicator of the condition of religion in America. For one thing, statistical trend data are simply unavailable for assessing some important dimensions of religious involvement that lend themselves to statistical treatment. But more important, statistical indicators are inadequate to provide a total diagnosis. To change the metaphor, Albert Einstein is reported to have remarked that it is not the function of science to *give* the taste of soup. It can only describe it; but the description cannot substitute for the taste itself. Likewise, we intend our analysis of trends to provide a description of the "taste" of American religious life since mid-century; however, we do not pretend to provide the "taste" itself. There is much about religion—that which, indeed, is most important to the person of faith—that defies statistical description. Nonetheless, the statistics that are available provide one important perspective by which to assess what has happened.

Another way of diagnosing the well-being of American religion is to consider its visible form, or embodiment, within the society. A key factor in this connection has been pluralism. American religion is not one but many; yet the various denominations have developed a rather remarkable pattern of living together with a relative absence of serious intergroup conflict. Why and how this is so is the focus of Part II. Martin E. Marty draws on history and geography to describe and analyze the patterning of American religious pluralism. Maps are included that show how church membership is distributed throughout the United States, county by county. As the maps reveal, denominations are not evenly distributed throughout the population. Rather they reflect earlier patterns of immigration and settlement as well as more recent geographical mobility within the nation. The maps tell us much about America's ethnic heritage and also provide important insights into American religious pluralism. By means of the maps, we are helped to see how geography has contributed to a relative absence of severe conflict between the different religious groups and why pluralism has not been as corrosive of religious and ethnic distinctiveness as one might suspect.

Once the diagnosis is complete, we turn in both Part III and the Afterword to prognosis. In Part III, Douglas W. Johnson focuses on the future of religion in America. The search for meaning and purpose, which has led persons to religious commitment and participation, will continue into the future. How the events likely to occur in the emerging future may influence the search for meaning and purpose and their implications for religious institutions are our concerns. The areas we consider range over a wide variety of factors—social, cultural, economic, scientific, and technological—that are likely to affect religious institutions and the personal search for meaning and purpose. The analysis reinforces what is implicit in the other chapters, namely that religious institutions do not exist in a vacuum. They exist in a complex environment that both shapes them and, in turn, is shaped by them. If we focus primarily on the former, it is because we believe that it is of considerable importance for those concerned about the future well-being of religion to be aware of the shaping influence of the sociocultural and geographical environment. In some cases, little or nothing can be done to alter these environmental effects; in others, however, the effects can be ameliorated or transcended. The analysis points to some ways in which the latter may occur.

A second prognosis regarding the future of religion in America is found in the Afterword by George Gallup, Jr.[1] Rather than asking, as Johnson does, how religion might respond to emerging sociocultural trends, Gallup assesses what appear to be some signs of renewal already visible on the horizon. In a thoughtful analysis of recent Gallup Poll data, he raises the possibility that there may be in the late 1970s the beginnings of a new religious revival.

In these ways, then, we try to assess the immediate past and present state of religion in the United States as well as the outlook for the emerging future. Much of what we consider focuses on the more traditional institutions of faith and the involvement in them of their constituencies. While we do not ignore the newer, often more exotic, religious movements that have become a part of the American scene in recent years, we have not made them a prominent part of our analysis. On the one hand, they are too new to lend themselves to statistical trend analysis, and on the other hand, we do not have the data to map them as we do for the other religious groups. Additionally, these newer movements have been treated extensively in a variety of books in recent years.[2]

Several organizations and individuals deserve special mention for their role in making this book possible. For making available to us the data on which the maps are based, we are grateful to Father Bernard Quinn of the Glenmary Research Center, Paul R. Picard of the Aid Association for Lutherans, and Constant H. Jacquet of the Office of Research, Evaluation and Planning of the National Council of Churches of Christ in the U.S.A. The cost of making the maps was borne by the Hartford Seminary Foundation. Particular appreciation is expressed to Constant Jacquet, editor of *The Yearbook of American and Canadian Churches;* to Anne E. Carroll and Suzanne E. Roozen for their painstaking efforts in the often tedious production of the maps; to Dean R. Hoge of the Catholic University of America and Wade Clark Roof of the University of Massachusetts for their helpful critique of a draft of the first section; and to Ellen P. Smith and Amy A. Beveridge for their yeoperson service in typing major portions of the manuscript. Anne E. Carroll is also to be thanked for assistance in preparation of many of the tables and figures. Finally, it has been a considerable pleasure to work with our editor at Harper & Row, John Shopp, whose constructive comments and suggestions have made a substantial contribution to the shape of this book.

NOTES

1. Mr. Gallup's article originally appeared in the *Journal of Current Social Issues,* 14 (Spring, 1977) 50–55, and is included by permission of the author and the publisher. While some of the poll data in Mr. Gallup's article is also considered in Part I, the concerns of the two analyses are different. One is concerned with diagnosis, the other with prognosis.

2. For those who wish to pursue further the study of the newer religious movements in American society, the following constitute a partial list of book titles: Jacob Needleman, *The New Religions* (Garden City, New York: Doubleday, 1970); Robert S. Ellwood, Jr., *Religious and Social Groups in Modern America* (Englewood Cliffs, N.J.: Prentice Hall, 1973); Irving L. Zaretsky and Mark P. Leone, eds., *Religious Movements in Contemporary America* (Princeton, N.J.: Princeton University Press, 1974); Charles Y. Glock and Robert N. Bellah, eds., *The New Religious Consciousness* (Berkeley: University of California Press, 1976); and Robert Wuthnow, *The Consciousness Reformation* (Berkeley: University of California Press, 1976).

I

Continuity and Change: The Shape of Religious Life in the United States, 1950 to the Present

JACKSON W. CARROLL

with the assistance of

DAVID A. ROOZEN

I

Introduction and Setting

When Alexis de Tocqueville, the French Catholic aristocrat, visited America in the early nineteenth century, he was constantly amazed at the vitality of American religion. While acknowledging the likelihood that some American involvement in religion stemmed from habit rather than conviction, he observed that ". . . there is no country in the world where the Christian religion retains a greater influence over the souls of men than in America; and there can be no greater proof of its conformity to human nature than that its influence is powerfully felt over the most enlightened and free nation of the earth."[1]

If de Tocqueville could visit this country in the late 1970s, he might still express amazement at religious phenomena. Were he to drive across the country by automobile, his radio could provide him with a steady flow of gospel music and preaching, punctuated by requests to listeners for donations, mail, and prayers for the success of the broadcast. A visit to the Boston Commons, Atlanta's Peachtree Street, or any of the nation's larger cities would allow him to witness the dancing of Hare Krishna devotees. Thriving religious bookstores would provide him with the fruit of a highly successful evangelical Christian publishing industry. He could also note the estimated five million Americans now involved in various forms of the "consciousness revolution," ranging from techniques adapted from Eastern mystics to est. All this and more he could encounter, and he might marvel anew at both the diversity and the apparent vitality of American religion. But what, he might ask, has happened within the more traditional institutions of faith? Are they too experiencing a surge of vitality apparent in these other expressions of religion? What is their condition?

It would be difficult for a visitor to overlook the traditional institutions since their buildings—synagogues and churches—are prominent features of the landscape. So much has been written in recent years about their impending demise, however, that the visitor might be tempted to assume that they were of little consequence. This has often been the response of those who study American religion—we have found it much more attractive to concentrate on the newer, more exotic movements. As important as it is to understand the latter phenomena, however, it is equally important that we not ignore the more traditional institutions. When almost 90 percent of the American population are willing to identify themselves as Protestants, Catholics, or Jews, no matter how much habit or social pressure may lie behind this identification, these institutions should not be lightly dismissed.

Our concern in the chapters in Part I of this book is to consider the shape of these religious institutions, that is, their condition as reflected in analysis of various religious trends. The time frame for our analysis is the third quarter of the twentieth century, a period of marked contrast and substantial change in American religion as well as in American society as a whole. Before reviewing some of these contrasts and changes as background for our analysis, we note briefly both the scope of our analysis and some limitations.

We have, of necessity, dealt primarily with trends in major Protestant denominations, both those that are theologically liberal and conservative, and in American Catholicism. Where possible, we have given attention to Judaism; however, as we shall point out, sources for statistical trend data on American Judaism are limited. We also have very little trend data on black Christians and none on other minority ethnic Christians, including the various branches of Eastern Orthodoxy. Even in our analysis of Protestant bodies, we have been selective, trying to include groups representative of the various denominational families. We deeply regret the omissions that lack of data and space limitations have made necessary.

Our inquiry focuses primarily on what has happened in the recent past and what is happening currently as reflected in various available statistics. We have chosen this particular approach partly because we are sociologists with a statistical bent. However, we also believe analysis of various statistical indicators and trends provides an important way, albeit only one of several, of viewing American religious life. What we have attempted is to bring information, much of which has been reported elsewhere, together in a comprehensive way and to provide an interpretation of some of the features of American religious life as it is reflected in the data. We are aware of the considerable limitations of religious statistics; nonetheless, we are convinced that in spite of the limitations, the data provide important insight into the issues we intend to address.

The statistics we report are those that reflect religious trends of the past twenty-five years; this is what we refer to by our term *trend data.* In recent years sociologists of religion have come to view religious commitment and behavior as multidimensional. Charles Glock and Rodney Stark, for example, have identified five dimensions of religiosity, or ways that people may express their religious commitment: the belief or ideological dimension, the practice or ritualistic dimension, the feeling or experiential dimension, the knowledge or intellectual dimension, and the effects or consequential dimension.[2] As they remind us, it is important to keep in view these different ways of expressing religious commitment when analyzing trend data.[3] Unfortunately, we do not have indicators for all of Glock and Stark's dimensions, and several of the trends for which we have data do not fit very well into any of their five divisions. Nevertheless, we have tried to group the various trends under categories that reflect differing kinds of religious behavior in an effort to see what has or has not changed over the past quarter of a century.

Following this introductory chapter, three chapters explore trends in religious identification, practice, and beliefs. By identification, we mean stated religious preference and actual church membership. Under the heading of religious practice, we include both objective and formal types of participation, such as church attendance and financial contributions, and informal devotional practices, such as private prayer and Bible reading. We also consider briefly what we call "technologies of the spirit," the various techniques for consciousness expansion, spiritual renewal, and self-fulfillment that are currently enjoying considerable popularity and are likely to have a significant influence on more traditional religion. In the chapter on beliefs, we consider changes

in the various religious beliefs of the American public for which trend data are available. In the final chapter of Part I, we summarize the major thrusts of the trend analyses and offer an interpretation of the trends in light of broader historical and sociocultural factors affecting the life of the churches. In these ways we try to provide a perspective on American religious institutions and participation in them—their present shape and how events of the past quarter of a century have affected them.

Before turning to an examination of the trends, we comment on the data we have used and their adequacy and review briefly some of the major features of the historical period that is the setting for the trend data.

DATA ON RELIGION

Statistical data are typically a source of considerable frustration to students of religion; thus we feel constrained to comment briefly on the problems of reliability, validity, and substantive importance of the data we report. Our figures come from two principal sources: the denominations themselves in their annual reports, summarized each year in the *Yearbook of American and Canadian Churches;* and various national public opinion polls, most of which did not have religion as a primary focus.

The denominational statistics often suffer from insufficient quality control over methods of record keeping and reporting. There are some congregations whose records are considerably unreliable and whose reporting to their denominational bodies thereby distorts the national statistics. While some of this unreliability may result from deliberate inflation of statistics, we suspect that it is more often the result of carelessness in record keeping or slowness in removing the names of moved or lapsed members from the rolls. For example, in a recent study of church membership trends undertaken by the United Methodist Church, pastors report each year that they have received approximately 10 percent more people (20,000–30,000 nationally) by transfer from other United Methodist Churches than they report having transfered out to other United Methodist Churches.[4] This means that there are a considerable number of people whose names are carried on at least two, possibly more, United Methodist rolls. How long such dual memberships are held is unknown. In any case, the data are thus inaccurate.

In addition, where church membership statistics are concerned, there is the vexing problem of differing definitions of membership from one denomination to another. For example, Southern Baptists, the largest Protestant body in the United States, practice adult baptism, and only baptized members—that is, adults or people usually 13 years or older—are counted as members. The Roman Catholic Church also counts all baptized people as members; however, its practice of infant baptism means that individuals from infancy onward are counted as members. Furthermore, in many instances Catholic and Jewish statistics reflect estimates of the number of Catholics or Jews living in a particular area. Thus differing membership definitions and differing ways of gathering statistics create problems of reliability and comparability.

For those concerned with trends, as we are here, there are further problems. Not only are there differences in definitions of membership *between* denominations, but there have been changes in membership definitions *within* particular denominations. For example, before 1926 there were several denominations reporting only heads of families as members. When this practice was changed to include all those confirmed, the number of members dramatically increased with little change in the actual number of people participating in those denominations. Since the concern here is more short range, there do not seem to be too many changes of this nature to bother us. However, several mergers of denominations have occurred during the period in which we are interested, and these are taken into account.

Also a problem for trend analysis is the way in which denominations that have not previously reported their statistics are added to the church membership totals. For example, the church historian Winthrop Hudson points out that in 1952 the Christ Unity Church, with 682,172 members, was included for the first time in the *Yearbook of American Churches*. Its addition alone accounted for more than one third of the overall church membership gain reported for that year.[5] Again, in some denominations (for instance, American Baptists and Disciples of Christ) local congregations have the option not to cooperate with the annual statistical reporting. A congregation may report one year, drop out of the reporting the next, and resume reporting a year or so later. Such a practice, if widespread, could obviously cause considerable fluctuation in the denomination's membership trends while representing no real gain or loss of members.

In sum, we use denominationally reported statistics of necessity, because they are a primary data source. Nonetheless, there are problems that necessitate caution in their interpretation.

We also rely rather heavily on public opinion poll findings. Unlike the denominational statistics, which come from churches and are primarily concerned with church members, the poll data are from cross-sections of the American population, both church affiliated and nonaffiliated. Thus they are somewhat broader in scope than the church statistics.

The research organizations responsible for gathering the data that we report from the public opinion surveys—the American Institute of Public Opinion

(AIPO),[6] better known as the Gallup Poll and as publishers of *The Gallup Opinion Index*; the National Opinion Research Center (NORC); and the Survey Research Center of the University of Michigan—are highly reputable organizations. They use careful methods of probability sampling and attempt to maintain quality control over the interview process. The findings are therefore generally reliable, especially for recent years.

The validity of the polls—whether they measure what they purport to measure and how adequate they are in either theory or practice—is more questionable. Interview questions for polls have to be relatively brief and yet preferably allow for a fixed range of responses. Thus the richness, complexity, and subtlety of the issues being addressed in the question are often sacrificed, and many areas of considerable interest in the study of religious beliefs or practice are dealt with superficially, if at all. For example, for a number of years, the Gallup organization has asked the question: "At the present time, do you think religion as a whole is increasing its influence on American life, or losing its influence?" As we shall see, there have been rather dramatic changes in the way this question has been answered over the past twenty years. But what is it measuring? What is meant by *religion* in the question? Is it organized religion, that is, the churches and synagogues? Is it the national religious bodies or local congregations? Or is it the personal religious beliefs or behavior of the American population? Is it all of these or none of these? In the last analysis, we are not sure. Thus the validity of such a question is itself somewhat questionable.

Other problems in the use of poll data include the time of year that polls are taken (a question on church attendance asked near Easter or Christmas will produce different results than if asked in mid-summer) and changes or variations in question wording. We have attempted to be sensitive to these and other problems and have taken them into account in our analysis.

Finally, most national public opinion polls are based on the responses of approximately 1500 people. While this number is adequate to give a picture of the American population as a whole, it does not always allow for a meaningful disaggregation of the data for a detailed analysis of particular subgroups. For example, a typical survey of 1500 respondents would contain only approximately forty-five Jews and thirty-four nonwhite Protestants—too few for detailed breakdowns.

We have spent some effort pointing out deficiencies in the data, not to discourage the reader, but to acknowledge their limits. At the same time, we wish to affirm the importance of the data in providing a perspective on American religion, indeed the only perspective available as far as statistical trends are concerned. While such information does not provide the precision of a sharp photograph, it enables us to discern the general contours of the landscape over the past quarter of a century, and that should prove important in assessing the condition of American religion during these years. We find helpful the comment of the sociologist and Catholic priest, Andrew Greeley, regarding the use of poll data for the study of religious change: "Like all survey research, the findings . . . tell us something, and they tell us something rather important, and relatively inexpensively. They give important hints but they tell us considerably less than everything we need to know."[7] His comment is appropriate, not only for poll data, but for church statistics as well.

HISTORICAL OVERVIEW: 1950–1977

The period we are considering represents a quarter century marked by rapid change and rather striking contrasts for both American society in general and American religion in particular. A brief review of some of these changes and contrasts will set the context for our analysis of the trends. We attempt neither to be exhaustive nor to interpret the significance of the events here. In Chapter 5 we return to some of these changes and contrasts as we seek to interpret the trends.

The 1950s were ushered in on a wave of post–World War II recovery, troubled, however, by the Korean War and the anxieties of the cold war. Business and industry boomed, and cities and suburbs grew dramatically. Both the strident anti-Communism of Joseph McCarthy and his associates and the era of "peace and prosperity" that marked the Eisenhower presidential years were phenomena typical of the decade. There were also important developments in the struggle against racial prejudice that were eventually to come to full expression in the 1960s. The 1954 Supreme Court decision striking down separate but equal schools, integration of the Little Rock schools, and the Montgomery bus boycott were but three such developments.

And in the churches there were also important changes. It was a decade of religious revival, although some have disputed that claim or questioned the authenticity of the revival.[8] As we shall see, the period was marked by rapid church membership growth, especially in the booming new suburbs. There was also a resurgence of evangelical fervor, spearheaded by the revival preaching of Billy Graham. Piety flourished along the Potomac with prayer breakfasts, the adoption of "In God We Trust" as the nation's official motto, and an uncritical tendency to give religious sanction and support to "the American way of life." There was also the immense popularity of the various purveyors of peace of mind—Norman Vincent Peale, Monsignor Fulton J. Sheen, and Rabbi Joshua Liebman—signalling perhaps a pervasive anxiety underlying the surface peace and prosperity. For Roman Catholics, the decade marked the end of the "siege mentality" that had previously characterized Catholic leadership, and Catholics became increasingly integrated into American society and influential in the culture.

Near the end of the decade there were growing signs of unrest. Blacks were challenging segregation in the churches openly and vigorously. Critics within the church were raising serious questions about the quality of church life and the authenticity of the revival. The need for renewal in local parishes was a common theme, heightened by the movement within Catholicism for liturgical renewal that came to fruition in the late 1950s. Also within Catholicism, Angelo Giuseppe Roncalli was elevated in 1958 to the papacy as John XXIII, and in early 1959 he announced his decision to call the Second Vatican Council to bring about renewal within the church.

If the 1950s witnessed considerable change, it was nonetheless minor contrasted with that of the 1960s. Those who lived through that decade may, like the authors, find it difficult to comprehend the number and variety of significant changes and upheavals that occurred. Consider the following: the election of the first Roman Catholic as President of the United States and his tragic death in 1963; the continuation and escalation of the cold war, including both the Berlin Wall and the Bay of Pigs; rapid technological advances, initiated earlier, but beginning to be implemented on an ever widening scale, inspiring hopes and fears of a technopolitan utopia; the full flowering of the civil rights movement—sit-ins, freedom rides, white citizens' councils, bombings, racial murders, the March on Washington, and the passage of the 1964 Civil Rights Act; the urban riots of the late 1960s and the assassinations of Martin Luther King, Jr., Malcolm X, and Robert Kennedy; antiwar protests over Viet Nam; the rise of student protests against both the military-industrial complex and the universities; the beginnings of the women's liberation movement; and, finally, the rise of the counterculture, including the search for alternative life styles, drug use, communes, and a variety of new religious movements.

In the churches there was also change and upheaval: the Second Vatican Council; the involvement of Christians, especially clergy and Catholic sisters, in civil rights and antiwar protests; radical theology and the proclamation of the "death of God," situation ethics, and the "new morality"; the Supreme Court decision against organized prayer in public school classrooms; the search for alternative forms of Christian community; the kindling of hopes for the ecumenical movement by the Consultation on Church Union (COCU) that held its first meeting in 1962; the stirrings of the charismatic or neo-Pentecostal movement within Roman Catholic and mainline Protestant churches; the Black Manifesto of 1969, calling for the payment by churches of reparations to blacks for past oppression; widespread activity, especially in social justice causes, by the national denominational and ecumenical bureaucracies during most of the decade; and, finally, the beginning of a partial dismantling of those bureaucracies by the end of the decade as grass-roots criticism and decline in support brought about restructure efforts and paring down of programs.

In the 1970s there has been a marked change. The upheaval and turmoil of the 1960s have given way to what appear to be disillusionment, cynicism, and a groping for direction; certainly these were significant themes of the 1976 presidential campaign. There has also been a turning inward to personal rather than social concerns. Perhaps the beginnings of this change in mood can be dated by the killings of student protestors at Kent State and Jackson State universities, where youth were stunned to learn that their elders would go so far as to shoot them. The country was profoundly relieved by the end of the Viet Nam war, but the war had left deep scars on the nation's psyche that were inflamed by Watergate and the first resignation of an American president, as well as by a variety of other disclosures of abuse of power by government agencies and personnel. Finally, there have been the energy and environmental crises, and severe economic inflation and recession coupled with high levels of unemployment.

This change in mood has not left the churches unaffected. Social activism, so visible in the 1960s, has virtually ceased among both Protestants and Catholics. There is pessimism among some people over the future of the church, especially the Catholic Church. Reflecting on a survey of American Catholics in 1972, sociologists William McCready and Andrew Greeley questioned whether or not we were witnessing the end of American Catholicism as it was known before 1960: "... There is evidence of the coming apart of the traditional, tightly bound organization of the Church ... the loyalty is gone, the creativity is gone and the meaning system is gone or at least going."[9] Among Protestants the pessimism has been equally widespread, especially in contrast to the cautious optimism that fed the activism of the early 1960s. Recently there has been considerable concern over membership losses in mainline Protestant churches while conservative churches have continued to experience growth.

Outside the established churches there have been such developments as the rise of the Jesus movement; the Unification Church of the Rev. Sun Myung Moon; the continued popularity of various Eastern religions;

and widespread participation in a variety of religious or quasi-religious "technologies of the spirit," such as biofeedback, psychosynthesis, est, and Transcendental Meditation. The churches have begun to be affected by these developments as members take part in groups using the newer technologies as well as non-Western meditation techniques. There has also been a recovery of spiritual disciplines within the Christian tradition.

The speed and extent of the sociocultural changes in America over the last three decades are unprecedented in modern times. Our brief overview has presented a backdrop for the extensive religious changes that the data indicate have also been taking place during this period.

NOTES

1. Alexis de Tocqueville, *Democracy in America*, vol. I (New York: Vintage, 1945, 12th Edition), p. 314.
2. Charles Y. Glock and Rodney Stark, *Religion and Society in Tension* (Chicago: Rand McNally, 1965), pp. 18–38.
3. Glock and Stark, pp. 69–72.
4. Warren J. Hartman, *Membership Trends, A Study of Decline and Growth in the United Methodist Church 1949–1975* (Nashville: Discipleship Resources, 1976), p. 16.
5. Winthrop Hudson, "Are the Churches Really Booming?" *The Christian Century*, 72 (1955), pp. 1494–1496.
6. Several of AIPO surveys were made available to us from the Roper Public Opinion Research Center through funds provided by the Russell Sage Foundation and administered by the Social Science Research Council's Center for Coordination of Research on Social Indicators.
7. Martin E. Marty, Stuart E. Rosenberg, and Andrew M. Greeley, *What Do We Believe?* (New York: Meredith Press, 1968), p. 116.
8. See, for example, S. M. Lipset, *The First New Nation* (New York: Basic Books, 1963); Winthrop Hudson, *Religion in America*, 2nd ed. (New York: Scribner's, 1973); Martin E. Marty, *The New Shape of American Religion* (New York: Harper and Brothers, 1958); A. Roy Eckhardt, *The Surge of Piety in America* (New York: Association Press, 1958); and Sydney E. Ahlstrom, *A Religious History of the American People* (New Haven, Conn.: Yale University Press, 1972). Some scholars, such as Lipset, reject outright the claim that there was a revival. Most acknowledge that there was a definite upsurge in religious interest and activity; however, they would perhaps be in agreement with Ahlstrom in his assessment that the revival "failed to sustain human religious needs" (p. 962). Ahlstrom believes that the primary role of the churches during this period was the provision of social identification for a mobile, uprooted people.
9. William McCready and Andrew Greeley, "The End of American Catholicism?" *America*, vol. 127, October 28, 1972, pp. 337–338.

2

Religious Identification

One of the important needs we have as individuals is for communities in which we may experience belonging and social support. It is in such communities that our basic identities are shaped and supported by others with similar interests and concerns. The nineteenth-century French sociologist Emile Durkheim made this insight central to his analysis of religion. In his view a basic function of religion is the incorporation of individuals into the community and the consequent overcoming of anomie, or normlessness resulting in a sense of confusion or loss of direction.[1] Will Herberg, the Jewish philosopher and social analyst, has written that the question:

"What am I?" . . . is perhaps the most immediate [question] that a man can ask himself in the course of his social life. Everyone finds himself in a social context which he shares with many others, but within this social context, how shall he locate himself? Unless he can so locate himself, he cannot tell himself, and others will not be able to know, who and what he is; . . . To live, he must "belong"; to "belong," he must be able to locate himself in the larger social whole, to identify himself to himself and to others.[2]

Later in his analysis, Herberg writes explicitly of the role of religion in the identification process:

To find a place in American society increasingly means to place oneself in one or another of these religious communities. And although this process of self-identification and social location is not in itself intrinsically religious, the mere fact that in order to be "something" one must be a Protestant, a Catholic, or a Jew means that one begins to think of oneself as religiously identified and affiliated.[3]

An example is the significance to Jews of their Jewish identity. Jewish identity is inherently tied to religion. As sociologists Marshall Sklare and Joseph Greenblum note, "Jewish tradition teaches that Jews are a group only by virtue of their having embraced the Torah, and thus religion is conceived of as the keystone of Jewish identity."[4] Yet, Jewish practice of religion is relatively low as far as synagogue attendance and religious observances in the home are concerned. What seems to be of critical importance to many contemporary Jews is not the practice of their religion, but the identity and sense of belonging that it provides. In his perceptive interpretation of American Judaism, the Jewish sociologist Nathan Glazer wrote:

. . . The strongest and, potentially, most significant religious reality among American Jews . . . is that the Jews have not stopped being Jews. . . . It is not that most Jews in this country submit themselves to the Jewish law; they do not. Nor can they tell you what the Jewish heritage is. But they know it may demand something of them, and to that demand, insofar as it is brought to them and has any meaning for them, they will not answer "No."[5]

It is the sense of Jewishness, Glazer maintains, that accounts for the flourishing of Jewish religious institutions in spite of the relatively low level of practice among Jews. Thus, for example, Sklare and Greenblum, whose study of Jews in a suburban community confirmed the low level of religious practice, found that four of five Jewish families (83 percent) in the suburb were present or past members of a synagogue.[6]

What is true for Jews seems also to be true for Protestants and Catholics. To be sure, levels of religious practice are higher for Protestants and Catholics than for Jews, as we shall see. But we suspect that a primary function of Protestant and Catholic religious institutions, as in Judaism, is in providing identity and belonging in a large and complex society. We agree with Andrew Greeley in his assertion that the ability of religion to play a quasi-ethnic role—providing a means of self-identification and belonging—is the secret of the survival of organized religion in the United States.[7]

To be sure, religious identification has become the focus of considerable bigotry and strife—the struggle of Protestants against Catholics in Northern Ireland is one dramatic and tragic example. The church historian Franklin Littell calls attention to the way that, in United States history, identification as a "child of the Reformation" has often become meaningful for otherwise nominal Protestants when " 'the Jewish threat' or 'the Catholic threat' . . . puts in an appearance."[8]

In this chapter we consider religion as a context for belonging and self-identification. Trends in religious preference—a self-reported identification—and trends in church membership are considered. We also take a look at the relation of religious preference to political office holding as an indication of the continuing importance of religious identification.

RELIGIOUS PREFERENCE

Public opinion polls regularly ask about religious preference. Responses are usually categorized as Protestant, Catholic, Jew, other, and none. Although such information is important to the analyst, it has several deficiencies. First, the five categories used by the polling organizations do not allow us to consider important variations within the main religious groups. Protestants vary considerably from denomination to denomination, and Catholics and Jews are also internally diverse. Second, the responses tell us about preference and not about actual membership. Third, the responses give no information about the degree of the respondent's preference: is she or he a strong or weak Protestant, Catholic, or Jew? Yet in spite of these deficiencies, the data provide us with useful information.

The trends in religious preference are summarized in Table 1. This table goes back to 1947, covering more or less the full period of the postwar religious revival. Several aspects of the table are of particular interest.

Table 1   Trends in Religious Preference, 1947–1975
(Percentage of the U.S. Population for a Sample of Adults)

Year	Total Expressing Some Preference	Protestant	Catholic	Jewish	All Others	None
1947	94	69	20	5	1	6
1952	98	67	25	4	1	2
1957	97	66	26	3	1	3
1962	98	70	23	3	2	2
1967	98	67	25	3	3	2
1972	95	63	26	2	4	5
1975	94	61	27	2	4	6

Religious preference percentages for all years except 1957 are based on a combined sample of at least four Gallup surveys administered during the year in question. The 1975 Gallup survey percentages are as reported in The Gallup Opinion Index, *Religion In America: 1976.* Report No. 130, 1976. The 1957 percentages are from a United States Bureau of the Census Current Population Survey (U.S. Bureau of the Census, *Current Population Reports*, Series P–20, No. 79, February 2, 1958). Percentages do not always total 100 percent because of rounding.

First, the overall percentage of the United States population expressing a religious preference has ranged between 94 and 98 percent for the twenty-eight year period, a remarkably high proportion regardless of the degree of individual preference. Between 1967 and 1975 there was decline (back to the 1947 level), possibly reflecting somewhat the changing mood of the country that we noted previously as characteristic of the late 1960s and early 1970s.

Among the other changes reflected in the table are a decline of eight percentage points in Protestant preference and three in Jewish. However, because of the small number of Jewish respondents in a typical survey, the Jewish percentage is subject to error and must be interpreted with caution. Catholic preferences have gained by seven percentage points, with the sharpest gain coming between 1947–1952. The "All Others" category has more than tripled in size during the period, although it is still quite small. These changes have been fairly constant during the period. We suspect that the 1962 figures for Protestants and Catholics, showing a Protestant gain and a Catholic loss since 1957, may reflect sampling error rather than actual changes in the trend lines.

What the table reflects overall is a population with a continuing willingness, whatever the reason, to identify itself in terms of one of the major religious communities. Further, while the Protestant majority in America is clearly intact, its size has eroded over the past twenty-eight years. Part of the change is due to the increased percentage of Catholics in the population and to increases among the "All Others" and "None" categories. However, how much of the growth in the last two categories is due to Protestant, Jewish, and Catholic defections is impossible to ascertain from the data.

The erosion of the Protestant majority is not simply a matter of numbers and relative size. It is also a matter of attitude or ethos. By the end of the first third of the century, there had occurred what might be called the end of the Protestant era in American life. It was the end of the hopes and efforts of most Protestants to maintain a Protestant America and the beginning of accommodation, often reluctant, to a pluralistic religious situation. By the mid-1950s, Herberg could assert that "Protestantism today no longer regards itself either as a religious movement sweeping the continent or as a national church representing the religious life of the people; Protestantism understands itself today primarily as one of the three religious communities in which twentieth-century America has come to be divided."[9]

In spite of the decline of Protestant hegemony, there are evidences of Protestantism's staying power in some areas of life. Political office holding is one area. Church historian Edwin Gaustad called attention to some aspects of this situation using data from 1967.[10] We have included the 1967 data and added 1973 and 1977

Table 2.   Political Leadership by Denominations, 1967–1977
(Percentages of the total number of Senators, Representatives, or Governors)

	Senate			House			Governors		
	1967	*1973*	*1977*	*1967*	*1973*	*1977*	*1967*	*1973*	*1977*
Methodist	24	18	20	16	15	14	20	12	10
Episcopal	15	18	17	12	11	11	16	10	8
Roman Catholic	13	14	13	22	23	27	18	24	30
Presbyterian	12	15	14	16	14	10	10	14	14
Baptist	12	8	9	10	11	10	12	10	10
United Church of Christ	6	7	4	5	5	4	10	6	6
LDS (Mormon)	4	4	4	1	1	2	4	2	2
Lutheran	3	3	2	2	3	3	6	6	6
Christian (Disciples of Christ)	1	1	0	3	2	1	4	4	2
Jewish	2	2	5	4	3	5	0	4	4
Unitarian–Universalist	3	4	3	1	1	2	0	2	4
All Others	4	6	8	7	10	10	0	6	2
None	1	0	1	1	1	1	0	0	2
	Senate			House			Governors		
SUMMARY	*1967*	*1973*	*1977*	*1967*	*1973*	*1977*	*1967*	*1973*	*1977*
Protestant	80	80	77	72	72	65	78	70	62
Catholic	13	14	13	22	23	27	18	24	30
Jewish	2	2	5	4	3	5	0	4	4
LDS (Mormon)	4	4	4	1	1	2	4	2	2
None	1	0	1	1	1	1	0	0	2

Source: Christianity Today, vol. 11, Dec. 9, 1966, pp. 276–77; vol. 17, Dec. 8, 1972, pp. 40–44; vol. 21, Dec. 3, 1976, pp. 56–57.

figures to give a ten-year perspective. The trends are shown in Table 2.

The summary percentages at the bottom of the table show Protestants declining by 3 percentage points in number of U.S. Senate seats over the decade, while Jews gained by the same amount, and Catholics stayed fairly constant. Protestant losses in the House of Representatives were slightly larger for the decade—7 percentage points—while Catholics gained 5 points and Jews, 1 point. It is in state gubernatorial positions that Protestant losses have been greatest; Protestant governors—78 percent of the total in 1967—declined by 16 percentage points. At the same time, Catholics increased by 12 points and Jews, who claimed no governors in 1967, had two governors (4 percent) in 1977.

How do these relative proportions in politics compare with the proportions of Protestants, Catholics, and Jews in the population? Comparing the 1975 religious preference figures in Table 1 (which are not likely to have changed significantly by 1977) with Table 2, we see that in 1977 the Senate was still disproportionately Protestant—77 percent of the Senate was Protestant, while only 61 percent of the American adult population identified themselves as Protestants. While 27 percent of the adult population identified themselves as Catholic, only 13 percent of the Senate was Catholic. Representation of Catholics and Protestants in the House of Representatives was approximately proportionate to the overall population. Gubernatorial proportions also were generally representative of the total population for both Catholics and Protestants. The proportion of Jews holding political offices in 1977 is considerably higher than

their size in the population. It is more than double in the Senate and double in governorships.

In 1975 six percent of the population expressed no religious preference; however, only 2 percent of the governors and 1 percent each of the senators and representatives in 1977 expressed no preference.

We have also included in the table the denominational distribution by type of office; however, when this distribution is considered, there are few notable changes over time other than the increase of Catholics in the House and governorships.[11] Methodists and Episcopalians seem to have lost the most ground in governorships and Presbyterians in the House. Otherwise, what is of most interest is the order of the denominations relative to each other and to their size in the population. For example, Methodists (including the several Methodist bodies) are approximately 7 percent of the population; yet, they constitute 20 percent of the Senate and also are overrepresented in the House and in governorships. Episcopalians (1.4 percent of the population), Presbyterians (1.9 percent), United Church of Christ members (0.9 percent), and especially Unitarian–Universalists (0.1 percent) are also very much overrepresented relative to their size in the population. On the other hand, Lutherans (4 percent of the population) are somewhat underrepresented except in governorships. When all types of Baptists are counted, they, too, are slightly underrepresented politically (though the election of a Southern Baptist to the presidency in 1976 may compensate for this.) The smaller, rapidly growing evangelical and Pentecostal groups are also underrepresented. Probably several factors lie behind this somewhat out-of-proportion representation by denominational groups.

First, Protestants generally have outnumbered Catholics and Jews in rural areas and small towns. Until recent court-ordered one person, one vote reforms, electoral districts made up of rural areas and small towns had more than their share of electoral "clout," which sent Protestants to Congress and to statehouses in inordinant numbers. This process has been and continues to be further supported by congressional seniority rules and the power of incumbency that keeps Protestants in office.

Second, social class affects the relative strength of denominations in political offices. Holding political office, especially at the national and state gubernatorial levels, is quite costly, and people with means have a distinct advantage. It should not be surprising, therefore, that religious groups whose members are typically upper-middle-class and presumably have greater means—for example, Episcopalians, United Church of Christ members, Presbyterians and Jews—are overrepresented in political offices. A cynic might say that Jesus' words apply more in politics than in religious life: "For to everyone who has will more be given..." (Matthew 25: 29, RSV).

Neither geography nor economic status, however, provides a full explanation. A third important factor seems to be cultural. The theological position of such denominations as Methodist, Episcopal, United Church of Christ, and Presbyterian is generally liberal and implies an ethical stance that takes seriously public as well as private moral issues.[12] These churches have what the sociologist Max Weber called an "inner worldly ascetic" religious orientation, by which he meant a religious belief system that emphasizes disciplined (ascetic) activity *in* the world as a response to God.[13] The world—including economic and political structures—is viewed as an arena the believer is called to work to transform for the greater glory of God. This orientation is partly responsible for most of these same denominations' (with the Methodists as a possible exception) assuming what Martin Marty has called "custodianship of the culture,"[14] which also implies political responsibility. American Judaism, like liberal Protestantism, has a "this-worldly" orientation (though not ascetic in Weber's sense) that is a factor in Jewish political involvement. Lutherans, however, have been less politically involved in spite of their numerical dominance in some states. Do they share less in the "inner-worldly ascetic" orientation? Weber thought so. He wrote of a "mystic component" in Lutheranism that gave less emphasis to "conspicuous social activity."[15] Furthermore, in the United States Lutheranism, like Catholicism, has been an immigrant church, less prone to feel custodianship for the dominant culture. This attitude may be changing to some extent, especially for Catholics, as their gains in political office holding suggest.

Another religious group openly espousing cultural custodianship through political involvement is the conservative evangelicals. Although there have long been Christians espousing right-wing political causes, evangelical Christians appear to be increasingly taking advantage of the fact they are a large and identifiable force within American life. A coalition of right-wing evangelical groups has begun a movement whose major goals are the election of like-minded evangelicals to political office, especially at the national level, and the evangelization of those politicians already in office. A campaign to pursue the former goal was launched in 1975, committed to the election of individuals espousing ultraconservative political views and "free enterprise" economic principles. In 1976 a Christian Embassy, funded by twenty businesspeople through the effort of Bill Bright of the Campus Crusade, was opened with the goal of evangelizing official Washington.[16] In addition to expressing their identity in political activity, some businesspeople of the evangelical right have also given expression to their religious identity by the publication of "The Christian Yellow Pages," a business directory in which advertising is limited to evangelical Christians.

Are such political and economic developments among evangelicals likely to be rather shortlived nativist attempts to hold back the tide of pluralism; that is, are they attempts by conservative white Anglo-Saxon Protestants to preserve their traditionally favored status in the face of increasingly visible and vocal ethnic diversity? Or do the evangelicals constitute a genuine new force in American society that is likely to persist? It is clearly too early to tell, although we suspect the former is more probable. Religiocultural imperialism, such as Protestants of all varieties have exercised in the United States, dies hard, but it is unlikely to remain strong indefinitely in an increasingly pluralistic society.

Before leaving the discussion of trends in religious preference, we take note of one study that shows these trends for nonwhites, approximately 90 percent of whom are black. Two sociologists, Norval D. Glenn and Erin Gotard, report data from a 1957 survey of the United States Bureau of the Census and from surveys in the early 1970s (combining data from three National Opinion Research Center surveys to secure a sufficient number of respondents for analysis).[17] The authors point out that this time period encompasses the major black protest activities of the 1960s, and that a number of social analysts were predicting widespread religious defections from predominantly black churches. Defections would occur, it was predicted, because blacks would judge traditional black churches to be too conservative and accommodative to the racial status quo.

Glenn and Gotard's data show that in 1957, 87.5 percent of nonwhites, aged 14 and older, identified themselves as Protestant. Of the Protestants, the large majority were Baptist (69 percent), with the remainder divided between Methodists (20 percent) and Other Protestant (11 percent). Catholics were 6.5 percent of the total, those with no preference were 3.5 percent, and all others, including Jews, made up 2.6 percent. In the combined 1972–1974 surveys, 83.8 percent of persons 18 years and older identified themselves as Protestants. This is a decline of less than four percentage points since 1957. There were slight decreases in Baptist and Methodist preferences and a small increase in the Other Protestant category. Catholics grew among nonwhites from 6.5 percent in 1957 to 8.9 percent in the early 1970s. There was a 1 percentage point increase among those with no preference. All others showed little change. In general, these results show that there was

very little change in self-reported religious preference among nonwhites from 1957 to the early 1970s. This lack of significant change generally parallels the data from whites, which Glenn and Gotard also summarize. The predictions of widespread religious defections among blacks seem not to be supported. Further data on church attendance trends for nonwhites, summarized in Chapter 3, add additional weight to this conclusion.

CHURCH MEMBERSHIP

We turn now from self-ascribed religious preference to trends in church membership. There are several ways of viewing the trends.

Figure 1 presents a comparison of Protestant, Catholic, and Jewish membership trends from 1947 through

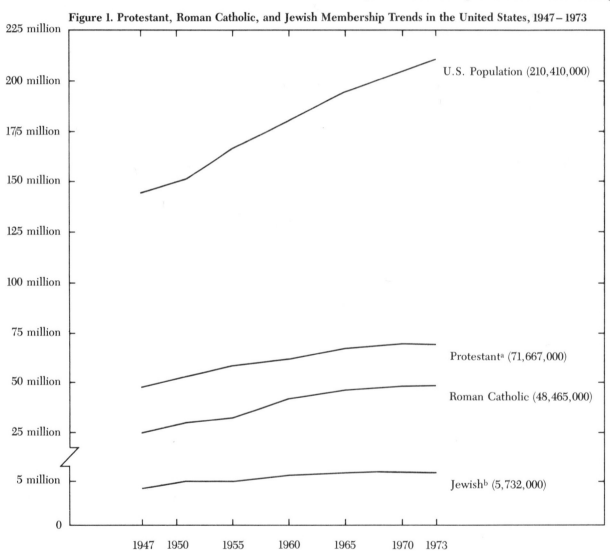

Figure 1. Protestant, Roman Catholic, and Jewish Membership Trends in the United States, 1947–1973

a. Protestant includes some bodies which, strictly speaking, are non-Protestant, such as Latter Day Saints (Mormons) and Jehovah's Witnesses.

b. Jewish includes Reform, Conservative, and Orthodox congregations.

Sources: U.S. Bureau of the Census, *Historical Statistics of the United States, Colonial Times to 1970, Bicentennial Edition, Part 2.* Washington, D.C., 1975.

George F. Ketchem, ed., *Yearbook of American Churches* (New York: Federal Council of Churches, 1949).

Constant H. Jacquet, ed., *Yearbook of American and Canadian Churches* (Nashville: Abingdon, 1975).

Morris Fine and Milton Himmelfarb, eds., *American Jewish Yearbook 1969, 1975*, Vols. 70, 76 (New York: The American Jewish Committee, 1969, 1975).

1973, as well as the trend of United States population growth during the same period. Thus we can compare the main religious groups with each other and with the total population.

Before comparing the trend lines, we may note that, proportionately, there are considerably fewer Protestant church members (approximately 35 percent) in the total population than there are people expressing Protestant religious preference (61–70 percent; see Table 1). There is much less discrepancy between the proportions for Catholics and Jews; however, in each case there are fewer members reported than there are individuals expressing Catholic or Jewish preferences. Why these discrepancies exist is a matter for speculation. Perhaps they result from the differences in membership definitions and ways of gathering statistics noted earlier. Many independent Protestant congregations, some of which are quite large, are not included in *Yearbook* membership figures on which Figure 1 is based. The discrepancy may also reflect the social pressure of the interview situation; that is, some people may feel it an embarrassment not to express a religious preference when asked by the interviewer.

Of major interest in Figure 1 is the gain or loss for each group compared with the others and with the total United States population. Catholic growth was especially pronounced during the late 1940s and in the 1950s, and it continued to exceed United States population growth through 1965. Although Catholics continued to grow into the 1970s, the rate of growth has been slightly less than that of the total population.

Protestants grew more rapidly than the total population throughout the post World War II period, down to 1955. During the 1955 to 1965 decade, Protestant growth generally paralleled that of the population. From 1965 to 1970, Protestants continued to grow, but at a rate slightly less than the total population; and from 1970 to 1973 the total number of Protestants showed a very slight loss (less than 1 percent). In subsequent paragraphs we talk more specifically about which Protestant denominations were responsible for this decline.

Jewish membership statistics, like Protestant and Catholic, show growth from 1947 to 1952 exceeding that of the population; however, unlike Protestants and Catholics, they show no gain from 1951 to 1955 (probably resulting from the method of estimating membership rather than reflecting an accurate reporting of members). From 1955 to 1960, Jewish growth was again greater than total population growth; however, from 1960 to 1970 the growth rate slowed considerably, less than that of the total population. From 1970 to 1973, there was a slight decline (approximately 2 percent).

These comparisons with total population growth will become more meaningful when, in Chapter 5, we try to account for membership gains and losses. As we will see, changes in the birth rate have a considerable effect on church membership, as they also affect other aspects of the society.

Figure 2 presents trends for twelve Protestant denominations, plus the trend for Roman Catholics for comparative purposes. Unfortunately there are no membership trend data for the three major branches of Judaism, Reform, Conservative and Orthodox. The twelve Protestant denominations were selected to give a broad sampling of groups ranging from the theologically more liberal to the more conservative. The reader should be aware, however, of the inadequacy of trying to represent wide internal diversity with such loose descriptive categories as "conservative" and "liberal."[18] We have corrected for several denominational mergers that occurred during this period by including membership data from all of the denominations entering into the mergers for all years reflected in Figure 2. The picture of membership trends is further detailed in Figure 3, which consists of bar graphs showing net percentage gain and loss figures for the same denominations in ten year intervals (1955 to 1965 and 1965 to 1975).

With one exception all the denominations represented had sizable membership gains through 1965. The exception, the American Baptist Churches, shows a slight loss between 1950 and 1955, and then a gain of 4.2 percent from 1955 to 1965. Although the largest percentage growth in membership occurred among several of the most conservative groups—Assemblies of God, Missouri Synod Lutheran, Southern Baptists, Church of the Nazarene—in addition to the Roman Catholic Church, nearly all the denominations showed substantial growth. The Episcopal Church, for example, which was to experience substantial decline from 1965 to 1975, had a gain of 20.2 percent from 1955 to 1965. This is a growth of just 7 percentage points less than the Southern Baptists.

For the 1960s, the picture is more complex. During the first five years of the decade, there was continued growth in all but one denomination, the United Church of Christ, which suffered a loss of 7.6 percent. That denomination was formed between 1957 and 1961 by a merger of the Congregational Christian Churches with the Evangelical and Reformed Church. A number of Congregational Christian Churches refused to join the merger, thus contributing to the membership loss. In the other major liberal denominations, the rate of growth slowed, while the conservative bodies, large and small, continued to grow at a more rapid rate. It was in the latter half of the 1960s, continuing into the middle 1970s, that all of the theologically liberal denominations began to experience membership declines.

Although the figures show the trends in five year intervals, the actual year-by-year data identify 1966 and 1967 as the years in which declines set in for the liberal denominations. Theologically moderate denomi-

Figure 2. Membership of Twelve Protestant Denominations and the Roman Catholic Church, 1950–1975

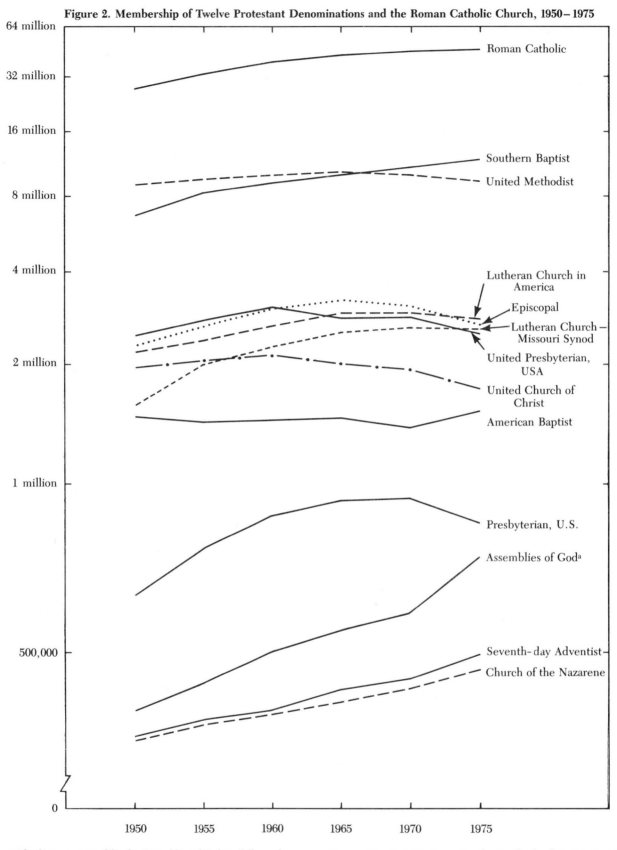

a. The figures reported for the Assemblies of God are full membership statistics.

Scale: In order to show churches of considerably different sizes on the same figure, the graph is drawn to a semi-logarithmic scale. Each higher point on the vertical scale doubles the one below it.

Source: Constant H. Jacquet, ed., *Yearbook of American and Canadian Churches 1977* (Nashville: Abingdon, 1977), pp. 246-247.

Figure 3. Percentage Change in Membership for 1955–1965 and 1965–1975 for Selected U.S. Churches

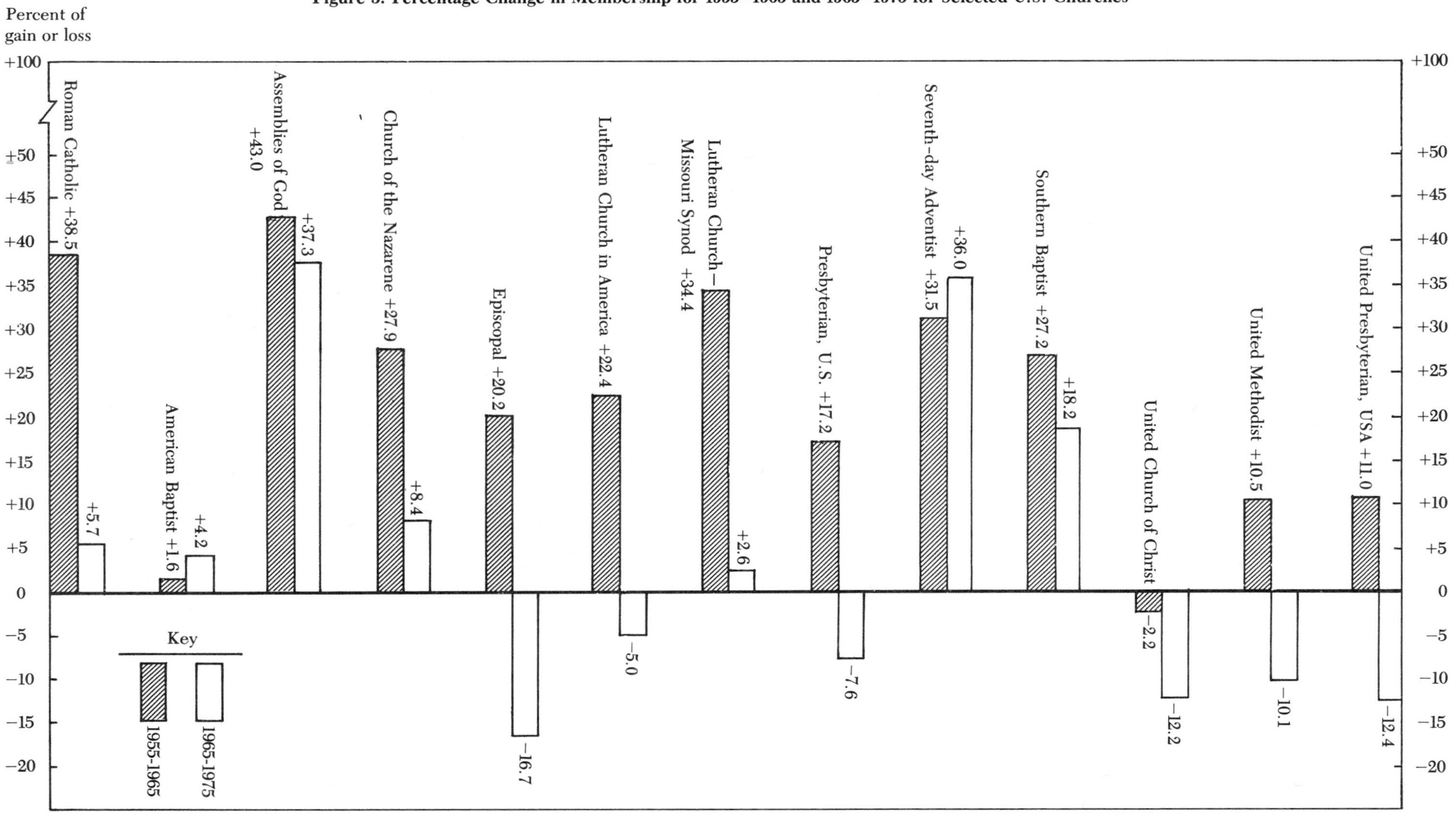

Percent of gain or loss

+100 +50 +45 +40 +35 +30 +25 +20 +15 +10 +5 0 -5 -10 -15 -20

United Presbyterian, USA +11.0 / −12.4

United Methodist +10.5 / −10.1

United Church of Christ / −12.2 / −2.2

Southern Baptist +27.2 / +18.2

Seventh−day Adventist +31.5 / +36.0

Presbyterian, U.S. +17.2 / −7.6

Lutheran Church—Missouri Synod +34.4 / +2.6

Lutheran Church in America +22.4 / −5.0

Episcopal +20.2 / −16.7

Church of the Nazarene +27.9 / +8.4

Assemblies of God +43.0 / +37.3

American Baptist +1.6 / +4.2

Roman Catholic +38.5 / +5.7

Key
1965-1975
1955-1965

+100 +50 +45 +40 +35 +30 +25 +20 +15 +10 +5 0 -5 -10 -15 -20

Source: Constant H. Jacquet, ed., *Yearbook of American and Canadian Churches*, (Nashville: Abingdon, 1977).

nations, such as the Lutheran Church in America and the Presbyterian Church in the United States also experienced some declines during this period, although their declines tended to lag behind more liberal groups by several years. Most of the conservative denominations continued to grow; though some of them, such as the Southern Baptists, did not grow as rapidly from 1965 to 1975 as they had in the previous decade. One conservative denomination that grew very little in the 1965 to 1975 period was the Lutheran Church—Missouri Synod. It was wracked with doctrinal controversy and a power struggle that led finally in 1976 to schism.

These trends to decline in the liberal denominations and growth among the conservatives are ones that National Council of Churches staff member, Dean Kelley, cited in his provocative book, *Why Conservative Churches Are Growing*.[19] Kelley also cited church school membership trends for several theologically liberal and moderate denominations (though not for the more conservative bodies) and found them in decline. Church school declines, however, tended to precede church membership declines by several years, suggesting that they are an advance indicator of church membership and attendance declines. In Chapter 5, we cite additional data on the relation of church school and church membership trends that support this suggestion.

That the changes in membership affected several denominations in similar ways during the same time period leads us to look for causes common to denominations of particular types and constituencies. We are not likely to explain trends by a factor that affected only one denomination, although a possible exception is the Roman Catholic Church, which experienced both Vatican II and the papal encyclical, *Humanae Vitae* (about which more will be said below). Each of these events was obviously unique to Catholicism and seems to have had a profound effect on church participation, although not on membership.

Before leaving the discussion of church membership trends, we take note of one other matter. The United Methodist Church—one of those denominations experiencing membership losses in recent years—has attempted to ascertain where the losses have occurred.[20] Members are added to the United Methodist Church by either confession of faith or transfer. Confession of faith includes both adolescents and adults who are joining the church, usually for the first time, as a result of having been "brought up" in the church from baptism or as a result of conversion. The transfer category includes those who transfer from other United Methodist Churches and from other denominations. Individuals may be removed from a church membership roll as a result of death, by transfer to some other United Methodist Church or another denomination, or by removal by action of the church, including a request for removal by the member.

As the United Methodists sorted out where their recent losses were occurring, they discovered that the primary area of loss was in the number of people received by confession of faith. Secondarily, a slight loss was through removal by church action, presumably of people long inactive, those with whom the congregation had lost touch, or those who requested withdrawal. Transfers in and out of the churches tended to balance one another, and the number of losses by death remained generally constant during years of growth or decline. Thus losses were not through a mass exodus but rather primarily through a decrease in those entering through traditional avenues.

These findings may be compared with those of two sociologists who studied sources of growth in a number of conservative churches in a large Western Canadian city, reported to be a major center of evangelical activity in Canada.[21] Unfortunately for our comparison, the two researchers, Bibby and Brinkerhoff, considered only gains and not losses of members as well. They found that 72 percent of new members over a five year period (1966–1970) came as a result of "reaffiliation"— that is, from people already members of an evangelical church when they first attended the particular conservative congregation they subsequently joined.[22] Another 18 percent of new members came from "birth-type converts," those who are children of evangelicals; and 9 percent joined through "proselyte-type conversion"— they were converts from outside the evangelical community.

Thus it seems that conservative church growth, at least in the groups studied, comes primarily through a kind of circulation process, by which evangelicals move from one conservative church to another. To a lesser extent, new additions are the offspring of members reared in an evangelical culture. Proselyte-type converts are typically "switchers" from other nonevangelical or conservative denominations; however, this is the least important source of new members. Bibby and Brinkerhoff conclude that conservative churches do a better job of retaining those already familiar with evangelical culture—both transfers and children of members—than moderate and liberal churches do in retaining their members.

This conclusion is plausible when considered alongside the United Methodist findings. Many United Methodists removed from membership rolls by congregational action are no doubt people who have moved without affiliating with another church or requesting a membership transfer if they have affiliated. In any event, the church has lost contact with them. Likewise, the considerable drop for United Methodists in the confession of faith category probably reflects failure to incorporate baptized children of church members into membership, although it may also reflect fewer children in the church family population due to a declining birthrate.

Thus if United Methodists are to some degree representative of other moderate-to-liberal denominations, it would appear that some of the membership declines of the 1960s are the result of a failure to hold on to and incorporate their members, especially the mobile ones, and their children. We will consider several other sources of losses and gains as we search for explanations for the change in Chapter 5. In summary, it is clear that, after a period of rapid membership growth during the 1950s and early 1960s, most major Protestant denominations experienced sharp losses during the middle to late 1960s, and these losses have continued into the 1970s. Similar losses were not experienced by theologically more conservative denominations.

NOTES

1. See Emile Durkheim, *Suicide*, trans. John A. Spalding and George Simpson (Glencoe, Illinois: Free Press, 1951); Durkheim, *The Elementary Forms of Religious Life*, trans. Joseph Ward Swain (London: George Allen and Unwin, 1915).
2. Will Herberg, *Protestant, Catholic, Jew* (Garden City, N.Y.: Doubleday, 1955), p. 12.
3. Herberg, p. 56.
4. Marshall Sklare and Joseph Greenblum, *Jewish Identity on the Suburban Frontier* (New York: Basic Books, 1967), p. 45.
5. Nathan Glazer, *American Judaism* (Chicago: University of Chicago Press, 1957), p. 139.
6. Sklare and Greenblum, p. 97.
7. Andrew Greeley, *The Denominational Society* (Glenview, Ill.: Scott, Foresman, 1972), p. 108.
8. Franklin Littell, *From State Church to Pluralism* (Garden City, N.Y.: Doubleday Anchor, 1962), pp. 145–146.
9. Herberg, pp. 124–125.
10. Edwin Gaustad, "America's Institutions of Faith," in *Religion in America*, ed. William C. McLaughlin and Robert N. Bellah (Boston: Houghton-Mifflin, 1968), pp. 125–129.
11. See *Christianity Today*, vol. 11, Dec. 9, 1966, pp. 276–277; vol. 17, Dec. 8, 1972, pp. 40–44; vol. 21, Dec. 3, 1976, pp. 56–57.
12. See Michael Parenti, "Political Values and Religious Cultures: Jews, Catholics and Protestants," *Journal For The Scientific Study of Religion*, vol. 7, Fall 1967, pp. 259–269, for a fuller discussion of the political significance of differing religious belief systems.
13. Max Weber, *The Sociology of Religion,* trans. Ephraim Fischoff (Boston: Beacon Press, 1963), pp. 166 ff.
14. Martin E. Marty, *The Fire We Can Light* (Garden City, N.Y.: Doubleday, 1973), p. 88.
15. Weber, p. 176.
16. For a detailed analysis of these efforts, see Jim Wallis and Wes Michaelson, "The Plan to Save America," *Sojourners*, vol. 5, April 1976.
17. Norval D. Glenn and Erin Gotard, "The Religion of Blacks in the United States: Some Recent Trends and Current Characteristics," *American Journal of Sociology*, vol. 83, September 1977, pp. 443–451.
18. Throughout, we use the terms *conservative* and *evangelical* interchangeably. Many who count themselves as conservative espouse a strongly evangelical or conversionist perspective; however, there is now considerable debate among evangelicals whether conversion is concerned solely with personal changes or whether it also includes social reform.
19. Dean Kelley, *Why Conservative Churches Are Growing* (New York: Harper & Row, 1972). See also Richard C. Wolf, "1900–1950 Survey: Religious Trends in the United States," *Christianity Today*, April 27, 1959, pp. 3–5.
20. See Warren J. Hartman, *Membership Trends, A Study of Decline and Growth in the United Methodist Church 1949–1975* (Nashville: Discipleship Resources, 1976).
21. Reginald W. Bibby and Merlin B. Brinkerhoff, "The Circulation of the Saints: A Study of People Who Join Conservative Churches," *Journal for the Scientific Study of Religion*, vol. 12, September 1973, pp. 273–283.
22. The reaffiliated category included not only transfers and previous members reactivating their membership but also what the authors refer to as "professions of faith." The latter category is not defined; thus it is not entirely clear how it differs from either of the types of members joining through conversion. We presume that it means an expression of renewal of a previous conversion experience.

3

Trends in Religious Practice

The question of religious practice moves us beyond personal identification or affiliation with a religious group to various types of involvement that require some action or response. Attendance at religious services; observing rituals in the home; participation in religious disciplines such as prayer, meditation, and scripture reading; involvement in the organizational life of a religious group; or contributions of money to the organization are examples of religious practices. As we noted in Chapter 1, Glock and Stark refer to such practice as the ritual dimension of religious commitment.

This dimension varies on a continuum from the more objective and formal types of religious practice, such as church attendance, organizational involvement, or financial support, to the informal and subjective types, such as private prayer or scripture reading. Trend data are more prevalent for the formal or objective types of religious practice, especially church attendance. The American Institute of Public Opinion (Gallup Poll) has, since 1939, gathered data on frequency of attendance. Giving to the churches, as reported in denominational statistics, is also fairly well documented •ver time. Trends in the more subjective aspects of religious practice are less well measured. We have only limited data on practice of prayer and meditation, Bible reading, and other forms of personal religious discipline. This lack is greatly to be regretted for a variety of reasons, not least of which is the possible light such information might shed on the current explosion of interest in the more subjective and personal disciplines of meditation and spiritual growth.

CHURCH ATTENDANCE

Church attendance is the most fully documented form of religious practice for which trend data are

available. Some may suggest that it is not as important an indicator of religious commitment as other forms of practice; however, its significance should not be taken lightly.

Although people attend religious services for a variety of reasons, some of which have little to do with religious commitment, it is in attendance that commitment can be shaped and renewed and that the support of a community of fellow believers can be experienced. People tend to participate most fully in those voluntary activities that seem rewarding in light of their own interests and needs. Thus increases or decreases in church attendance reflect to a considerable extent the degree to which people find that attendance meets their interests and needs.

Attendance is also quite obviously important for the churches. American churches are voluntary associations. As such, they depend very much for their existence on the voluntary participation and support of members, and attendance is one of the most significant forms of participation and support.

Some would also claim that church attendance is basic to the life of the nation. One such group is the Religion in American Life campaign, directed by a lay committee with support from the Advertising Council of America. Its objective is "to emphasize the importance of all religious institutions as the foundations of American life and to urge all Americans to attend and support the church or synagogue of their individual choice.[1] A rather blatant statement linking religion and Americanism appeared regularly during the 1950s and early 1960s in an advertisement on the church page of *The Dallas Times Herald:*

The Church for All, All for the Church. The Church is the greatest factor on earth for the building of character and good citizenship. It is a storehouse of spiritual values. Without a strong Church, neither democracy nor civilization can survive. *There are four sound reasons why every person should attend services regularly and support the Church. They are:* (1) For his own sake. (2) For his children's sake. (3) For the sake of his community and nation. (4) For the sake of the Church itself, which needs his moral and material support. Plan to go to Church regularly and read your Bible daily.

It is easy to be cynical about these statements, and clearly there is strong opposition from the Judeo-Christian prophetic tradition to such blatant identification of nation and religion. Furthermore, religious groups in America are by law independent of the state and have often been in vocal opposition to American political and economic policies and practices. Nonetheless, it is true that the Judeo-Christian tradition has been of crucial importance in shaping many of the core values and beliefs of American society—values that are sometimes referred to as America's civil religion.[2] Consequently, participation in churches and synagogues frequently functions to reinforce a commitment to American society and its core values. Attendance is thus of significance not only for individual members and the churches but potentially also for society as a whole.

We should note, however, that for Judaism, synagogue attendance has traditionally been less central than church attendance for Christianity. The home, with rituals designed for observance by the family, has been the center of Jewish religious practice. In their study of Jews in an American suburb, Sklare and Greenblum commented on the traditional significance of the home in contrast to the synagogue:

Unlike a synagogue, where procedures are necessarily a compromise between contending conceptions (or where someone may attend a religious service to be "seen" or because one has been invited by a relative or friend), religious practice in the home is a more nearly perfect reflection of individual conviction and desire. And unlike the house of worship, where practice may be influenced by a religious specialist, the home has no professionals.[3]

From their research, Sklare and Greenblum suggest that this traditional emphasis on the home as the central institution of Jewish cultic practice may be declining in importance as compared with synagogue participation. They interpreted increased synagogue attendance reflecting the need of Jews, facing increasing assimilationist pressures, to have a place where they can learn how to be Jews and to conduct Jewish home observances and other practices they were neglecting.[4] Nevertheless, the synagogue's traditionally less central role in contrast to church attendance for Protestants and Catholics should be kept in mind as we compare attendance trends.

Figure 4 shows church and synagogue attendance trends from 1955 to 1975, based on Gallup Poll surveys. As we noted earlier, question wording and season of the year are important factors affecting the validity and reliability of such data. The question always asked in Gallup surveys is: "Did you, yourself, happen to attend church or synagogue in the last seven days?" The answer to that question does not tell us how regular the respondents are in attendance but only if they happened to attend in the past week. Moreover, attendance generally "peaks" in the Lenten season and "bottoms out" in January and again in mid-summer.[5] Since 1955 the Gallup organization has met this problem by using several different surveys at different times of the year and averaging the results, thereby correcting for seasonal variation. Because attendance figures prior to 1955 are based on single surveys and are therefore likely to be unreliable, we have chosen to include only the trends from 1955 through 1976.

The trends in Figure 4 are shown for all faiths combined: Protestants, Catholics, Jews, and all others. They are also shown separately for Protestants, Catholics and Jews. We can see that the total reported attendance at church and synagogue was highest in the middle to late 1950s when approximately 49 percent of the population reported having attended. From 1958 to 1971, there was a slow but consistent decline to 40 percent, where it remained through 1975. In 1976, however, there was the first increase—two percentage points—in eighteen years. It is obviously too soon to tell if this is the beginning of a new upturn in attendance that will continue. The overall average church attendance for the twenty-one-year period is 44 percent.

Since Protestants constitute a high proportion (approximately 60 percent) of those expressing a religious preference, the total trend line in most instances closely parallels that for Protestants. Protestant attendance has been considerably lower than Catholic attendance throughout the twenty-one-year period; however, changes during this time have not been as dramatic for Protestants as for Catholics. From a high of 44 percent in 1957–1958, Protestant attendance declined to a low that has fluctuated beween 40 and 37 percent since 1964. In other words, from its peak during the religious revival, Protestant attendance declined between five and seven percentage points during the early 1960s, remained relatively constant between 1964 and 1975, and, in 1976, climbed back to its 1963 level of 40 percent.

Attendance trends within Protestantism differ from denomination to denomination, although only limited data are available to trace these differences. A comparison of five Protestant denominational families for selected years between 1966 to 1976 showed Lutherans having the highest overall attendance (between 37 and 41 percent). Episcopalians were lowest, ranging between 20 and 37 percent in attendance. Methodist and Presbyterian attendance varied between 30 and 38 percent, and Baptists were most consistent, ranging between 37 and 39 percent for the period.[6]

Although Catholic church attendance is always considerably higher than Protestant during the period covered by Figure 4, it shows a much greater decline than

Figure 4. **Percentage of Adherents Attending Religious Services in an Average Week, 1955–1976**

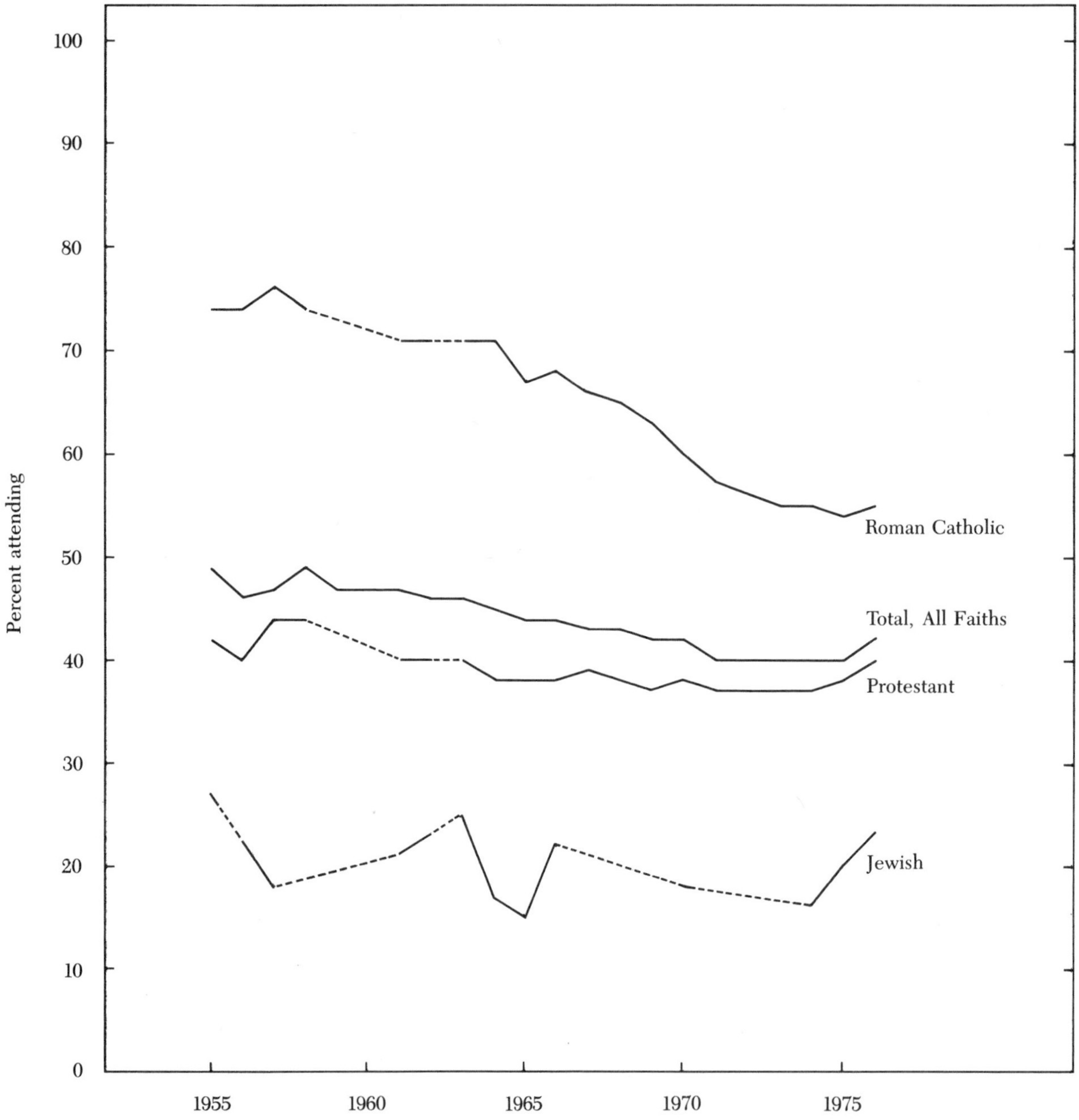

ᵃA dotted line indicates missing data for certain years.

Sources: Hazel Gaudet Erskine, "The Polls: Church Attendance," *Public Opinion Quarterly* Vol. 28 (Winter 1964), pp. 669–679.

George H. Gallup, *The Gallup Poll: Public Opinion, 1935–1971* (New York: Random House, 1972).

The Gallup Opinion Index, *Religion In America: 1975*, Report No. 114, 1975.

The Gallup Opinion Index, *Religion In America: 1976*, Report No. 130, 1976.

The Gallup Opinion Index, *Religion In America: 1977*, Report No. 145, 1977

that of Protestants. From a high of over 75 percent attending during 1957, Catholic attendance dropped to a low of 54 percent in 1975. The decline has been particularly acute since 1963. The Gallup trend figures for Catholics have been confirmed by another study of Catholic practices, that by Greeley, McCready, and McCourt, who report a decline in weekly mass attendance from 71 percent in 1966 to 50 percent in 1975.[7]

Those Catholics going to church "practically never" or "not at all" increased from 6 to 12 percent during this period.

Because Jewish figures are less reliable, some of the attendance fluctuation for Jews shown in Figure 4 is probably due to sampling error that increases considerably with small numbers. Nevertheless, it is evident that there have been changes. Nathan Glazer cites a 1947 public opinion poll that put Jewish attendance at services at least once a month (a different way of asking the question of attendance than that used by Gallup) at 18 percent.[8] The 1955 Gallup figure (averaged over several times a year) is 27 percent. Even allowing for sampling error, this indicates an upswing in Jewish attendance as Jews were caught up in the postwar religious revival. Perhaps it reflects also the increased importance of the synagogue in contrast to home observances that we noted previously. Since 1955, it is evident that there have been considerable fluctuations in the percentages of Jews reporting synagogue attendance. How to interpret such fluctuations is problematic. One possibility is to imagine a "best fitting" straight line that passes through the actual trend line, that is, an imaginary line that averages out the actual up and down fluctuations. If this is done, then we can infer that there has been a decline in Jewish attendance from the middle 1950s at least down to 1974. During 1975 and 1976, there have been increases. While these increases may also simply be fluctuations due to sampling, they may reflect the start of an upward trend. As with Protestants and Catholics, it is too soon to tell if this is true.

If the "best fitting line" interpretation of the Jewish attendance trend is plausible, then Jewish attendance shows a somewhat similar pattern as that for Protestants, although neither experienced as sharp a decline as Catholics. It may be that some of the same factors that we will consider in Chapter 5 to explain Protestant declines will also be applicable to Jewish changes.

Has the change in attendance over the past twenty-five years been even across the population, or are there some groups or types of people who are primarily responsible for the trends? We have included several subgroup analyses for selected years in Table 3.

The breakdown by sex reveals that women are more frequent attenders at religious services than men. This finding has emerged in virtually every study of church attendance with which we are familiar. Moreover, as Table 3 reveals, this difference has been relatively constant (from 8 to 10 percentage points) over the entire period. Though the attendance of both men and women has declined, the rate of decline has been essentially similar for both.

If sex differences do not explain the sources of attendance declines over the past two decades, what about age? Table 3 shows clear age differences in attendance throughout the period. For most of the period, the youngest age group surveyed (21–29) has had the lowest percentage of attendance. The middle (30–49) and older (50 and older) age groups have had roughly similar proportions attending with a slight edge overall going to the middle age group. These differences reflect important individual and family life cycle differences. What is significant is that the decline in church attendance since 1955 has not been even for all age groups. The youngest age group has a much more marked decline in attendance than the two older groups, a decline of 17 percentage points from 1955 to 1975.

This decline occurred during a time when the number of people in the 21–29 age group of the population was increasing dramatically, especially during the late 1960s and early 1970s, as a result of the "baby boom" following World War II. The overall size of the 50 and older age group was also on the increase during this period; however, the attendance rate of this group remained relatively constant, averaging about 46 percent of those surveyed. The middle age group declined in attendance by 11 percentage points over the past two decades, a decline greater than that of the oldest group, but considerably less than that of the youngest group.

Differences in attendance also seem to vary by educational level, though not as sharply as by sex or age. In all three levels of education summarized in Table 3, there have been declines in attendance over the past two decades. The greatest declines have been among the college educated and the least among those with only grade school education. We suspect that these educational differences in participation reflect the age-group trends. Younger people, who have increased in number, have also attended college with greater frequency; thus the declines in attendance by college-educated people likely reiterates the decline in attendance among the younger age group.

In some analyses of attendance by region of the country, using survey data from only one year, it has been reported that the "Bible belt" regions of the South

Table 3. Church Attendance for Selected Groups and Years
(Percentages of the U.S. Population for a Sample of Adults)

	1955	1961	1963	1964	1965	1967	1968	1969	1970	1975
National	49	47	46	45	44	43	43	42	42	40
Sex:										
Male	43	—	41	40	40	41	39	38	38	35
Female	54	—	51	49	48	49	48	46	46	45
Age										
21–29	47	43	41	39	37	—	34	33	32	30
30–49	52	47	47	47	47	—	46	45	45	41
50+	45	48	47	50	44	—	44	44	45	46
Education										
College	53	52	53	50	48	48	47	46	46	40
High School	49	47	46	44	44	44	43	42	41	39
Grade School	47	44	43	43	40	43	41	41	41	43
Region										
East	52	49	52	—	49	46	46	45	43	40
Midwest	49	49	48	—	44	48	45	46	47	44
South	51	47	46	—	44	47	44	40	44	43
West	38	36	35	—	34	34	32	35	33	29

Dashes indicate no data available for that year.
Sources: George H. Gallup, *The Gallup Poll: Public Opinion, 1935–1971.* New York: Random House, 1972.
The Gallup Opinion Index, *Religion In America: 1976.* Report No. 130, 1976.

and Midwest are leaders in church attendance, followed by the "cosmopolitan" East, with the "secularized" West bringing up the rear.[9] The Gallup trend data only partly support this pattern. Clearly the level of attendance is lowest in the West, but only in recent years did attendance in the East fall below that of the South and Midwest. Although attendance in all regions has declined, the decline has been greatest in the East and least in the Midwest. Catholics, who greatly outnumber Protestants in the East, very likely account for much of the Eastern decline.

The various differences in attendance reflected in Table 3 suggest some of the factors warranting consideration in interpreting the trends. Age in particular seems to be a significant factor and, to a lesser degree, education and region. We also saw that denominational differences among Protestants, probably reflecting theological differences, seem to be sources of differences in attendance patterns.

In Chapter 2, we cited information on religious preference trends among nonwhites from a study by Glenn and Gotard. This study also reports church attendance data from three points in time for nonwhites. From 1956 to 1966, attendance among nonwhite Protestants declined from 46.6 to 38.0 percent. From 1966 to 1973, nonwhite Protestant attendance increased by 5.6 percentage points to 43.6 percent.[10] Previously we noted the prediction that blacks would reject the church during the upsurge of civil rights activity of the 1960s. It may be that some of the attendance decline among nonwhites reflects this rejection; however, it is unlikely to be the sole cause of the decline. Since white Protestant attendance also declined during this period (though not so much as nonwhite), it seems that more general causes of attendance declines affecting both white and nonwhite Protestants were also at work. Furthermore, the increased attendance of nonwhite Protestants from 1966 to 1973, while white Protestant attendance declined very slightly, does not seem to reflect disenchantment by blacks with the church. In fact, if attendance trends may be taken as an indicator of the "health" of religious institutions, predominantly black denominations (in which most black Protestants are members) are in better "health" than predominantly white Protestant denominations.

FINANCIAL CONTRIBUTIONS TO THE CHURCH

Another important form of religious participation in American society is that of financial contributions to religious organizations. That these contributions should be included as an indicator of religious commitment might be interpreted as expressing the immensely practical nature of American religion. A story by comedian Bob Hope illustrates it well: "Once I was flying in a plane that was hit by lightning!" Hope said. " 'Do something religious,' a little old lady across the aisle suggested. So I did—I took up a collection."[11]

Why a person gives to religion is a complex issue. A 1975 study notes that giving to the church in the Middle Ages was seen primarily as a way of earning merit for one's redemption—"salvation at a price."[12] Not until the seventeenth century did reasons for giving shift away from a primary concern with one's own redemption to a concern for the welfare of others. When a large sample of United States and Canadian church members were asked in 1971 why they gave to the church, the majority listed "gratitude to God," followed by the beliefs that giving is a "part of worship" and that it is a "privilege to share."[13] We suspect that such factors as guilt, habit, and social pressure also play a role in patterns of giving to the church. Whatever the reasons, giving is clearly one way of participating in religion. Furthermore, if there is truth to Jesus' words that where one's treasure is, there is his heart also (Matt. 6:21), giving is an important indicator of personal religious commitment.

Giving is also important for the ongoing life of the religious organization for some of the same reasons that attendance is important. As voluntary associations independent of direct state support, religious organizations are very much dependent on the contributions of their constituents to support a wide range of activities. The magnitude of giving to religion makes this clear. Despite declines in giving to religion over the past decade, as of 1975 approximately 43 percent of all philanthropic giving in the United States went to religious causes.[14] The 1977 *Yearbook of American and Canadian Churches* summarizes contributions to forty-three United States denominations during the preceding year, not including Roman Catholics, Jews, and Orthodox Church members. The forty-three churches reported total contributions for 1974 of almost $5.7 billion, of which approximately $4.5 billion was spent for local congregational expenses and almost $1.2 billion for benevolences such as world missions or denominational support of institutions of higher education.[15] With this amount of money at issue, it is little wonder that the offering, rather than the sacraments or sermon, sometimes seems to be the high point of the worship service.

But what has been happening to giving to religion over the past twenty-five years? Has it also undergone decline? We have two ways of attempting to answer the question.

First, let us look at the overall pattern of giving in the private sector, including giving to religion. The Commission on Private Philanthropy and Public Needs, a privately initiated and funded citizens' panel to study philanthropic giving in the United States, reports that individual giving to all nonprofit organizations declined about 15 percent from 1960 to 1972, with the biggest decline in giving to religion, including giving to parochial schools.[16] The commission attributes most of the overall decline in giving to what has happened to religious giving. From 1950 to 1960, the period of the religious revival, giving to religion grew from approximately 53 to 56 percent of total philanthropic giving; however, between 1960 and 1974 it declined to just over 43 percent of the total. At the same time, the share of giving to health and welfare causes and to civic and cultural affairs increased from 1960 to 1974. Other giving, including giving to education, increased during the 1960s but has declined since 1970.

Our second set of data on giving sheds further light on the situation. Table 4 contains figures for per-capita giving to selected Protestant denominations from 1950 through 1975, adjusted to 1967 constant dollars to control for the effects of inflation. The pattern of giving in these selected denominations supports the overall trend we have noted. For most denominations there was a considerable increase in giving during the 1950s, generally greater than the percentage increase in per-capita disposable income (that income available after taxes and other general governmental payments such as fines and penalties). These were "boom" years for giving to religion. With few exceptions (for instance,

The Episcopal Church), the rate of increase in giving slowed in the early 1960s, and several denominations experienced decreases in giving (based on 1967 dollars) between 1965 and 1970, most of which have continued through the early 1970s. During this same period, per-capita disposable income increased steadily if not dramatically. Thus most denominations included in the table lost ground in giving, especially during the late 1960s and early 1970s, when compared with the trend in disposable income.

The differences and pattern of change among the various denominations are somewhat complex and make interpretation difficult. Several observations may be made. First, there are considerable differences in the amount of per-capita giving to theologically liberal denominations and to two of the conservative denominations included in the table—the Church of God (Anderson, Indiana) and the Church of the Nazarene. At the same time, another conservative group, the Southern Baptist Convention, is among the lowest in per-capita giving. The considerable difference in size of the denominations is certainly a factor. Both the Church of God and the Church of the Nazarene are relatively small. Southern Baptists, however, have the largest membership of all Protestant groups, and with such large numbers there is considerably more likelihood for

Table 4   Per Capita Giving by Full, or Confirmed, Membership to Selected Protestant Churches and Per-Capita Disposable Income, 1950–1975
(Adjusted to 1967 constant dollars)

Denomination	1950	1955	1960	1965	1970	1975
Church of God (Anderson, Ind.)	——	135.92	148.76	177.72	182.35	186.59
Percentage Change from the previous column		——	+9.4	+19.4	+2.6	+2.3
Church of the Nazarene	145.14	156.61	160.41	178.09	190.94	187.27
Percentage Change	——	+7.9	+2.4	+11.0	+7.2	−1.9
Episcopal	58.87	60.52	72.70	112.99	96.83	106.60
Percentage Change	——	+2.8	+20.1	+55.4	−14.3	+9.16
Lutheran Church in America°	49.26	68.08	82.23	83.90	83.33	79.16
Percentage Change	——	+38.2	+20.8	+2.0	−0.6	−5.3
Lutheran Church—Missouri Synod	68.75	95.18	108.39	112.84	107.88	99.20
Percentage Change	——	+38.4	+13.9	+4.1	−4.4	−8.75
Southern Baptist	39.58	55.54	62.75	62.65	65.97	71.93
Percentage Change	——	+40.3	+13.0	−0.1	+0.5	+8.3
United Church of Christ°	51.52	71.48	83.88	83.91	79.91	77.04
Percentage Change	——	+38.7	+17.3	+0.03	−4.8	−3.72
United Methodist°	37.25	53.45	62.93	60.58	67.10	62.97°°
Percentage Change	——	+43.5	+17.7	−3.7	+10.8	−6.5
United Presbyterian, USA°	55.30	84.63	95.03	101.30	99.44	105.45
Percentage Change	——	+53.0	+12.3	+6.6	−1.8	+6.04
Per Capita Disposable Income in 1967 Dollars	1982	2077	2183	2577	2903	3136°°
	——	+4.8	+5.1	+18.0	+12.6	+8.0

°Corrected for merger by including members of merged denominations for each time period.
°°1974 figure.
Dashes indicate no date available for that year.
Sources: Statistics of Giving, United Stewardship Council, Hillsdale, Michigan, 1950; *Statistics of Giving*, Joint Department of Stewardship and Benevolence, National Council of Churches, New York, 1956; *Statistics of Church Finances*, Department of Stewardship and Benevolence, National Council of Churches, New York, 1961, 1966; *Church Financial Statistics and Related Data*, Commission on Stewardship, National Council of Churches, New York, 1971, 1977.

a larger percentage of inactive (or at least noncontributing) members.

Second, the 1975 figures show that one of the conservative denominations, the Church of the Nazarene, lost ground in per-capita giving from their 1970 figure. During the same time giving to two of the most liberal denominations, the Episcopal Church and the United Presbyterian Church, increased. Actually, however, the United Presbyterians barely recovered from losses during the late 1960s to record only a slight improvement over the 1965 figure. The Episcopal increase for 1975 is still short of the 1965 level of giving with inflation taken into account.

Third, the losses sustained in the late 1960s by several denominations, including the Episcopal and United Presbyterian Churches, may have resulted in part from negative reaction by some members to the denominations' involvement in controversial social action efforts. To express their anger, some members may have voted with their pocketbooks. While such a reaction provides a partial explanation for the giving trends, as we illustrate more fully in Chapter 5, we do not find it wholly adequate. Most denominations, whether involved in controversial social action or not, experienced slower rates of increase or actual decline in per-capita giving during this period and on through the early 1970s.

Finally, the relationship between membership growth and growth in per-capita giving is not entirely clear. Through 1960, there seems to have been a strong positive relationship between growth in membership and per-capita giving. In the late 1960s and especially from 1970 to 1975, the relation is much less clear. The Church of God (Anderson, Indiana) and the Church of the Nazarene, both fast growing denominations, did not show corresponding increases in per-capita giving from 1970 to 1975, and giving to the Nazarenes actually decreased. Both the Episcopal and United Presbyterian Churches sustained membership loss during the same time, but their per-capita giving increased.

We are not left with a uniform explanation of the trends. What is apparent are the declines in per-capita giving that have been experienced by several denominations since 1965. Such declines have considerable impact on the work of national denominations and local congregations, both in services provided to members and to outreach efforts at home and abroad.

TRENDS IN DEVOTIONAL PRACTICES

We noted previously that the practice or ritualistic dimension of religion has a subjective or private area as well as the relatively objective or public behavior that we have considered so far. The former includes prayer, Bible reading, and other forms of devotional practice. Unfortunately, there is relatively little information that permits an examination of trends.

Three Gallup surveys[17] have reported the percentage of the population indicating that they have read the Bible within the past year—hardly a very rigorous test of the importance of Bible reading! In 1952, 67 percent reported Bible reading during the past year; that percentage declined to 62 percent by 1970 and then rose slightly, to 63 percent, by 1974.

A more demanding measure of trends in Bible reading is available in two studies of American religious beliefs and practices conducted for the *Catholic Digest* in 1952 and 1965.[18] The studies used representative samples of the United States population. While they cover only two points in time, they report, among other things, the percentage of individuals reading the Bible at least once a week. For Protestants surveyed, there was an increase of seven percentage points, from 40 to 47 percent, from 1952 to 1965. During the same period Catholic weekly Bible reading increased from 22 to 37 percent, a fifteen point increase. Although only 148 Jewish respondents are included in the survey, Jewish weekly Bible reading also shows an increase, from 14 percent in 1952 to 31 percent in 1965.

During the same period, however, the data show a decline among Catholics (from 88 to 82 percent) and Jews (from 45 to 17 percent) reporting a belief that "the Bible is really the revealed Word of God." Protestants remained constant at 85 percent. Thus among Catholics and Jews weekly Bible reading paradoxically increased at the same time that belief in the Bible as the revealed Word of God declined. What the Catholic changes seem to reflect is the spirit of Vatican II: an increased acceptance by lay people of responsibility for their own spiritual journeys, including Bible reading and interpretation, and a questioning of many traditional forms of authority, including the authority of the Bible.

Before considering other forms of devotional practice, we note one additional analysis of trends in Bible reading for a particular segment of the society—college students. Sociologist Dean R. Hoge summarizes several studies of students that show a decline in Bible reading since the early 1950s. At Haverford College, for example, Bible reading "several times a week" fell from 15 percent in 1952 to 3 percent in 1966.[19]

Data on personal prayer are even more scarce, with the *Catholic Digest* surveys our primary source. In both the 1952 and 1965 surveys, only 8 percent of those questioned reported that they never prayed; an additional 5 percent in 1952 and 9 percent in 1965 reported infrequent prayer. For each group the 1965 figures represented an increase in those never or infrequently praying (from 3 percent in 1952 to 8 percent in 1965 for Catholics, from 11 percent in 1952 to 14 percent in 1965 for Protestants, and from 28 percent in 1952 to 51 percent in 1965 for Jews). At the other end of the spectrum, those who reported praying three times a day or more decreased sharply from 1952 to 1965 for Jews (from 9 percent to 5 percent). For Catholics the decrease was less significant (from 28 percent to 25 percent). There was a slight increase for Protestants (from 21 percent to 23 percent). The primary reason given for praying in both years was to ask God for favors, help, strength, and guidance.[20]

During the period from 1952 to 1965, the largest declines in daily prayer were in the younger segments of the population. There was a decline of 20 percentage points for those between ages 18 and 24, and of 18 points for those between 25 and 34. These figures reflect declines similar to those found by Hoge in his analysis of college students. While the changes in those reporting the practice of prayer were not identical in all of the colleges surveyed, the direction of the changes—decline—was consistent.[21]

Even when we note the declines in the number of people reporting praying on a regular basis, the rather high percentage that continue to pray at least daily is remarkable. As psychologists of religion Michael Argyle and Benjamin Beit-Hallahmi suggest, prayer and other private religious acts are probably a good index of genuinely religious activity, "since non-religious motives are less likely to interfere." They note that in England, for instance, only 14 percent of the population attend church weekly, whereas 46 percent report saying daily prayers. The differences are of a similar magnitude in the United States.[22]

The Greeley, McCready, and McCourt study also provides trend data regarding the devotional practices of Catholics. Since it covers the decade from 1963 to 1973, it allows an assessment of the effects of the rather striking changes that took place in the Catholic Church after Vatican II. During that decade there were marked declines in a variety of traditional forms of religious devotion. The declines in weekly church attendance among Catholics that we previously noted are confirmed by the authors. In addition, they discovered that the percentage of Catholics practicing monthly confession declined from 38 to 17 percent; those visiting the church to pray at least once a week declined from 23 to 15 percent; and those saying daily private prayers fell from 72 to 60 percent. The percentage of Catholics attending a retreat within the preceding two years fell from 7 percent to 4 percent; those making a Day of Recollection, from 22 percent to 9 percent; and those making a mission, from 34 percent to 6 percent.

While more customary forms of religious practice have declined, practices such as charismatic or pentecostal prayer meetings, informal home liturgies, and marriage encounter sessions have increased; for instance, 60 percent of Catholics reported having taken part in charismatic prayer meetings. We concur with the authors that these changes in Catholic practice are dramatic and unprecedented.

We cannot close this subsection on trends in devotional practices without again mentioning briefly the burgeoning participation in the technologies of the spirit, which we referred to earlier. These are the various techniques, or technologies, employed to foster spiritual growth or, if a less religious description of the goals is preferred, to awaken inner experience. Unfortunately, there is little quantitative data available on these technologies, and none that allows us to assess trends.

Recent studies by sociologist Robert Wuthnow[23] provide some information gathered in interviews with a randomly selected sample of the population of the San Francisco Bay Area in 1973. The Bay Area is a particularly fertile seed bed for new religious movements and, as such, is probably atypical of the United States as a whole. Wuthnow estimates that, since the middle 1960s, over three hundred new religious movements have appeared in the Bay Area.

A list of thirteen new religious and quasi-religious movements was presented to Wuthnow's respondents. Each group on the list was known by at least some of the respondents, ranging from a high of 52 percent knowing about Synanon to a low of 6 percent knowing about est. The proportion of people reporting actually having participated in these groups is much smaller, ranging from a high of 7.9 percent in yoga to a low of 0.6 percent in the Christian World Liberation Front, a Berkeley-based part of the Jesus movement. Small though such percentages are—certainly even smaller if the sampling had been nationwide—the groups maintain themselves and possibly grow.

They are continuing to grow. Several of the technologies have been "packaged" and "marketed" over a wide area, thus becoming available to even larger audiences. A 1976 Gallup survey handed a card listing several movements to a representative sample of Americans and asked: "Which, if any, of these are you involved in or do you practice?" Four percent professed involvement in Transcendental Meditation, 3 percent in yoga, 2 percent in the charismatic movement, 2 percent in mysticism, and 1 percent in Eastern religions.[24] When the percentages are projected to estimate the approximate number of devotees in each movement, the figure becomes rather large; for example, 4 percent participation in Transcendental Meditation projects into approximately six million people. Only the United Methodist Church and the Southern Baptist Convention, among Protestants, have larger memberships, and the projected number for Transcendental Meditation is approximately the same as the estimated Jewish population of the United States. These size comparisons are made to indicate the magnitude of the appeal of these movements rather than to imply that such groups necessarily compete with established churches for members. Many participants in the new movements are also active participants in churches.

Another Gallup survey estimated that as many as

thirty-two million Americans express a belief in astrology, holding that their lives are governed by the position of the stars.[25] Twice as many women as men were among those professing belief in astrology; there were also virtually as many churchgoers as nonchurchgoers, which would likely also be true among those involved in some of the movements emphasizing spiritual disciplines. It would most certainly be true for charismatics and probably also for many involved in mysticism, yoga, and Transcendental Meditation. To borrow a descriptive phrase used in another context,[26] we might conclude that there are quite a few Americans who are "indiscriminately pro-religious."

Our interest in these movements is to make three points about them that are relevant to our concern with religion in America.

First, they have their greatest appeal among youth, especially among the more highly educated youth. Wuthnow found that non-Western movements, such as yoga and Krishna Consciousness and neo-Christian movements, such as Campus Crusade and the Children of God, were especially attractive to individuals between ages 16–20. The 21–30 age group were more likely to be attracted to non-Western groups such as Transcendental Meditation and Zen, and to movements such as Synanon and Scientology. Est was most attractive to the age groups from 31 to 50.[27] None of this is especially surprising. It is common knowledge that most of the new religious and quasi-religious movements have their greatest appeal to youth. But these findings form part of an emerging picture of the present youth generation of which we have had other glimpses previously. This generation, particularly those who are well educated, are less likely to join churches or synagogues or attend traditional religious services than the youth of the past might have been.

A second point is the considerable emphasis these movements give to inner change leading to self-fulfillment or self-realization. Most of the technologies, religious or humanistic, make self-fulfillment a primary concern. Social transformation, the major theme of the 1960s, is "out" in the 1970s; inner transformation is "in," or at least it is made a prerequisite for social transformation. As a popular magazine described them somewhat critically, the various technologies feed "on the romantic notion that inner experience alone can transform reality and that anyone can knead his life into a perfect work of art."[28]

Finally, there seems to be an increasing diffusion of these techniques into the life of the churches. Both laity and clergy are among the growing numbers of people taking part in workshops on personal growth and meditation techniques. Seminaries and other agencies conducting continuing education programs for laity and clergy are finding workshops in spiritual growth to be among their most popular offerings. Added to this is the

spread into mainline churches of the charismatic movement, which emphasizes personal experience of the Spirit.

For many mainline churches, especially Protestant ones, this diffusion has no doubt brought something of a jolt. During the 1950s and 1960s emphasis on spirituality and intense religious experience was not among the primary concerns of mainline Protestantism, especially the more liberal denominations. Such an emphasis was incongruous with the dominant secular rationality of the age and the concern for social change. Though the new technologies show a concern with techniques and results as did the positive-thinking movement of the 1950s, the similarities generally end there, and our hunch is that most mainline congregations of that period, and especially their clergy, would have been embarrassed by the recent concern with spirituality and religious experience. What the effects of the diffusion of these techniques will be is of considerable importance for the future shape of traditional religious organizations.

NOTES

1. Cited in A. Roy Eckhart, *The Surge of Piety in America* (New York: Association Press, 1958), p. 25.
2. See, for example, Robert Bellah, "Civil Religion in America," *Daedalus*, Winter 1967; and Martin E. Marty, *A Nation of Behavers* (Chicago: University of Chicago Press, 1976), pp. 180–203.
3. Marshall Sklare and Joseph Greenblum, *Jewish Identity on the Suburban Frontier* (New York: Basic Books, 1967), p. 49.
4. Sklare and Greenblum, 1967, p. 64.
5. In an analysis of church attendance patterns over a twenty-year period, Gallup reports the following distribution by months (in percent of the population):

January: 41	July: 43
February: 47	August: 42
March: 47	September: 43
April: 48	October: 46
May: 44	November: 43
June: 44	December: 45

(Gallup Opinion Index, *Religion in America, 1975*, Report No. 114, 1975, p. 2).
6. Gallup Opinion Index, *Religion in America, 1977*, Report No. 145, 1977, p. 32.
7. Andrew M. Greeley, William C. McCready, and Kathleen McCourt, *Catholic Schools in a Declining Church* (Kansas City: Sheed and Ward, 1976), pp. 29–30. The question about attendance asked of respondents in the Greeley, *et al.*, survey was worded differently from that asked in Gallup polls; thus, the percentages are slightly different. The overall downward trend in attendance, however, is quite similar.
8. Nathan Glazer, *American Judaism* (Chicago: University of Chicago Press, 1957), p. 113.
9. See Jackson W. Carroll and David A. Roozen, "Religious Participation in American Society: An Analysis of Social and Religious Trends and Their Interaction," photocopied report, (Hartford, Conn.: Hartford Seminary Foundation, 1975), pp. 104–106.
10. Norval D. Glenn and Erin Gotard, "The Religion of Blacks in the

United States: Some Recent Trends and Current Characteristics." *American Journal of Society,* vol, 83 (1977), p. 445.

11. Cited in Marty, *A Nation of Behavers,* p. 202.

12. Commission on Private Philanthropy and Public Giving, *Giving in America, Toward A Stronger Voluntary Sector* (Washington, D.C.: Commission on Private Philanthropy and Public Needs, 1975), pp. 62–63.

13. Douglas W. Johnson and George W. Cornell, *Punctured Preconceptions* (New York: Friendship Press, 1972), p. 35.

14. Commission of Private Philanthropy and Public Giving, p. 71.

15. *Yearbook of American and Canadian Churches,* (Nashville: Abingdon Press, 1975), pp. 252–253.

16. Commission of Private Philanthropy and Public Giving, pp. 71–74.

17. The surveys are AIPO 509 (1952), AIPO 821 (1970), and reported in the Gallup Opinion Index, *Religion In America, 1975,* Report No. 114, 1975, p. 7.

18. Martin E. Marty, Stuart E. Rosenberg, and Andrew M. Greeley, *What Do We Believe?* (New York: Meredith Press, 1968).

19. Dean R. Hoge, *Commitment on Campus* (Philadelphia: Westminster, 1974), pp. 65–66.

20. Marty et al., pp. 236–245.

21. Hoge, pp. 65–66.

22. Michael Argyle and Benjamin Beit-Hallahmi, *The Social Psychology of Religion* (London: Routledge and Kegan Paul, 1975), p. 3.

23. Robert Wuthnow, *The Consciousness Reformation* (Berkeley: University of California Press, 1976), esp. pp. 30–42; and Wuthnow, "The New Religions in Social Context," in *The New Religious Consciousness,* ed. Charles Y. Glock and Robert N. Bellah (Berkeley: University of California Press, 1976), pp. 276–293.

24. Reported in *The Hartford* (Conn.) *Courant,* November 18, 1976.

25. *The Hartford Courant,* November 18, 1976.

26. Gordon W. Allport and J. M. Ross, "Personal Religious Orientation and Prejudice," *Journal of Personality and Social Psychology,* vol. 5 (1967), pp. 432–443.

27. Wuthnow, "The New Religions," pp. 285–286.

28. "Getting Your Head Together," *Newsweek,* September 6, 1976, p. 62.

4

Trends in Religious Beliefs

Most people, if they were asked what the central dimension of religion is, would point to religious beliefs. Religious beliefs not only reflect conceptions of God, the universe, human nature, and the purpose of life, but they become interpretive frameworks, or perspectives, that are potentially significant for attitudes and behavior in other areas of life—social, cultural, economic, and political. The range of beliefs, what their consequences are for personal and social existence, and how beliefs and their consequences change over time are key questions in the study of religious trends.

It is, therefore, regrettable that data from two or more points in time on the religious beliefs of the American public are so sparse. There have been several important studies in recent years using survey data of a cross-section of the population to describe religious beliefs at a single point in time; however, the studies lack continuity. We can hardly fault the researchers for this lack, since there are so few previous studies on which to build. Nonetheless, we are left with a decided gap in our understanding of trends in religious beliefs. This gap prevents us from providing authoritative answers to several important issues relating to beliefs.

One such issue is secularization. Are we entering a post-Christian era? Have traditional Christian beliefs become less and less tenable in an ethos dominated by scientific rationality? What is the future of belief and of the churches that are its institutional carriers? Some scholars, such as Rodney Stark and Charles Y. Glock, assert that there has been a serious demise of core Christian belief which, if it continues, will leave "churches of the present form with no effective rationale for existing."[1] Others, including Andrew Greeley, strongly dissent from this analysis. Even if there has been a lessening salience of traditional beliefs, Greeley

believes churches fulfill other important functions as well, especially meeting "belonging" needs of their constituents.[2]

Another issue for which adequate trend data are needed is the emergence of what some, such as Martin Marty, have called a two-party system within Protestantism. There is, on the one hand, "private Protestantism," with its emphasis, as Marty says, on "individual salvation out of the world, personal moral life congruent with the ideals of the saved, and fulfillment or its absence in the rewards and punishments in another world in the life to come." On the other hand, there is "public Protestantism," made up of those who have been heavily influenced by European post-Enlightenment theological and social thought, and who believe that salvation includes social as well as individual transformation.[3] Over roughly the last century this two-party conflict has manifested itself in a variety of ways. Some of its more recent manifestations have been helpfully analyzed by cross-sectional surveys, but there is a need for more adequate trend data.

The inadequacy of data in large part is the result of the considerable difficulty in measurement of so complex a variable as religious beliefs. How, in a self-administered questionnaire or interview, can the variety of religious beliefs be summarized statistically? Further, there is the problem of salience. A person may indicate agreement with a particular belief statement, but agreement is not necessarily a test of the importance of the belief for the individual's view of life. These are not insurmountable obstacles to obtaining measures of belief, but they make such measurement, especially on a national scale, almost prohibitively expensive. Thus we are left with a limited number of trend studies of beliefs that we can summarize here.

Furthermore, we are not at all certain how much correspondence there would be between the belief profile trends of the general public and the theological trends mentioned earlier. The theological debates of the past twenty-five years have taken place, for the most part, in the academy—theological seminaries and university departments of religion—rather than in the parish churches. Though some of the more controversial debates have been reported in the media and discussed in sermons and lectures in the churches, they may not have seriously affected the overall beliefs of the church-going public. A study in depth of trends in the public's religious beliefs that measured both content and salience might reveal some correspondence to the theological ferment taking place in academic theological circles. The public's theology may not be as sophisticated or self-conscious, but large numbers of lay people may have been responding to the same general sociocultural ethos and asking questions similar to those raised by the academics.

A hint that this connection may exist came in 1963, with the publication of Anglican Bishop John A. T. Robinson's book, *Honest to God*. The book made understandable for a lay audience some theological themes debated in academic circles for a number of years. The book was liberating for many laity, as it helped bring to the surface troubling questions and issues that previously had been more often felt than expressed openly. Thus a sensitive measurement of the beliefs of the broad lay public over time might reveal a wrestling with issues of belief and unbelief comparable to that of the academic theologians.[4] Meanwhile, we can only speculate about such matters while reporting the data we do have.

BELIEF IN GOD

The first belief trend we consider has to do with Americans' belief in God. Findings from several studies are summarized in Table 5. As can be seen from the Gallup Polls, based on national samples, and the Detroit area studies, there is little variation over time in the American public's profession of belief in God, and that profession is made by over 90 percent of the population at each given time. The percentages decline only slightly between 1952 and 1965 in the two *Catholic Digest* surveys, which list only those who say they are "absolutely certain there is a God." A similar question of certainty of belief was asked in the Detroit studies in 1959 and 1971 of those who had responded to a previous question that they believed in God. In this case, in both years and especially in 1971, there is a decided drop in certainty of belief (from 68 to 48 percent).

This last finding illustrates an important point. Question wording in the 1959 Detroit area survey had implied that it was acceptable for a person to answer that he or she was "uncertain" about belief in God. The

Table 5   Trends in Belief in God, 1947–1975, from Selected Surveys
(Percentages of those polled)

1. *Gallup Polls:*°	1947	1953	1967	1975
Do you personally believe in God? (% "yes")	94	98	98	94

2. *Detroit Area Studies:*°°	1958	1959	1971	
a. Do you believe there is a God or not? (% "yes")	96.6	93.2	94.0	
b. Certainty of belief in God (% very sure)		68	48	
c. Asking what God would have one do in everyday decisions:				
Often ask	35		38	
Sometimes ask	46		41	
Never ask	19		21	
d. Possibility of being a good American without belief in God (% saying one can)	57		77	

3. *Catholic Digest Surveys‡*	1952	1965		
a. Percent absolutely certain there is a God:				
Total sample	87	81		
By religious preference:				
Catholic	92	88		
Protestant	87	85		
Jewish	70	39		
Other or none	55	45		
b. How people think of God:				
As a loving Father	79	73		
As supernatural power	17	19		
Other	5	7		
Don't believe or don't know	1	3		

°*Source:* American Institute of Public Opinion Surveys no. 407: November 1947; no. 513: March 1953; no. 750: August 1967. The Gallup Opinion Index, *Religion In America: 1976*, Report no. 130, 1976.
°°*Source:* Otis Dudley Duncan, Howard Schuman, and Beverly Duncan, *Social Change in a Metropolitan Community* (New York: Russell Sage, 1973), pp. 68, 70.
‡*Source:* Martin E. Marty, Stuart E. Rosenberg, and Andrew M. Greely, *What Do We Believe?* (New York: Meredith Press, 1968), p. 220. Used by permission of Hawthorn Books, Inc.

question regarding certainty of belief began by stating that "many people, including saints and great religious leaders, have had doubts . . . about God's existence."[5] Although the *Catholic Digest* also asked about the person's certainty of belief in God, it made no comment either way about the acceptability or unacceptability of an "uncertain" response. Thus it is possible that these differences in question wording rather than any real difference in the populations surveyed were responsible for the differences in the percentages. To admit lack of certainty, where one is not sure that it is acceptable to do so, may be difficult for a large portion of the American public. The social pressure of the interview situation may lead some people to give what seems to them to be a socially desirable answer to the question of belief (and certainty of belief) in God. This, plus the often simplistic, either–or way the question of belief in God is asked, should cause us to be somewhat skeptical about the overwhelmingly affirmative responses to the belief in God question. Pressure to give religiously acceptable answers may be decreasing.

In any case, we note in the *Catholic Digest* responses that Catholics have the highest certainty of belief for both years surveyed, followed relatively closely by Protestants. The large drop in certainty among Jewish respondents may reflect sampling error; if this is not the case, then clearly Jewish belief in God has declined significantly from 1952 to 1965.

We have not shown age-group trends from the *Catholic Digest* data in Table 5; however, they are revealing. While the percentage of all age groups expressing absolute certainty of belief in God declined slightly over the thirteen-year period, there was a decided drop (from 87 to 71 percent) in those in the 18–24 age group.[6] Considering the general tendency to give affirmative responses, this decline of 16 percentage points in the period between the two studies is a rather significant change.

It is interesting to compare the proportion of Americans expressing belief in God with that of other nations. A 1976 Gallup report summarized international responses to the question "Do you believe in God or a universal spirit?"[7] As compared with the United States figure of 94 percent, only India was higher, with 98 percent expressing belief; Japan was lowest, with 38 percent. In Western Europe as a whole, 78 percent expressed belief. Scandinavian countries were lowest among Western European nations, with 65 percent affirming belief. A 1948 Scandinavian survey showed 81 percent expressing belief in God. Britain and France had 76 and 72 percent, respectively who responded affirmatively in 1976, virtually the same as in 1968 and, for France, an increase of 6 percentage points since a 1948 survey. While there are enormous problems with such cross-cultural measurement of beliefs, the differences between the United States percentages and those of the Western Europeans, with whom we share most in cultural heritage, are striking. It would be tempting to cite these differences as proof that the United States is less secular than Western Europe, including Great Britain. Clearly the differences cited lend weight to such a claim, but alone they are insufficient evidence. It may be that American religion is no less secular than its European counterpart in spite of the considerable differences in belief in God. To determine this, we would need to know considerably more about how other religious beliefs and practices differ. We would need to know what belief in God means and the role it plays in the lives of those espousing it and in the society as a whole. These are important issues, but in the absence of

more adequate data, it would take us too far afield to consider them here.[8]

Returning to the trend data on American belief, it can be noted that people not only differ in the degree of certainty of belief, they also vary considerably in their conceptions of God. Such important differences are overlooked in the typically simplistic way the question of belief in God is usually asked. Sociologist N.J. Demerath, III, reports a study of the beliefs of college students, in which 86 percent of the sample affirmed belief in God when simple yes–no response categories were used. Later in the questionnaire, 45 percent responding (including one third of those saying "yes" to the earlier question) gave basically agnostic answers to a question regarding their conception of God.[9]

The only trend data on conception of God are from the *Catholic Digest* surveys. The data are summarized in Table 5. There was a decline of 6 percentage points in those thinking of God as a loving Father, with a 2 percentage point increase in those conceiving of God as a supernatural Power. As before we have omitted from Table 5 the age breakdown, but the data once again reveal differences related to age. It is the youngest age groups that show the largest decline in belief in God as a loving Father (from 80 percent in 1952 to 67 percent in 1965 for the 18- to 24-year-olds; and from 80 percent to 68 percent for the 25- to 34-year-olds).[10]

Two other questions related to belief in God are also included in Table 5. In the Detroit area studies respondents were asked, "When you have decisions to make in your everyday life, do you ask yourself what God would want you to do?" Over one third of the respondents in both 1958 and 1971 indicate that they do this often, and more than 40 percent say that they do so sometimes. Social scientists who conducted the study see these responses as reflecting habits of personal piety that continue, even though people seem "to feel less constrained to endorse conventional or official doctrines."[11]

The other data from the Detroit area studies indicate a considerable increase between 1958 and 1971 (20 percentage points) in those who do not make belief in God a necessary mark of being a good American. This seems to indicate an increasing theological rejection of the religious nationalism that highlighted the cold war mentality of the 1950s, and also the recognition of the growing religious pluralism of American society.

LIFE AFTER DEATH

A second aspect of belief for which trend data are available is that of life after death. Belief in life after death is variously expressed in Christian creedal affirmations as eternal life, the immortality of the soul (which is in actuality not a biblical conception but rather reflects Greek influence), or resurrection from the dead. However expressed, it is clearly a central theme of Christian orthodoxy; and, although its subtlety and profundity are impossible to capture in a single question of a public opinion survey, it has proved in various recent studies of beliefs to be a highly reliable measure of Christian orthodoxy.[12] Trend data reflecting belief in life after death are summarized in Table 6.

The Gallup Poll figures summarized in the table indicate responses to the question, "Do you believe in life after death?" Percentages for those answering "yes" were available for five years; complete responses (including "no" and "undecided") were available for only three of the years. The table shows that over two thirds of those sampled affirmed belief in a life after death in each of the five years. The proportion increased to almost three fourths of those surveyed during the 1950s, the period of the religious revival, declined by only one point by 1968 (to 73 percent), and dropped to 69 percent in 1975. While the percentage expressing belief shows an increase and then a slight decline, there has

been a steady increase from 1957 to 1975 of those saying "no."

In the Detroit area studies, the percentage expressing belief in life after death declined and the percentage expressing disbelief grew in almost equal proportions from 1958 to 1971. The percentage uncertain remained relatively constant.[13]

The *Catholic Digest* data, though based on a different wording of the question, are essentially similar to the Gallup findings, showing little decline in those saying "yes" between 1952 and 1965. The percent saying "no" increased only slightly. The breakdowns by religious preference show both Catholics and Protestants with high levels of belief and little decline. The Jewish respondents reveal considerable decline (from 35 to 17 percent). This sharp decline may reflect sampling error, but it is true that life after death is not a tenet of traditional Jewish belief. Overall, these data do not suggest significant increase in secularization unless the increased percentage saying "no" reflects a growing candor in the acknowledgement of unbelief, which may be a possible indication of secularization.

Several other questions on belief in life after death in the *Catholic Digest* surveys may be noted (data not shown here). Heaven was viewed by 72 percent of the respondents in 1952 and 68 percent in 1965 as a place where those who have led good lives are eternally rewarded. However, only 58 percent in 1952 and 54 percent in 1965 also believed in a Hell where the unrepentant are eternally damned, and only 12 and 17 percent, respectively, believed that there was any real possibility of going to Hell themselves. While these beliefs do not show much change over the time between the two surveys, they do seem to tell us about the content of beliefs about life after death. Evidently, it is easier to believe in a Heaven where the good are rewarded than in a Hell where the evil are punished. It is especially difficult to contemplate one's own fate as punishment in Hell. Of course, there is no way of knowing the extent of belief in earlier times in a literal Hell or the degree to which people feared damnation for themselves. We suggest that such beliefs would have been more widely held in the past and that there has been some erosion of belief, especially in the nether side of life after death.

In one other pair of questions in the *Catholic Digest* surveys, respondents were asked, "Which do you think you, yourself, are most serious about—trying to live comfortably; or preparing for life after death?" Although no significant changes occurred over time, the responses are quite interesting. Forty-six percent of the respondents in 1952 and 1965 said that they were most serious about trying to live comfortably, while only 20 percent (21 percent in 1952) said that they were most serious about preparing for life after death. Another 30

Table 6   Trends in Belief in Life After Death
(Percentages of those polled)

1. *Gallup Polls*°	1948	1957	1960	1968	1975
Believe in life after death:					
Yes	68	74	74	73	69
No		13		19	20
Undecided		13		8	11
2. *Detroit Area Studies*°°	1958	1971			
Believe in life after death:					
Yes	74	65			
Uncertain	12	13			
No (excludes those who do not believe in God)	14	22			
3. *Catholic Digest Surveys*‡	1952	1965			
Think soul will live on after death:					
Yes	77	75			
No	7	10			
Don't know	16	15			
Yes response by religious preference:					
Catholic	85	83			
Protestant	80	78			
Jewish	35	17			
Other or none	43	37			

°*Source:* Hazel Gaudet Erskine, "The Polls: Personal Religion," *Public Opinion Quarterly* vol. 29 (Spring 1965), p. 147.

Bradley R. Hertel and Hart M. Nelson, "A Post-Christian Era?" *Journal for the Scientific Study of Religion* vol. 13 (December 1974), p. 413; American Institute of Public Opinion Survey no. 625, February 1960; The Gallup Opinion Index, *Religion In America: 1976,* report no. 130, 1976.

°°*Source:* Otis Dudley Duncan, Howard Schuman, and Beverly Duncan, *Social Change in a Metropolitan Community* (New York: Russell Sage, 1973), p. 68.

‡*Source:* Martin E. Marty, Stuart E. Rosenberg, and Andrew M. Greeley, *What Do We Believe?* (New York: Meredith Press, 1968), p. 246. Used by permission of Hawthorn Books, Inc.

percent in both years indicated an equal seriousness about both. When asked which they thought they should be more serious about, 53 percent in 1952 and 46 percent in 1965 indicated life after death. In 1952 22 percent and in 1965 25 percent answered trying to live comfortably. While the only trend evident in the two questions is the decline of seven percentage points from 1952 to 1965, the overall pattern is interesting. Adjustment to this life was more important than preparation for life after death for almost half of the American public, and the two were of equal importance for an additional 30 percent. Although there seemed to be some unease about this (for example, the belief that preparing for life after death *should be* more important), living comfortably in this life clearly held a high value. Nothing leads us to suspect that the trend has reversed itself. It more likely has intensified.

Again, we have no comparable data from the past to suggest that this would have been different in earlier periods of our history; however, we suspect that there was a long-term change. One possible piece of evidence that this may be the case is found in an analysis by sociologists Louis Schneider and Sanford Dornbusch of themes in popular devotional and inspirational literature between 1875 and 1955.[14] Schneider and Dornbusch conclude that belief in an afterlife, while never a prominent theme in this genre of literature, seemed to even less central in the years following World War II. They detected since that time an intensified emphasis on the importance of religion for facilitating adjustment to this life. N.J. Demerath, III, noting Schneider and Dornbusch's conclusions, cites an analysis of the themes of hymns that found fear replaced by love and gratitude.[15] These studies, together with the data from the *Catholic Digest* surveys, suggest that belief in life after death, especially the fear of hell, has lost considerable power over the years.

Even if we are correct in assuming that there has been a long-term decline of the belief (or at least in some of its negative dimensions), we should nevertheless reiterate that, during the period of time that we are considering and for which we have trend data, there has

been relatively little change. And what change there has been seems to lie with specific groups. One further bit of evidence helps to locate where changes have occurred in belief in life after death over the past quarter of a century.

Table 7 contains the results of surveys from three years categorizing belief in life after death by age. Unfortunately, the age categories for the 1975 survey differ slightly from the preceding years, making comparisons difficult. Nonetheless, some indication of the effects of both age and time can be discerned in the table.

In the 1957 data there are no significant differences related to age with the exception of those age 65 to 75, who are slightly more likely to express belief; however, somewhat weakly in 1968 and more strongly in 1975, age differences are apparent. The under-30 population is increasingly less likely to acknowledge belief in life after death than the older groups (especially the oldest). Furthermore, those under 30 are more likely to express disbelief (saying "no") than uncertainty. This is further evidence that youth's recent attitude toward religion is not typical of the American population as a whole.

In addition to age differences, time differences are also evident. This is especially true among the under-thirty group—a decline of 11 percentage points from 1957 to 1975 in those indicating belief, and an increase of 12 percentage points in those indicating disbelief. There is less decline in those affirming belief among the older groups, but there are also increases in acknowledgement of disbelief rather than uncertainty. As we noted earlier, this may signify an increasing candor in the expression of disbelief. If so it is possibly an indication of secularization or at least of an apparent decrease in social pressure for conforming to prevailing belief patterns.

BELIEFS ABOUT JESUS CHRIST

Although belief *in* Jesus Christ is a core Christian doctrine, and beliefs *about* Jesus Christ are among those that tend to divide Christians into various parties, there

Table 7   Belief in Life After Death, by Age
(Percentages of those polled)

Age	1957			1968			1975°		
	Yes	*No*	*Undecided*	*Yes*	*No*	*Undecided*	*Yes*	*No*	*Undecided*
21–31	75	13	12	71	22	7	64	25	11
32–42	73	14	13	74	17	9	72	17	11
43–53	74	13	13	72	22	6			
54–64	70	13	16	75	17	8			
65–75	78	9	13	75	15	10	71	19	10
76 and over	75	12	12	83	7	10			

°Age categories for the 1975 data are *under 30, 30–49, 50 and older.*

Sources: Bradley R. Hertel, and Hart M. Nelson, "A Post-Christian Era?" *Journal for the Scientific Study of Religion* vol. 13 (December 1974); p. 413.

The Gallup Opinion Index, *Religion In America: 1976*, report no. 130, 1976.

are almost no national trend data on these beliefs. An exception is questions asked in the *Catholic Digest* surveys of 1952 and 1965.[16] Only one percent of the total sample in either year said that they did not believe Jesus Christ ever actually lived. Seventy-five percent in 1952 and 72 percent in 1965 indicated that they believed "he was God." Among neither Roman Catholics nor Protestants was there any significant change over time; however, in both years, more Catholics than Protestants (by 15 percentage points) ascribed to the belief. Age differences in belief were not great, but there was a decline of eight percentage points in belief among the 18- to 24-year-olds.

One other question can be cited, though it has more to do with the authority of the Pope than with belief about Jesus. In two national surveys of Catholics, respondents were asked if they believed that Jesus handed over the leadership of his church to Peter and the popes. In 1963, 70 percent thought that it was "certainly true" that he had done so; ten years later, only 42 percent agreed. Thus there appears to have been a substantial attrition among Catholics in belief in the pope as vicar or representative of Christ. This was further apparent in the 1973 survey, when only 32 percent of the Catholics believed it "certainly true" that the pope is infallible when he speaks on faith and morals.[17] These changes occurred over the period when Vatican II was having its major impact on the church.

BELIEFS ABOUT THE INFLUENCE OF RELIGION

We turn finally to a question that indicates a belief about the influence or consequences of religion than about religious belief per se. It is the question that has been asked in quite a number of Gallup surveys since 1957: "At the present time do you think religion as a whole is increasing its influence on American life or losing its influence?" Earlier we pointed out the vagueness of the word *religion* in such questions. What does it mean—Organized religion? Local churches? National denominations? Personal religious beliefs and behavior? All of these or none of these? Some scholars refuse to take the question seriously because of its vagueness. Another has suggested interpreting the question as a projective test of sorts, for which respondents supply their own meaning but which gives us an indication of the saliency of religion for them.[18] Whatever the meaning of *religion* in the question, the changes in responses have been dramatic over the eighteen years from 1957 to 1975. Table 8 shows the overall responses by year. We have not included breakdowns by various groups; however, where they provide insights into the change, we will note them here.

In 1957, near the peak of the postwar revival, 69 percent of the American public (66 percent of the Protestants and 79 percent of the Catholics) believed

Table 8 Trends in Belief About the Influence of Religion on American Life
(Percentages of those polled)

	1957	1962	1965	1967	1968	1970	1974	1975
Increasing	69	45	33	23	18	14	31	39
Decreasing	14	31	45	57	67	75	56	51
No difference	10	17	13	14	8	7	8	7
No opinion	7	7	9	6	7	4	5	3

Sources: American Institute of Public Opinion Surveys nos. 580, 655, 706, 742, 760, 779.

The Gallup Opinion Index, *Religion In America: 1975*, Report No. 114, 1975.

The Gallup Opinion Index, *Religion In America: 1976*, Report No. 130, 1976.

religion was increasing in its influence on American life. Only 14 percent believed that it was losing its influence. By 1970 the percentages had reversed. Seventy-five percent of the total population (including 75 percent each of the Protestants and Catholics) believed that the influence of religion was decreasing, while only 14 percent believed it was increasing. That is a remarkable change, and the fact that the percentages during these years increased and decreased in the same direction rather than erratically gives us some confidence that the changes were real. Since 1970 the trend appears to have started a reversal. In 1974 and 1975 a growing number of people believed the influence of religion was increasing, though the percentages were still far from the 1957 high.

When the responses over time are broken down for various groups, several interesting patterns occur.[19] Though more Catholics than Protestants believed that the influence of religion was increasing in 1957, by 1974 they were less likely to believe in an increase (34 percent for Protestants and 30 percent for Catholics). This is further indication of the considerable changes Roman Catholics have undergone in recent years.

Of particular interest are age differences. The sharpest declines in belief in the increasing influence of religion through 1970 were initially in the under-30 age group (from 67 percent in 1957 to 20 percent in 1967, to 14 percent in 1970). By 1968 there were only small differences among all the age groups. However, when the trend reversed in the 1974 and 1975 surveys, the youngest group led all age groups in believing religion's influence was increasing. In 1975, 44 percent of those under 30, 35 percent of those 30-49, and 40 percent of those 50 and older believed in an increasing influence of religion. Given our previous findings that suggest a lessened interest in religion among youth, these results seem surprising.

Do these statistics signal a return by youth to traditional forms of religion—especially Christianity? It is tempting to think that this is so; however, we are reminded of the popular song, "My Sweet Lord," by George Harrison. Upon first hearing the song, a Christian would be tempted to identify it as an affirmation of devotion to Jesus Christ—until one listened closely and heard the muted but distinct Hare Krishna chant in the background. Thus the changes in the youth population's belief in the influence of religion may not express a vote of confidence in the churches at all, but rather young people's attraction to nontraditional, often non-Christian religious expressions.

Apart from these trends among various subgroups, what do the overall changes reflect? We can only speculate. The 1960s were exceptionally turbulent years. Is it that amidst the rapid changes, especially scientific advances, religion was seen as a conservative, out-of-date institution that was losing its influence? Or could it be that, as the decade progressed, loss of confidence in the influence of religion was part of the general loss of confidence in most social institutions? Or do the declines reflect a negative reaction to the visible involvement of some clergy and laity, as well as national denominational boards and agencies, in controversial civil rights and antiwar activities? And does the present reversal toward belief in an increasing influence of religion reflect a turn back to religion among youth and adults, of which the various religious movements and interest in spirituality in and outside the established churches are a part? Are the changes a part of a generally conservative trend in society as a whole? There may be some truth to several or all of these suggestions, though they remain, of necessity, matters of speculation. We consider several of these possibilities in Chapter 5 as we try to account for the overall trends that we have noted.

A NOTE ABOUT THE TWO PARTIES

At the beginning of this chapter we made reference to Martin Marty's thesis of a "two-party" system within Protestantism, which is reflected in sharp differences in theological perspectives. Several cross-sectional studies have pointed to the considerable differences existing among the various denominations,[20] within particular denominations,[21] and between clergy and laity.[22] The two-party system also contributes to the contrasts between conservative and liberal church growth drawn by Dean Kelly in *Why Conservative Churches are Growing.*[23]

The trend data reviewed in this chapter are not, in our judgment, adequate to shed much light on the issue of beliefs. One of the data sources we cited heavily, the *Catholic Digest* surveys, has broken down the interview responses for several Protestant denominations; however, the number of people interviewed in most denominations was quite small, considerably increasing the probability of sampling error. Therefore, we chose not to report the denominational differences for the belief items.

In spite of the likelihood of sampling error, we should note that the various breakdowns by denomination in the *Catholic Digest* surveys appear to reflect a conservative–liberal spread across the denominations. Although the degree of conservatism or liberalism varies from one belief question to another, there are generally three discernible groups. At the conservative pole on almost all issues were Baptists and a group designated as "other denominations," presumably including most of the smaller sects. The middle positions were usually occupied by Methodists, Lutherans, and Presbyterians, with the order varying on particular issues. The liberal pole typically belonged to Episcopalians and Congregationalists (United Church of Christ). This ranking varies somewhat from that suggested by Glock and Stark, who distinguished four groups: (1) *fundamentalists* (Missouri Synod Lutherans, Southern Baptists, and a number of small sects); (2) *conservatives* (American Lutherans and American Baptists); (3) *moderates* (Disciples of Christ and Presbyterians); and (4) *liberals* (Congregationalists, Methodists, and Episcopalians).[24] Both rankings reflect the two-party system; however, they point to the need for treating the parties as positions along a continuum from liberal to conservative, or public to private, rather than as a simple dichotomy.

The growing number of self-conscious evangelicals within most denominations makes it likely that the two-party conflict will intensify in the years ahead. To be sure, there are significant differences among various evangelical (conservative) Christians, especially over the importance of individual as opposed to social-change efforts. Nevertheless, there is an increasing awareness among evangelicals of their common identity as born-again Christians. Whether such a common awareness will transcend and supercede existing denominations and create a new alignment of Protestants remains to be seen. In any event, further research on this important issue needs very much to be done, using a sufficiently large sample size to allow detailed analyses within and between denominations. Similar analyses of Roman Catholic differences are also needed. The two-party system in Protestantism may have its analogues within Catholicism. Controversies among Catholics over abortion, for example, and over moves of some bishops to de-Romanize the American church seem to reflect a Catholic version of the two parties. There is also further work needed on differences and similarities of the various ethnic traditions within Catholicism in the United States.

NOTES

1. Rodney Stark and Charles Y. Glock, *American Piety* (Berkeley: University of California Press, 1968), p. 223.

2. Andrew Greeley, *The Denominational Society*, (Glenview, Ill.: Scott, Foresman: 1972), pp. 127–155 (especially p. 138).

3. Martin E. Marty, *Righteous Empire* (New York: Dial Press, 1970), pp. 178 ff.

4. A measure of beliefs developed by Richard A. Hunt ("Mythological-Symbolic Religious Commitment: The LAM Scales," *Journal for the Scientific Study of Religion*, vol. 2 (March 1972), pp. 42–52) attempts this by allowing respondents to give a literal, symbolic, or antiliteral response to a number of Christian belief statements. Limited use of Hunt's scales has revealed them able to distinguish rather clearly among those who hold beliefs literally, those who reinterpret them symbolically, and those who reject them totally. While the scales do not lend themselves easily to adaptation in broad public opinion polls, they are one of several recent attempts to develop more sophisticated and sensitive approaches to the measurement of beliefs.

5. Otis Dudley Duncan, Howard Schuman, and Beverly Duncan, *Social Change in a Metropolitan Community* (New York: Russell Sage, 1972), pp. 69–70.

6. Martin E. Marty, Stuart E. Rosenberg, and Andrew M. Greeley, *What Do We Believe?* (New York: Meredith Press, 1968), p. 216.

7. Gallup Opinion Index, *Religion in America*, Report No. 130 (1976), pp. 12–16.

8. Examples of the view that there is little difference in the degree of secularization between Europe and America are Thomas Luckmann, *The Invisible Religion* (New York: Macmillan, 1967), and Bryan Wilson, *Religion in Secular Society* (Baltimore, Md.: Penguin Books, 1966). Arguing against this position and affirming that the genius of American religion has been its ability to incorporate the sacred and secular in a synthesis is Andrew M. Greeley, *The Denominational Society* (Glenview, Ill.: Scott, Foresman, 1972), pp. 127–155.

9. N. J. Demerath, III, "Trends and Anti-Trends in Religious Change," in *Indicators of Social Change*, ed. Eleanor B. Sheldon and Wilbert E. Moore (New York: Russell Sage, 1968), pp. 377–378.

10. Marty et al., p. 220.

11. Duncan et al., p. 69.

12. See, for example, Gerhard Lenski, *The Religious Factor* (Garden City, N.Y.: Doubleday, 1958); Stark and Glock, *American Piety;* and Bradley R. Hertel and Hart M. Nelsen, "Are We Entering a Post-Christian Era? Religious Belief and Attendance in America?" *Journal For the Scientific Study of Religion*, vol. 13 (December 1977), pp. 409–419.

13. In 1959 the Detroit area researchers asked the "life after death" question differently from 1958 and 1971, indicating that an "uncertain" response was permissible. Twenty-seven percent of the respondents gave the "uncertain" response, compared with 12 percent in 1958; 66 percent gave "yes" responses, compared with 74 percent in 1958. The wording of the question undoubtedly affected the answers. See Duncan et al., pp. 68–69.

14. Louis Schneider and Sanford Dornbusch, *Popular Religion: Inspirational Books in America* (Chicago: University of Chicago Press, 1958).

15. Demerath, p. 439. The hymn theme reference is to B. F. Crawford, *Religious Trends in a Century of Hymns* (New York: Carnegie Press, 1938).

16. Marty et al., pp. 224–226.

17. Andrew M. Greeley, William C. McCready, and Kathleen McCourt, *Catholic Schools in a Declining Church* Kansas City: Sheed and Ward, 1976), p. 33.

18. Demerath, p. 389.

19. See Gallup Opinion Index, *Religion in America*, Report No. 114, 1975, pp. 12–13.

20. See Stark and Glock, *American Piety*.

21. See Dean Hoge, *Division in the Protestant House* (Philadelphia: Westminister, 1976); and Wade Clark Roof, *Community and Commitment* (New York: Elsevier, 1978).

22. See Jeffrey Hadeen, *The Gathering Storm in the Churches* (Garden City, N.Y.: Doubleday, 1969).

23. Dean M. Kelley, *Why Conservative Churches Are Growing* (New York: Harper & Row, 1972).

24. Charles Y. Glock and Rodney Stark, *Religion and Society in Tension* (Chicago: Rand McNally, 1965), pp. 120–121.

5

Interpreting the Trends

How can we characterize the trends presented so far? And how do we make sense of the shape of American religious life that the trends reveal? This chapter addresses these two questions. We begin by making several summary observations about the trends.

A REVIEW OF THE MAJOR TRENDS

First, in the mainline Protestant churches, especially those that are moderate to liberal in theological and social perspective, there has been a pattern of initial growth followed by decline in most of the dimensions of religion for which we had data. A relatively similar pattern is also the case for Catholics and Jews. In most indicators—especially attendance and giving—the general tendency was growth during the 1950s, peaking somewhere between 1958 and the early 1960s. For most of the 1960s and into the early 1970s, there were declines of varying magnitudes in the several indicators. It is too soon to tell, but in the late 1970s there seemed to be a "bottoming out," if not a reversal, of some of the declines.

Most of the declines have been relatively small, much smaller than many of the radical critics of the churches and synagogues have suggested. Data can often be interpreted from contrasting points of view. Critics of organized religion and pessimists may see in the trends support for a long-term and continuing decline of American religious life; others may see them as temporary and not at all inexplicable in light of the turbulent period through which the nation has passed.

A second observation is that the declines have been greatest among youth and young adults (the under-30 age groups). Where we were able to separate out age-group trends, it was the under-30 group that had declined in attendance, Bible reading, prayer, belief in

God, and belief in life after death. Only in two instances were there countertrends. Youth were more likely to be participants in the newer religious movements outside the traditional religious institutions. And, after leading the declines through the 1960s in those believing religion's influence was decreasing, in 1974 and 1975 youth were most likely to believe its influence was increasing.

Do these declines among young people reflect a temporary phenomenon, a youth moratorium on various forms of social participation, including traditional religion? And will these youth return to religion once their moratorium is over? Or do the data reflect a more basic shift in the values and life styles of youth that has long-term implications for traditional religion?

A third inference from the trends is the apparent increase in openness in expressing an instrumental approach to religion. We have seen some evidence of a tendency to view religion as useful for some personal or social end rather than as an expression of devotion to God alone. Thus one is religious or participates in religion *in order to* gain peace of mind (as in the 1950s, "cult" of positive thinking), promote family solidarity ("the family that prays together stays together"), or achieve self-realization (as in some of the technologies of the spirit of the 1970s). Or perhaps, as we have noted, one participates in religion for the well being of the nation. We also pointed to an increase in the concern for adjustment to this life, in contrast to preparing for life after death.

This instrumental approach is not necessarily a new trend; there have always been strains toward it in religion. Magical practices may be interpreted as an extreme form of the instrumentality of religion, and magic has been around as long as religion. What seems to be on the increase is an openness in taking such an approach to religion.

Finally, growth seems to have occurred most frequently among two kinds of religious expressions. On the one hand are the conservative or evangelical Protestant churches. In several instances, especially church membership and giving, there is evidence that they have grown while the more liberal, mainline Protestant denominations have declined. On the other hand, growth has also occurred in the various nontraditional, often non-Christian, religious movements and in related quasi-religious movements that provide the technologies of the spirit. These movements, for the most part, are outside the mainline churches and synagogues, although some of them include participants who are also members of mainline groups. Thus both conservative and nontraditional religious expressions have grown, while mainline Protestantism, Catholicism and Judaism have declined. Much of the decline of Catholicism may be due to factors internal to the Catholic Church, as we will consider below. But what are the appeals of the conservative and nontraditional religious expressions? Or, conversely, why the declining appeal of the mainline religion?

To attempt to provide some answers to these and other important questions raised by the several trends is the task of this chapter. As we attempt this, we need to register several cautions.

First, the data we have summarized do not allow for very precise analysis of cause and effect. In many cases we have not had access to the raw data, and this prevents us from carrying out some of the more refined types of analysis that might have been desirable. Thus much of what follows involves making inferences about apparent relationships between variables that appear to make sense.

Second, we do not believe that the trends we have summarized can be reduced to any single cause, however tempting that may be. Single cause explanations of the trends—for example, secularization (however defined), demographic shifts, rejection of the social activism of the mainline churches in the 1960s, decline of strictness in these same churches, and so forth—attract attention. But to explain general trends by any one of these factors alone oversimplifies an exceedingly complex set of relationships. Thus we look not to single factor explanations but to the impact of multiple factors whose interrelationships we cannot always trace out or understand. Furthermore, we believe that identifying some of the multiple factors affecting the trends will help those concerned about the trends identify both the factors over which they have no control and those that are amenable to change. Four factors, or rather four sets of factors, will be considered.

FACTORS BEHIND THE TRENDS

Age Structure and Family Life Cycle

We begin by considering the effects on religious participation of age, including the changing age structure of the population and the family life cycle, which is obviously related to age.

The relationship of age to various forms of religious participation has been well documented in previous chapters. To take but one example, church attendance was lowest for youth and young adults, and it increased through middle and older adulthood. This pattern makes sense when we think of it in terms of the "typical" family life cycle and its relation to religious participation. A recent article by the sociologist of religion Widick Schroeder summarizes this relation:

The "typical" American Protestant begins his involvement in an American church in Sunday School. This "American" institution . . . is a central enterprise in the typical American Protestant church. Volunteer teachers give generously of their time and talent, and parents prod their offspring into relatively frequent attendance, particularly in the grammar school years.

The typical American Protestant reduces his church participation markedly in late adolescence and early adulthood. During this period of his life, a person is leaving his family of origin and is making the transition to the adult world. . . .

After people form families of their own, they are likely to increase their involvement in church life. As did their parents before them, people in their late twenties or early thirties are likely to desire religious instruction for their children. Consequently, they are apt to reaffiliate as their children reach Sunday School age, for they feel some increased responsibility to participate in the institution to which they are sending their children for religious instruction. Finally, as their children mature and leave this family of origin, some parents are inclined to reduce their involvement or to disaffiliate themselves.[1]

Schroeder restricts his description to the "typical" Protestant; however, it also seems to apply to Jews as well. In their study of Jews in an American suburb, Sklare and Greenblum found that the presence of children in the home was strongly associated with the parents' decision to join a synagogue. Parental satisfaction with the synagogue was typically based on its attractiveness for children and youth and its ability to nurture in the children a sense of Jewish identity. When the children had left the home, many parents continued to participate in the synagogue. Their motivation for participation shifted from parental responsibility for their children's religious nurture to an expression of their own sense of belonging to the Jewish community and their recognition of the synagogue as a central institution of Jewish life.[2]

While the life-cycle explanation for church and synagogue involvement seems to hold for Protestants and Jews, it apparently does not apply as well to Catholics.[3] Why there is a difference between Catholics and the other two groups is not clear. Apparently norms supporting church involvement as a family responsibility are not the same in the differing religious traditions.

Our data in Table 3 showed only the relation between age and church or synagogue attendance, without controlling for religious preference. Furthermore, the relation between age and attendance is not the same as that between family life cycle and attendance, which focuses not only on age but on the presence or absence of school-age children in the home. Even with these limitations, there is a reasonable similarity between Schroeder's typical Protestant family life cycle description and the pattern of church attendance by age group in Table 3, although the older adults in our data seem to participate more regularly than Schroeder's picture suggests.[4] More important, the family life cycle portrait also helps to interpret the trends in participation that we observed. To appreciate the relation between age and attendance, however, we need one further set of data—trends in the age structure of the population for this period, which are summarized in Table 9.

As Table 9 shows, there was spectacular growth during the 1950s in the under-20 age group—children, adolescents, and youth—a slight decline in the 20–34 age group, and increases in both the older age groups, especially those 65 and older. Growth in the 65 and older group was almost equal to that of the under 20 group. As Schroeder notes, growth was considerable in those age groups from whom church members (and attenders) were most likely to be drawn, especially children (therefore also likely involving their parents) and older adults. Growth was less among age groups least likely to join or attend a church, especially young adults. This corroborates an earlier finding by the anthropologist Dennison Nash. Comparing the size of church membership from 1950 through 1966 with the number of families with children under 18 in the total population, Nash found a very high correlation between the two variables. He concluded, as did Schroeder, that the swelling of the church membership rolls during this period was due in large part to parents who were involved out of a desire to have their children participate in Sunday school and other aspects of church life.[5]

In 1958 the birth rate began a sharp decline that has continued through the mid-1970s; however, it may have begun an unexpected increase at the time of this writing. During the 1960s the under-20 age group grew by only 11 percent, while the 20–34 age group grew by almost 25 percent. Moreover, there was only an 8 percent increase in the 35–64 group. In the first half of the 1970s, there was a decline in the under-20 group, while the number of 20- to 34-year-olds continued to increase sharply.

Thus just as much of the rapid growth in religious membership and participation during the 1950s seems attributable to population growth in those age groups most likely to participate—parents and their children—so also do the declines in membership and participation that set in in the 1960s seem to reflect age-structure changes. Older youth and young adults, those least likely to participate, grew rapidly, while the growth in the parent and child age groups slowed considerably.

There are two other pieces of evidence that support our interpretation of the trends. One is a comparison of church membership trends with those of the national Parent–Teacher Association (P.T.A.).[6] From 1955 to 1960, P.T.A. membership increased by 30.5 percent, Catholic Church membership increased by 26 percent, and Protestant church membership by almost 9 percent. All three groups continued to grow, but much more slowly, during the early 1960s. Beginning in 1965 P.T.A. membership began to decline, paralleling in many respects the declines in several mainline Protestant denominations. Indeed, from 1970 to 1974 P.T.A. membership losses (− 25 percent) considerably outstripped church membership losses, and one news story reports 1977 P.T.A. membership lower than that of 1951.[7] It appears that age structure and family life cycle factors are operative in the P.T.A. as well as in the churches.

More corroborative evidence comes from two studies by denominations of membership trends. Schroeder's portrait of the typical family life cycle mentioned the prominent role of the Sunday school in attracting parents of school-age children. In United Methodist and Episcopal studies of church membership trends, there appears to be a sequential attendance and membership pattern. Changes (either growth or decline) in Sunday school attendance are followed within a year by similar changes in Sunday school enrollment. Within two to three years, corresponding changes occur in attendance at Sunday worship. Within five or six years, church membership changes can also be observed.[8] These patterns lend support to the interpretation of membership and participation changes by age structure and family life cycle changes, clearly suggesting that parental church membership and participation are related to having children of school age (who might attend Sunday school) present in the home.

It would be appealing to leave interpretation of trends to this rather straightforward and, we believe, important explanation. Yet there are several questions that may be raised. Why, for example, the rather dramatic rise in the birth rate that began about 1940 and then sharply declined beginning about 1958? Or again, why were the early to mid-1950s marked by rather high levels of religious participation by older youth and young adults in contrast to their "typical" participation patterns? And, once youth and young-

Table 9 Percentage Change in United States Population by Age Groups, 1950–1974 by Decade

	Under 20	20–34	35–64	65 and over
1950–1960	+34.6	− 4.7	+15.1	+34.5
1960–1970	+11.0	+24.8	+ 7.7	+20.4
1970–1974	− 2.3	+14.2	+ 1.6	+ 8.6

Source: Adapted from U.S. Department of Commerce figures.

adult participation began to decline in the late 1950s, why did it continue to do so at a greater rate than that of elders throughout the 1960s and into the 1970s? Factors other than age structure and family life cycle are also important.

Values and Religious Participation

We believe that the religious trends also reflect broad shifts in more general values and attitudes, which, in turn, reflect the impact of historical circumstances and events. Dean R. Hoge, in his analysis of college students cited earlier, points to a cluster of value commitments and attitudes that were widespread during the early to middle 1950s. Along with commitment to orthodox religious beliefs and high rates of participation, college students exhibited: a fear of communism or subversion; a tendency to conform to the norms and expectations of others rather than to risk expressing individuality; commitment to family life; commitment to military duty and patriotic war; low interest in political activity; and low level of criticism of college education.[9] The entire cluster of values and commitments suggests a focus more on personal and private concerns than on social and public concerns.

The students' values reflect a response to the underlying anxiety occasioned by such circumstances as the postwar economic boom and its attendant stress and insecurity; an unprecedented (at that time) high population mobility; life in the new suburbs; and, above all, the stress of the cold war, in which communism was frequently portrayed as the anti-Christ. In such an ethos, religious commitment was seen as a bulwark for the family and for the nation. The general concern of parents for their children to have the benefit of Sunday school was probably heightened under the circumstances.

This same cluster of attitudes and value commitments, which includes a commitment to family life, may also account in part for the sharp rise in the birthrate in the 1950s. The economist Joseph J. Spengler argues that fertility is one way in which young adults express their satisfaction or lack of satisfaction with family life. Thus the baby boom in the 1950s is in part the reflection of a high commitment to family life.[10]

If the trends in religious belief and participation of the 1950s were related to these more general values, we believe the same to be true for the trends of the 1960s and beyond. That there were profound shifts in values and attitudes as we moved from the 1950s into the 1960s is easier to demonstrate than to explain; nevertheless, the attitudes and value commitments of the former decade were virtually stood on their head in the 1960s, for a significant segment of the population. By the middle to late 1960s, there were among many youth and young adults: little fear of communism or subversion, but rather considerable rejection of the capitalistic system; little emphasis upon conformity to social norms and considerable emphasis on individual freedom and autonomy; little commitment to traditional family life and considerable experimentation with new forms of marriage and family styles that would enhance freedom; widespread refusal to accept military duty and revulsion against notions of a patriotic war; considerable political activism to bring about social change; and radical critique of educational and other institutions. And, as happened in the 1950s, religious beliefs and practices changed along with these values.

But the shift in values that occurred in the early 1960s was not as evenly distributed across the population as the value changes of the previous decade. The new values seem to have been much more readily adopted by youth and young adults. Older adults (over age 30) appear to have maintained, to a considerable extent, commitment to the family and other values suggestive of traditional forms of involvement. A national study of the values of adults in the late 1960s found 62 percent indicating family as a major value commitment. This same group also expressed concern over what they perceived as a declining interest in religion.[11] To be sure, there were some older adults who were also affected by the value changes and whose religious commitment declined, but the value changes appear to have been greatest among youth and young adults.

Several factors may cause these differences. One is the impact of the peculiar historical events of the period. As we noted in Chapter 1, the 1960s were a decade filled with events that brought exceptional change and upheaval, and the impact of such events on value commitments was likely to have been great. This, however, is not an adequate explanation, since adults would have experienced the same historical changes. A second factor seems to be what analysts of social change call a cohort difference. This term refers to entrance into the young adult population of a new generation (a new cohort) very different from the preceding young adult population that the new cohort replaced. Perhaps, as Margaret Mead suggests, youth of the 1960s, born since World War II, had different life experiences during their formative years and were better able to recognize the contradictions and destructive potential of what their elders had wrought than the generation that preceded them could.[12] This may explain why they reacted differently from their predecessors to the historical circumstances that coalesced to shape the 1960s. Third, social conditions, including mass communications and the concentration of greater numbers of youth than ever before on college and university campuses, facilitated the diffusion of these values and attendant symbols and styles that were self-consciously different from those of their elders.

Yet another change of mood set in near the beginning

of the 1970s, as we suggested in Chapter 1. The radical social protests receded and in their place came increasing cynicism and disillusionment about the possibilities of change. Thus there has been a shift away from a concern with the social and public and a renewal of interest in the personal and private.

But this shift is not back to the values and commitments of the 1950s, because social conditions are not the same. Rather, the 1960s themes of individual freedom, autonomy, and tolerance of diversity continue, but without a correlative social emphasis. Now personal fulfillment, not social change, is the goal. Comparing survey data on student values of the late 1960s with those of the 1970s, pollster Daniel Yankelovich summarized the trends as follows:

Just a few years ago, the country was reduced to near panic by what seemed to be the wholesale alienation of college youth. . . . [Now] most college students accept the necessity for hard work as a fact of life. They do not shirk it or shrink from it. At the same time what they regard as a proper payoff for hard work has shifted dramatically.

Students specifically reject a nose-to-the-grindstone philosophy of life. They do not subscribe to the old credo that if they work hard, stay out of trouble, and put their responsibilities to family and others ahead of their own personal satisfactions, then they will be rewarded with a good living, economic security, enough money to buy possessions, a nice place to live, and a good education for their kids. What they see instead is the active pursuit of a career as a means to self-fulfillment, with money, security, and possessions included in the overall scheme, partly taken for granted, partly demanded as a matter of right, but subordinate to the main goal of finding just the right life-style for expressing their psychological potential.[13]

The freedom and self-fulfillment themes seem to be part of the widespread appeal of some of the new religious and quasi-religious movements that we considered in Chapter 2 and the instrumental orientation noted earlier in this chapter. These themes, however, are not relevant to more traditional forms of religious participation. In an analysis of a large cross-sectional sample survey of the United States population, we found that a cluster of value and attitude statements emphasizing freedom, autonomy, and tolerance (we called it a "New Morality Index") was negatively related to church attendance. Although youth and young adults were more likely to score high on the New Morality Index, there were some older adults who also had high scores, and their attendance was similarly low. Furthermore, the Episcopal Church, followed by the Presbyterian Church, had a greater percentage of members ascribing to these values than did other denominations; Baptists had the least.[15]

Unfortunately, we do not have trend data on these values; thus we do not know how widespread they may have been in the past or what their past effects on religious participation have been. If, however, they persist and become increasingly widespread, as some students of long-term religious and social change suggest, their consequences for the churches may be profound.

The Effects of Denominational Activities

The two sets of factors considered thus far in interpreting the trends are essentially external to the churches; that is, they are part of the context in which the churches function. We turn now to factors that are more or less internal, beginning with the policies and practices of the churches at the national level.

A frequently offered interpretation of the decline in membership and participation of the 1960s is that it reflected a negative reaction to the social activism of the churches. The criticism was particularly strong of the various social action programs undertaken by the denominational bureaucracies and by ecumenical agencies such as the National Council of the Churches of Christ (NCC). These agencies, both denominational and ecumenical, engaged in a number of visible and controversial activities to promote racial justice and to oppose the war in Viet Nam. Several activities on behalf of racial justice may be cited as illustrations.

The Commission on Religion and Race of the NCC played an active role in the Selma (Alabama) march of 1964; recruited and trained volunteers for voter registration and other civil rights activities in the South; appealed strongly for the passage of the Civil Rights Act of 1964 and the Voting Rights Bill of 1965; and played a considerable role in the work of the Delta Ministry, an important grass-roots organization for economic and social development among impoverished rural sharecroppers in the South. Several of these activities were undertaken in cooperation with Catholic and Jewish agencies.

In addition to NCC activities, several denominational agencies joined in 1968 to create the Interreligious Foundation for Community Organization (IFCO), to provide a channel through which church funds and other money could reach black and other minority communities and grass-roots organizations. In 1967 the Episcopal Church created a General Convention Special Program as a response to needs of the poor in urban areas. Grants were made to a wide variety of local community groups, both church and nonchurch related, that were attempting to address urban issues. Many of the issues addressed were highly controversial, and some of the groups funded were reported to be vocally antichurch. An agency of the United Presbyterian Church in the U.S.A. contributed $10,000 in 1971 to the Angela Davis Marin County Legal Defense Fund. The Fund had as its purpose to assist in Ms. Davis's trial for conspiracy in connection with a courtroom kidnapping and subsequent shoot-out in which a judge and three others were killed. Ms. Davis had previously gained widespread national publicity as a leading black spokesperson against racism. She was also an avowed Marxist whom the regents of the University of California at Los Angeles had tried to fire from her teaching position. Thus it is not surprising that the denomination's support of her defense fund was controversial.

What were the consequences for the churches of these and similar actions? This is a difficult question to answer, since clear data are not available. Two points, however, may be made.

First, there was considerable negative reaction from the denominational constituencies to those activities that were highly visible and widely publicized. The reactions ranged from a massive outpouring of letters of protest to the Angela Davis contribution, to attempted withdrawals of entire organizations from parent bodies. Other forms of protest were withholding giving to national denominations and redirecting giving to noncontroversial projects that met the approval of local church constituencies.

The United Presbyterian experience in the Angela Davis affair seems to have resulted in such redirected giving rather than in any significant cancelling of giving in general to the church.[15] The declines in giving from 1965 to 1970 (see Table 4) may have stemmed from a negative reaction to social action, but they preceded the Angela Davis experience. On the other hand, the Episcopal Church's General Convention Special Program seems to have resulted in cutbacks in giving; one Episcopal rector reported a loss of $20,000 in pledges in a five-day period as a result of negative reactions to this program.[16] The sharp declines between 1965 and 1970 in per-member contributions to the Episcopal Church, noted in Table 4, no doubt reflect this negative response. One national study of Protestant church members estimated that approximately 6 percent of members withheld funds because of the social involvement of the churches.[17]

Although giving appears to have been affected by social involvement, we are not inclined to attribute much of the membership and attendance loss directly to this negative reaction. The declines, especially among Protestants, are too constant over the years to reflect responses to particular actions by the denominations. Furthermore, attendance declines set in before social involvement of the churches became a major issue.

The second point regarding the effects of social activism by the national denominations on participation concerns a less direct but, in our opinion, more important influence. The 1950s was a period of considerable growth in church membership and participation. It was also a period when church extension—organizing new congregations—was a major priority of the home mission boards of most denominations. Millions of dollars were raised for new church building. A history of the

first twenty-five years of the National Council of Churches reports that 3,198 new local churches were established from 1954 to 1957. A National Council of Churches projection for the future called for 2,000 new churches per year for the next twenty years.[18]

What was the fate of these projections in the 1960s and 1970s? By the beginning of the 1960s, one after another criticism began to be leveled at the churches for their "sell-out" to the "numbers and success game," and for their irrelevance in the urban crisis and the struggle for racial justice. Responding to these emerging social issues and to the criticisms, denominational leaders shifted priorities. Among the major changes of the more liberal denominations was a shift from new church development to the programs of social and economic justice mentioned above. The shift was dramatic: In 1960 new church construction totaled $889 million; in 1970 the total had dropped to $494 million, a decline of almost 44 percent.[19] The United Presbyterian Church, which had started an average of 70.1 new churches per year from 1950 through 1962, established only 29.8 per year between 1963 and 1973, and a large number of these were ethnic churches. On the other hand, the Southern Baptist Convention, which has not shown membership decline, averaged 95.2 new churches per year between 1963 and 1973.[20]

New churches do not necessarily mean large increases in overall membership. They are, however, successful in attracting members of the denomination who move to new areas. Over 57 percent of the members of new Methodist churches established between 1950 and 1958 were already Methodists who transferred their membership to the new churches.[21] Nevertheless, the retention of many mobile members or, correspondingly, their potential loss had new churches not been established, indicates the significant role of new church development.

Thus the shift in priorities away from new church development to support of social concerns seems to be an important factor in understanding trends in membership and participation during the 1960s. We are not criticizing here the shift in priorities. Rather, our concern is to point out that membership losses in many denominations during the 1960s were more likely a result of the shift in priorities than of a wholesale defection in protest to social action. Had the churches been able to manage both social activism and new church development, the declines might not have been so severe. In actuality, however, what might be called a "no-growth theology" took hold, and social involvement came to be set in sharp opposition to church extension, not only on economic but also on theological grounds.

The actions of national denominations that we have considered thus far apply clearly to Protestant bodies, and they are no doubt also partly applicable to Catholicism. However, declines in Catholic religious practice that were considered in Chapter 3 must be explained primarily by factors unique to Catholicism. Church attendance declines for Catholics began in 1958, as did Protestant declines (see Figure 4). The trends for both religious bodies were roughly comparable until the middle to late 1960s, when Catholic attendance began a sharp slide and Protestant attendance generally levelled off. Clearly, something unique to Catholicism took place.

In an analysis of these changes, Andrew Greeley and his associates used data from national samples of Catholics in 1963 and 1973 to test several theories about the declines: (1) that the changes during this period reflected basic demographic and educational changes in Catholicism, as Catholics became more Americanized and acculturated; (2) that the declines were part of a reaction against the Second Vatican Council by ordinary Catholics angered at the changes engendered by the Council; (3) that the changes resulted from the "meat on Friday" syndrome—that is, that there was so much relaxing of traditional Catholic requirements that the whole structure of obligations, including Mass attendance, was called into question; and (4) that the declines were triggered by a negative reaction to the papal administration of Paul VI, especially by his 1968 encyclical, *Humanae Vitae*, which reaffirmed traditional proscriptions against birth control despite widespread expectations to the contrary.[22]

Tested against the data from the national samples, the first three theories were not sustained. A part of the decline was explained by cohort differences, that is, by differences between generations of Catholics in the population. The younger generation—those born since 1944—were lowest in their religious practices. In addition to cohort differences, however, the most powerful explanation of the declines was found in the fourth theory. As Greeley and his colleagues express it, "The decline in Catholic religiousness . . . is in part the result of a joint decline in the acceptance of the pope as a leader in the church and acceptance of the church's sexual ethic."[23] The two are obviously linked; the authors suggest that people first disagree with the church's sexual teaching, reject the authority of the leader who reaffirms that teaching, and then become estranged from other aspects of the church's teaching and practice. The Second Vatican Council, rather than contributing further to the declines, seems to have mitigated them by giving encouragement to some Catholics who otherwise would have been even more alienated by the Encyclical. The point made by Greeley and his associates is well illustrated in a recent cartoon. A group of bishops, having reaffirmed the Pope's teaching in the Encyclical, are standing in the door of a church. One bishop says to the others: "Well, we've solved the birth-control problem, the abortion problem and the sex problem—now, what do you suggest we do about the attendance problem?"[24]

Thus it is not simply changes external to the churches that have affected the trends. Decisions and actions of the churches themselves at the national and international levels have also been at work.

Local Factors and Religious Trends

The factors we have considered so far in interpreting the trends have been general social changes or the actions of national church bodies. As important as these factors are in explaining the trends, it is important to remember that people join and participate in *local* churches and religious groups. What leads them to join and participate, or decide not to do so, are often very particular, highly local factors—for example, the perceived or experienced quality of a particular local church or synagogue's life, the influence of a particular minister or rabbi, or stability or change in the community surrounding the church or synagogue. Such local factors may outweigh the effects of broader ones, mitigating, counteracting, or exacerbating them.

Because local factors are often unique to their settings, we cannot easily generalize about them in explaining the trends we have noted. In fact, unless the factors at the local level are common to a large number of churches and synagogues within the same time period, they are not likely to be of help in trend analysis. It is possible, however, to identify some local factors that seem to be generally operative and important for interpreting the trends. We restrict our discussion to churches; much of what we describe, however, is also applicable to synagogues.

First, there are the effects of changes in the immediate communities in which churches are located, and attendant changes in the residents of the communities. Consider the following scenario:

Congregations—expecially Protestant congregations, which are based on voluntary membership—are, in their early years, reflective of their immediate communities, tending to draw members from the immediate geographical area. Furthermore, because most American neighborhoods are generally homogeneous economically and socially, congregations typically reflect this homogeneity. Like attracts like, so that in some cases a given denomination may have several distinct local churches in the same town or city, each with a style or ethos reflecting something of the particular characteristics of its dominant membership. Thus there may be in the same small town several United Methodist churches—one that is predominantly white middle class, another that is also predominantly white but with a blue-collar constituency, and another that is predominantly black. The shared Methodist heritage may be all that the churches have in common.

As time passes, communities change. Their residents move or die, new residents move in, often with socioeconomic characteristics, cultural backgrounds, and life styles that differ from the previous residents. Or businesses or industry may be established and alter the residential character of the community. New suburbs may be developed. Such changes obviously do not leave the churches unaffected. Some older churches are able to incorporate newcomers effectively, especially when the newcomers do not differ significantly from older members in their cultural backgrounds and life styles. New congregations may be established to attract the new residents, or some of the older congregations may move to a new location where the residents are thought to be similar to the membership of the church. And others—probably most congregations—remain in their settings, trying to hold on to their mobile membership, which lives increasingly distant from the church building.

This scenario, based on both social ecology and social status factors, is fairly descriptive of what has happened in community after community across the country. These community changes, in turn, are the result of other broader changes, such as massive rural to urban migration (apparently beginning to abate in the mid-1970s), economic and social changes that have profoundly affected life in many central cities, and the rapid growth of suburbs and exurbs (small communities beyond the suburbs). The effects of such changes on church membership and participation trends have been considerable.

These effects have been documented for one Protestant denomination, the Reformed Church in America, in research by denominational administrator Douglas A. Walrath.[25] Walrath developed a typology for classifying churches based on the community or setting in which they are located, and used the typology in a five-year trend study of churches in the synod of Albany, New York. The study, lasting from 1969 to 1974, included churches selected to represent each of the types. Membership and participation changes varied considerably according to type. Losses in membership were heaviest in city churches, including churches in midtown, urban neighborhoods and older city suburbs. These churches contained 35 percent of the synod's membership, but they accounted for 62 percent of its membership losses. The losses were next heaviest in churches in rural villages (250 to 2,500 people) and in villages historically independent but now strongly related to an urban area. These churches, with 24 percent of the synod's members, accounted for 16 percent of its membership losses. The remaining types, including both rural churches in the open countryside and churches in the newer suburbs, accounted for 41 percent of the synod's membership and 22 percent of the membership losses. Attendance rates followed essentially similar patterns, with city or city-related churches experiencing the greatest attendance declines. Only churches in the newer suburbs showed attendance gains. Church school participation rates were generally similar in direction, but they were even more dramatic in the magnitude of the

losses. A comparison of growing and declining United Presbyterian churches reports similar findings.[26]

A key element in such trends has been changes in the social setting of the churches, including population and land-use changes. As communities changed in the makeup of their residents or in the type of activity occurring there, so also have the churches changed, sometimes growing but more often declining.

It is not simply changes in the community surrounding the church that affect membership and participation rates; it is also the way churches are able to relate to the people who are their members or potential members. This is why our hypothetical scenario calls attention to social status differences as well as to the social setting of the churches. People whose choice of residence reflects their sociocultural background or their present circumstances bring expectations to the church that reflect in part who they are socially and culturally. These expectations influence the way people perceive and experience the life of a particular congregation, and participation (or lack of it) is strongly conditioned by the degree to which their expectations are met.

Ethnic minorities, for example, blacks or Hispanics, moving into a formerly all-white, Anglo-Saxon neighborhood, are unlikely to find that the United Church of Christ congregation down the street, whose members now commute to the church from the suburbs, meets their expectations. Unless the congregation alters its style to meet the newcomers' expectations, they are likely to look elsewhere for a church or not to participate anywhere.

Where a new suburb develops in a formerly rural fringe area, members of the existing churches in the area are often quite different in socioeconomic and cultural background from the newcomers. The newcomers may be more affluent, more highly educated, and employed in occupations quite different from those of the older residents and church members. Their expectations for the church are likely also to be different from what currently exists in the community churches; and, unless the newcomers "capture" leadership in the churches and have some influence in shaping the program to meet their needs, they are likely not to participate. If they participate at all, it will be in new congregations developed with them in view, or they will commute some distance to churches in their former community or residence. Thus it is not only community changes but also changes in the social and cultural characteristics of members and potential members that affect the trends in membership and participation. Walrath's study was able to point to the effects of both of these types of factors on membership and participation changes.

Whether associated with community change or not, many new social and cultural characteristics have developed during the past twenty-five years, as our analysis of value changes has already made clear. Consequently, the expectations people have for the church have generally become more diverse. Warren Hartman identified several distinct church "audiences" in his study of United Methodist Church members,[27] including a group giving top priority to fellowship needs, another with strong evangelistic concerns, a third whose primary interests were in acquiring a better knowledge of the faith through study, and a fourth group deeply concerned about the ministry of the church in society. A fifth or residual group gave equal priority to more than one of the concerns. Our earlier analysis suggests the addition of at least one other audience—those interested in spiritual renewal.

How local churches have been able to respond to these diverse audiences has been a major factor in their pattern of growth or decline. When growing United Presbyterian churches were compared with those that had lost membership, the growing congregations were most likely to describe their relationship to the life styles and values of their communities as "identifies with," "similar," "involved with," or "supportive of." These churches have apparently been able to respond creatively to community change and the diversity of audiences.[28]

Another strategy seems to be to decide, in essence, to be a "one-audience" church. That is, the style of the church—its theological emphasis, programs, and general ethos—will have primary appeal to a single constituency, frequently based on social class and status. One probable reason for the success of suburban churches in the 1950s was their ability to relate to constituents who were relatively homogeneous in their circumstances and life styles. Evidently this continues to be the case, as the studies by Walrath and the Presbyterian Church point out. Similarly, we suspect that conservative church growth of recent years has been in denominations and local churches that have had a single focus.

The Institute of Church Growth, an evangelical group that has gained considerable attention in recent years, states the "homogeneous unit principle" as a major axiom of church growth. To maximize growth potential, a church should as nearly as possible reflect in its composition the patterns and life styles of the community in which it exists. "Show me a growing church," writes C. Peter Wagner, Director of the Institute, "and I will show you a homogeneous unit. There may be some exception to this rule, but I have not found one yet. . . ."[29] We are inclined to criticize such a claim on theological grounds, as the homogeneous unit principle implies exclusiveness and separation between peoples, or uncritical captivity to a particular cultural style. Nevertheless, the principle makes sociological sense, and such homogeneity is probably one factor behind some of the growth trends that we observed.

Conversely, some of the declines we observed can be explained by local churches that have had little sense of

identity with diverse constituencies. They have tried unsuccessfully to satisfy them with "a little something for everyone," but without a central focus to provide meaning. Martin Marty describes such churches as "Protean" or "boundaryless": "Protean . . . institutions lack fixity or boundaries, and are marked by fluidity and flow. . . . They lack identities or centers."[30] Where this is the case, few people find their expectations adequately met by the church, and membership and participation declines set in. We might add that such lack of boundaries is no more theologically defensible than the cultural captivity of homogeneous churches. Indeed, a boundaryless church is as much culturally captive to pluralism as a homogeneous church is to a particular audience, whether it be an audience of middle Americans or one of upper-middle-class intellectuals.

It is unlikely that any church or religious group will fully escape the influence of its cultural setting, nor should it desire to escape it fully. It is through its social and cultural forms that a religious group's message is embodied and proclaimed in each new time and place. This is especially true for Jews and Christians who share a theological heritage that takes the world and events of human history with great seriousness. Yet, they also share an Old Testament prophetic heritage that is strongly critical of religious institutions whose beliefs and practices are so identified with their culture that they are indistinguishable from it. The tension between being in the culture but not being fully identified with it is the fine line that a church or synagogue must walk as it attempts to be faithful to its purpose.

It is not easy to walk this line. The variety of factors affecting participation in churches and synagogues makes clear how much the destinies of these organizations are shaped by broad trends and events beyond their control. To admit this need not lead to paralysis or despair. Rather, it can lead to a search for ways to respond constructively, creatively, and in faithfulness to the purpose of these religious institutions within the limited but crucial range of possibilities open to them. Some of the possibilities are suggested by Douglas Johnson in Part III as he surveys trends that are likely to affect religion in America.

We began by asking about the shape, or condition, of religion in America since 1950, particularly that of the traditional institutions of faith. The trends that we have reviewed reveal both continuity and change, growth and decline, strength and weakness. These have not been easy years for religious institutions. Nonetheless, the trends also reveal a resiliency within these institutions and considerable continuing support for them within the population that augers well for their future.

NOTES

1. Widick Schroeder, "Age Cohorts, the Family Life Cycle, and Participation in the Voluntary Church in America: Implications for Membership Patterns, 1950–2000," *Chicago Theological Seminary Register*, vol. 65 (Fall 1975), p. 18.

2. Marshall Sklare and Joseph Greenblum, *Jewish Identity on the Suburban Frontier* (New York: Basic Books, 1967), pp. 181–198.

3. See, for example, Bernard Lazerwitz, "Some Factors Associated with Variations in Church Attendance," *Social Forces*, vol. 39 (May 1961), pp. 301–309; and Jackson W. Carroll and David A. Roozen. "Religious Participation in American Society: An Analysis of Social and Religious Trends and Their Interaction," photocopied report (Hartford, Conn.: The Hartford Seminary Foundation, 1975), pp. 94, 95, 121.

4. Our data may obscure the pattern of participation for the oldest age group by grouping all people over age 50 together. The oldest group may, as Schroeder suggests, reduce their participation because of physical infirmities or a general disengagement from social relationships. See Howard M. Bahr, "Aging and Religious Disaffiliation," *Social Forces*, vol. 49 (1970), pp. 59–71.

5. Dennison Nash, "A Little Child Shall Lead Them: A Statistical Test of an Hypothesis that Children Are the Source of the American Religious Revival," *Journal For the Scientific Study of Religion*, vol. 7 (Fall 1968), pp. 238–240.

6. See the *World Almanac* (New York: Newspaper Enterprises, Inc., 1955, 1960, 1965, 1974) for P.T.A. membership data.

7. "National PTA Seeking Ways to Add Numbers, Rejuvenate," *The Hartford (Conn.) Courant*, February 23, 1977.

8. The Methodist study is reported in Warren Hartman, *Membership Trends, A Study of Decline and Growth in the United Methodist Church 1949–1975* (Nashville: Discipleship Resources, 1976), p. 29; Episcopal trends are in Ruth Doyle, "Church Membership and Church Participation Trends in the Episcopal Church, 1950–1975" (unpublished paper prepared for a Hartford Seminary Working Group on Church Trends), 1977.

9. Dean R. Hoge, *Commitment on Campus* (Philadelphia: Westminster, 1974), p. 186.

10. Joseph J. Spengler, "Values and Fertility Analysis," *Demography*, vol. 3, no. 1 (1966), pp. 109–130. Cited in Hoge, *Commitment on Campus*, p. 178.

11. Dubois S. Morris, Jr., ed., *Perspectives for the '70s and '80s* (New York: National Industrial Conference Board, 1970), pp. 116–117.

12. Margaret Mead, cited in Lyle Schaller, *Understanding Tomorrow* (Nashville: Abingdon, 1976), p. 29.

13. Daniel Yankelovich, *The New Morality: A Profile of American Youth in the Seventies* (New York: McGraw-Hill, 1974), pp. 21–22.

14. Carroll and Roozen, p. 122.

15. Dean R. Hoge, *Division in the Protestant House* (Philadelphia: Westminster, 1976), pp. 113–114.

16. Paul A. Mickey and Robert L. Wilson, *What New Creation?* (Nashville: Abingdon, 1977), p. 105.

17. Douglas W. Johnson and George W. Cornell, *Punctured Preconceptions* (New York: Friendship Press, 1972) p. 116.

18. Nathan H. Vanderwerf, *The Times Were Very Full* (New York: The National Council of the Churches of Christ in the U.S.A., 1975), p. 39.

19. The figures for both years are expressed in 1967 constant dollars to correct for inflation and make them comparable. Source for the figures is the U.S. Bureau of the Census, *Historical Statistics of the United States, Colonial Times to 1971, Bicentennial Edition* (Washington, D.C.: U.S. Government Printing Office, 1975), p. 624.

20. Presbyterian figures are reported in *Membership Trends in the United Presbyterian Church in the U.S.A.* (New York: United Presbyterian Church in the U.S.A., General Assembly Mission Council, 1976), p. 107. Southern Baptist figures are from Don F. Mabry, "A Study of the Number of New Churches and the Net Gain in Churches of the Southern Baptist Convention," mimeographed paper (Atlanta: Atlanta Home Mission Board, 1974), p. 5.

21. Hartman, p. 37.

22. Andrew M. Greeley, William C. McCready, and Kathleen McCourt, *Catholic Schools in a Declining Church* (Kansas City: Sheed and Ward, 1976), pp. 103–153.

23. Greeley et al., p. 129.

24. Oliphant, *The Washington Star*, November 15, 1976.

25. Douglas A. Walrath, "The Congregations of the Synod of Albany, Reformed Church in America, Part V: 1974 Sample Survey," Schenectady, N.Y., 1974.

26. *Membership Trends in the United Presbyterian Church*, pp. 29–30.

27. Hartman, pp. 46–47.

28. *Membership Trends in the United Presbyterian Church*, p. 29.

29. C. Peter Wagner, *Your Church Can Grow* (Glendale, Calif.: Regal Books, 1976), p. 117.

30. Martin E. Marty, *The Fire We Can Light* (Garden City, N.Y.: Doubleday, 1973), p. 10.

II

Patterns of Religious Pluralism

MARTIN E. MARTY
and DOUGLAS W. JOHNSON

6

The Maps of Religious Groups: Introduction

DOUGLAS W. JOHNSON

The thirteen maps reproduced in this book are based on membership information collected in 1973 and 1974 from officials of each of the religious groups listed below. The membership statistics are for 1971, the latest available figures at the time of the survey. The maps show the membership spread in the United States of each of the religious groups. The statistics were analyzed for each county of every state and the percentage of the county's population adhering to each denomination was determined. The counties are colored (in the case of black-and-white maps, shaded) according to a key showing the percentage of the county's population that belongs to each denomination.

A glance at these maps reveals the geographic distribution of the thirteen denominations or families of denominations. More than that, a careful examination of the maps can uncover much about the history of these religious groups since they were planted or formed in America, and indeed much about the history of immigration, industrialization, and politics in the United States. Compare, for instance, John Kennedy's Massachusetts and Jimmy Carter's Georgia on the Roman Catholic (Map 7) and Baptist (Map 1) maps. As would be expected, Catholics are exceptionally strong in Massachusetts and Baptists exceptionally strong in Georgia. The opposite situation also indicated on the maps—the relatively small number of Catholics in the old South of Georgia and the relative weakness of Baptists in Massachusetts—is an important background to religion's role in the Kennedy and Carter presidential campaigns. The results of immigration patterns are

clearly evident in the upper Midwest on the Lutheran map (Map 4). Here is a great concentration of Lutherans, where large numbers of immigrants from the Lutheran homeland in Germany and Scandinavia settled.

Each of the thirteen maps represents a religious denomination or family of denominations that is distinct in its history, organization, practice, and, in some cases, theology. Denominations that are grouped under one family designation are generally similar in historical background and to some extent similar, but by no means identical, in organization, practice, and theology. The denominations represented are:

Map 1. BAPTIST CHURCHES
American Baptist Churches in the U.S.A.
Baptist Missionary Association of America
Free Will Baptists
General Association of General Baptists
North American Baptist General
Conference
Seventh Day Baptist General Conference
Southern Baptist Convention

Map 2. CHRISTIAN CHURCH (DISCIPLES OF CHRIST) AND THE CHRISTIAN CHURCHES AND CHURCHES OF CHRIST

Map 3. THE EPISCOPAL CHURCH

Map 4. LUTHERAN CHURCHES
The American Lutheran Church
Lutheran Church in America

The Lutheran Church—Missouri Synod
Wisconsin Evangelical Lutheran Synod

Map 5. METHODIST CHURCHES
Free Methodist Church of North America
The United Methodist Church

Map 6. PRESBYTERIAN CHURCHES
Associate Reformed Presbyterian Church
(General Synod)
Cumberland Presbyterian Church
The Orthodox Presbyterian Church
Presbyterian Church in the U.S.
Reformed Presbyterian Church, Evangelical Synod
The United Presbyterian Church in the
U.S.A.

Map 7. THE ROMAN CATHOLIC CHURCH

Map 8. UNITED CHURCH OF CHRIST

Map 9. ADVENTIST CHURCHES
Church of God General Conference (Oregon, Illinois)
Seventh-day Adventists

Map 10. MENNONITE CHURCHES
Evangelical Mennonite Brethren
Conference
Mennonite Church
Mennonite Church, The General
Conference

Map 11. MORAVIAN CHURCHES
Moravian Church in America (Unitas
Fratrum)
Unity of the Brethren

Map 12. PENTECOSTAL CHURCHES
Church of God (Cleveland, Tennessee)
Pentecostal Holiness Church
United Pentecostal Church International

Map 13. REFORMED CHURCHES
Christian Reformed Church
Reformed Church in America

On January 10, 1973, all the denominations listed in the *Yearbook of American Churches 1971* were contacted by letter and invited to participate in the study on which the maps are based. The study was sponsored by the Office of Research, Evaluation and Planning of the National Council of the Churches of Christ in the U.S.A. (New York); the Department of Research and Statistics of the Lutheran Church—Missouri Synod (St. Louis); and the Glenmary Research Center (Washington, D.C.), a Catholic agency.

When replies came into the offices of the National Council of Churches, additional information was given those who asked for it, and a preliminary letter of instructions was sent to those who indicated a desire to participate. In the meantime, the computer center at Concordia Teachers College, River Forest, Illinois, prepared a complete set of prepunched county-coded computer cards, to be used for recording the data. Since some denominations do not have churches in every state, denominations were asked to indicate whether cards would be needed for every county in the nation or just for those in certain states. County-coded cards for the states requested were then sent to participating denominations, along with detailed instructions for recording the data.

The county cards were returned to the computer center for key punching and verification. During this process I and the other two directors of the study, Paul R. Picard and Bernard Quinn, were in frequent contact with the participating denominations in working out problems and difficulties. Information received up to December 31, 1973, was included in the study. The next step was to run a series of computer edit tests to check for errors and to produce the printout of tables that is published in Douglas W. Johnson, Paul R. Picard, and Bernard Quinn, *Churches and Church Membership in the United States: 1971* (Washington, D.C.: Glenmary Research Center, 1974). A copy of the letters and instruments used for gathering and recording the data will be found in the appendix to *Churches and Church Membership*.

The maps were developed from the tables in *Churches and Church Membership*. After further additions and corrections were made, based on correspondence with the participating denominations, the maps were checked for accuracy by a team from Hartford Seminary Foundation. Regrettably, maps could not be prepared for all the major religious groups in the United States because statistics were not available from some groups. Omissions are discussed at the beginning of Chapter 7.

The county population reported in the 1970 United States census is used as the base for figuring the percentage membership for each denomination in that county. Thus the maps can be said to give as accurate a picture as possible of the membership of these thirteen religious groups at the time of the last census. Although membership in these groups may have increased or decreased since 1971, the year for which statistics were reported, it is unlikely that the geographical distribution represented on the maps has altered significantly.

7

The Career of Pluralism in America

MARTIN E. MARTY

INTRODUCTION

Americans, long bemused and befuddled by their religious pluralism, have come increasingly to understand it and even relish it. The idea that many religious groups would and would have to coexist was unfamiliar to most people who settled early America. For a millennium and a half the ancestors of the new American majority, residents of the British Isles or the European continent, had known only the experience of Christendom. From the early fourth century onward, the Christian faith had been established by law throughout the Roman empire or "the whole known world." It was culturally and socially impossible not to be Christian on Christian soil. The single exception, the Jews, lived a ghetto existence, set apart from the society at large.

The privileged position of Christians led them to act differently than when they had been exiles, outsiders, and potential victims of persecution. They began to throw their weight around and to persecute the left-over non-Christians. They could use the force of the sword to have their way, to enforce decrees of Christian powers. They contributed to the establishment of a single symbol system. The common people could look at church windows or flags and banners and know what it was that these were imparting in a Christian frame of reference.

The world didn't stay quite as neat as this picture of early Christendom suggests. By the eleventh century the church had split in two, in a great schism that separated Eastern from Western empires and churches. Still, the average believer and citizen had no experience of what we would now call pluralism. People who were under a different kind of churchly jurisdiction normally lived hundred of miles away. Even the Protestant Reformation of the sixteenth century did not completely change the picture. Territories or nations either remained Roman Catholic or turned one kind of Protestant or another. *Cuius regio eius religio*, the principle that the religion of the civil ruler became the faith of the people, was agreeable to most Protestants in their sixteenth-century settlements.

The map of Europe was becoming more crazy-quilted in the process of modernity. From the sixteenth until the nineteenth, and sometimes even the twentieth, centuries the situation was what might be called a host culture–guest culture. One faith would dominate and be established by law, but it had to begin to make allowance for nonconformists and dissenters. By the eighteenth century in many nations, it was also possible to publicly disavow any faith. But the host–guest picture differs significantly from the American style of pluralism, based on the principles that "any number can play," that all are protected by law, and that none are to be legally privileged.

The founders of most American colonies brought with them their European habits, and in nine of the thirteen colonies they established a single church as late as the time of independence. But the interaction of people in colonies, and later states, the growth of mobility, the rise of many new denominations in the face of religious freedom, and the arrival of wave upon wave of immigrants served to compromise and almost kill the old idea of territorialism. Something happened to the religious map in the process. The lines could never be neat again. There would be no legally established monopolies. Increasingly, the grinding and mixing processes of American life would ensure that no single church body dominated in a region. Enter many American towns and you will see a sign on which great numbers of churches are listed, all of them friendly competitors greeting the visitor or newcomer.

The description of change from territorialism to pluralism can be overstated, however. More of the old patterns survived than most imagine could have survived. During the past quarter century, two maps of religious dominances have appeared in America, which have served to disturb the serenity of those who had come to think of America as a blurry blend of all faiths in similar proportions almost anywhere. Thoughtful people began to revise their opinions about the character of religious pluralism. There *were* surprisingly broad areas in which one church dominated. It was also clear that some large and old denominations were spread thin across the map and in the process had lost certain kinds of power.

The first of these maps, in Edwin Scott Gaustad, *Historical Atlas of Religion in America* (New York: Harper & Brothers, 1962), presented data from 1950. A revision of this map with data from 1971 appeared, along with a detailed statistical presentation by Johnson, Picard, and Quinn, in *Churches and Church Membership in the United States: 1971* (1974). The revised map was also included in the revised edition of Gaustad's *Historical Atlas of Religion in America* (New York: Harper & Row, 1976). A glance at these maps will give an idea of the character of American pluralism and the location of religious centers of power. Each county of the nation is colored to match the religious group that has the largest number of adherents.

The viewer of the map will find that there are five nations within a nation, religiously speaking. First, there is a very well-defined Latter-Day Saints empire, the state of Utah. In no county in that state, according to the 1974 map, does any other religious group outnumber the Mormons. Meanwhile the Mormons have also spilled over the state lines to become dominant in northern Arizona, northwestern Colorado, western Wyoming, southern Idaho, and eastern Nevada. The second area where a single religion dominates is the South. Except for the southern tips of Texas, Louisiana, and Florida, the vast majority of southern counties are dominated by Baptists of the Southern Baptist Convention. Third follows an upper Midwest Lutheran complex, beginning in southern Wisconsin and arcing through Minnesota and the Dakotas into the Northwest and down into Iowa and Nebraska in the southern part of Lutherandom. Fourth is a wide area in which there are large numbers of Methodists, though seldom do they

dominate as thoroughly as do the first three groups mentioned. The Methodist band or belt might be described as the South of the North and the North of the South, the path of the revivalists from Pennsylvania and Virginia west to Colorado. Fifth and finally, America's largest single church population, the members of the Roman Catholic Church, concentrate in a number of territories. It is they who occupy the southern tips of Texas, Louisiana, and Florida, outposts beyond Baptist country. The Southwest would appear to be theirs so far as dominances are concerned. In only one county of California are they outnumbered by members of any other church. New York and New England, with the exception of a dozen counties, make up an area of Catholic preponderance. Finally, in only five counties that border all the Great Lakes are Roman Catholics outnumbered by any other group. In short, urban white America is largely Roman Catholic.

These two general maps from the past quarter century reveal the strength of religious groups relative to each other, not to the U.S. population as a whole. This means that if approximately 60 percent of Americans are church members, in a typical county as few as 30 percent of the people—half of that 60 percent—would be enough to assign that county to a dominant group. Where no one denomination could reach the 50 percent church membership mark but did have over 25 percent, the map makers indicate its strength as well. Not many counties had less than 25 percent of the church members concentrated in a single group.

For all their strengths, the maps based on this approach did have several deficiencies. As just hinted, they did not show the strength of a church population relative to the total number of residents, including nonchurch members. Second, while statistics were available in the Johnson, Picard, and Quinn volume, they had not yet been translated to graphics, so it was hard to learn from the map anything about any group except the largest in each county. Both these deficiences are remedied in the thirteen maps in this book.

Before turning to the present maps, the reader should be presented with a couple of cautionary words about their use or misuse. The first has to do with the regrettable omissions. Black denominations do not have systematic practices of reporting statistics to national headquarters, and estimates of their strength are based on such hazardous speculations that it was felt advisable to omit them rather than to skew the more reliable figures that came from reporting groups. This means, however, that only blacks who are members of largely white denominations are represented on this map. Were blacks in their own historic denominations added to the maps, they would tend to reinforce the Baptist and Methodist areas of dominance and might qualify the picture of Catholic majorities in some urban centers outside the south. The largely urban Eastern Orthodox churches and some of the rapidly growing Protestant groups like the Assemblies of God did not make statistics available. The Jewish groups, planning an eventual report of their own, were not yet prepared to make statistics available at the time the present survey was made.

The second problem has to do with definitions of membership. Suffice it to say here that as far as possible the mapmakers have tried to use consistent and fair means of measuring what is a church member from group to group.

Finally, since the United States Census does not include church membership data, all the statistics on religion deal not with the place of members' residence but with the place of their membership. We have no way of knowing how many of the church members affiliated with institutions in a particular county live in that county. We can only know how many members are reported by the churches that are located in each county. However, this fact does not greatly distort the larger picture, since the regional implications would not change. It is hard to picture many people being active members of a church more than one county line away.

With these qualifications in mind, we can now turn to the maps that show where the members of various denominations are to be found and their strengths relative to the population in the nation's counties.

MAP 1. BAPTISTS

What can one say about the Baptists except that they break most of the rules about patterns of dominance and growth in American religion. They do have an empire, throughout the South. In some respects they are "the catholic church of the South," if by catholic we mean positively interested in shaping and stamping a culture. But far from seeing that endeavor lead to compromises that would cut into growth patterns, the Southern Baptist Convention remains disciplined, assertive, generally doctrinally conservative, often rather rigid, and consistently capable of retaining the loyalty of old members while aggressively programming means to recruit new ones.

The Southern Baptist Convention by no means represents all of the Baptist bodies, though it is the only geographically dominant one. Were we able to chart the black Baptist churches, one of which alone claims over five million members, we might see more Baptist dispersion through the northern cities. But the northern (largely white) American Baptist Churches know no such areas of dominance. The American Baptist Churches in the U.S.A., the official name of the northern group, reported 1,502,759 members in 1973, compared to 12,295,000 in the Southern Baptist Convention. This figure by itself outnumbers the whole Methodist cluster in America—and does not include a large number of small Baptist churches which did not participate in the data gathering.

If once upon a time the Baptists were a typical lower class church of the dispossessed, and if they still minister to many poor whites, particularly in the South, it should also be noted that the southern churches have known prosperity. Numerous social analysts have shown how, particularly since World War II, much of the American power shift has been toward the South and the West. The contrast between "Yankee" and the new "cowboy" style can be overdrawn, but it is true that the shift has brought new affluence to the South, along with large numbers of people below the 37th parallel. "Texas Baptist millionaire" is almost a cliché comment on the new blend: people who desire an other-worldly Gospel in religion and a very worldly style of life outside that sphere.

So at least in the South there is a Baptist "culture." In middle-sized cities there may be no country club; the church owns a swimming pool, gymnasium, and recreational facilities. Huge evangelistic rallies can be the major cultural events in many cities. Religious groups on campuses are not by and large in the hands of adaptive liberals but in the control of revivalist-minded evangelicals. In many places it would not be judicious for a non-Baptist to run for political office and expect to win.

The Baptists in the North have respectably held their own. It can be seen that the entire Northeast and the middle Midwest (Ohio, Indiana, Illinois, southern Michigan, and Wisconsin) have in most cases a Baptist representation up to 5 percent. On the Lutheran turf of the further northwest part of the Midwest, they appear very rarely. A presence on the West Coast and in the Southwest, Baptists still draw their strength from the South.

In the South the Baptists have the largest collection of counties colored dark blue (over 50 percent of the population being theirs) of any Protestant group. The number of counties that attract more than 15 or 25 percent of the people is astounding. How did they get there?

The Baptists in America are a largely native growth. Few of the people called Baptist derive from continental Anabaptism; Mennonite, Amish, and Brethren groups do that. Nor did English Baptists of the seventeenth century send many people over. The New England Congregationalist churches began to split during a revival of the 1730s and 1740s called the First Great Awakening. The more disciplined revivalist groups were as fiercely autonomous in their sense of Congregationalism as their host churches had been. But they came to favor adult baptism by immersion as a sign of the disciplined intent. They were in on the great late-colonial battles for religious freedom. Linking with the earliest Baptists, who with Roger Williams had converged on Rhode Island, they began to move southward.

By the time of the Revolution they had worked their way into Virginia and elsewhere in the South, there to gather strength until the opening of the West. When that occurred more or less simultaneously with a Second Great Awakening, another major revival early in the new century, they were well poised to make their move. While the older colonial bodies kept insisting on an educated ministry and thus succeeded in nearly paralyzing themselves, the Baptists were ready to ordain people who experienced what seemed to be a genuine call, even if they had no special training. Congregations were independent; the polity was not centrally organized, as the Methodists' had been, but somehow the Baptists spread without much planned movement.

Late industrialization in the South helped the Baptists. There was no large and bewildering intrusion of continentals: Catholics, Lutherans, Jews, Eastern Orthodox. The favored local churches tended to be kin to Baptists in cultural styles. Combining congregational-centrism, revivalist fervor, the common touch, and a genius for promotion, the Baptists have kept their momentum as no other large group has. Cut off the South and America would know Baptists pretty much as it knows the United Church of Christ or the Disciples of Christ. But the South is not to be cut off; it is the great Protestant concentration and a new national power center. From it Baptists are continuing to spread across the rest of the map, showing few signs of slowing down and even fewer signs of internal stress.

MAP 2. CHRISTIAN CHURCH (DISCIPLES OF CHRIST) AND THE CHRISTIAN CHURCHES AND CHURCHES OF CHRIST

All maps are designed to help lead people to places; but maps also have to be partly misleading. (A map is not a territory, it only points to one; maps are flat, and the world is not. Maps like those in this book have to include some details but leave others out.) The map you see here has to be misleading because it includes two sets of churches that, on paper, have had many family resemblances but in reality have drifted far apart. They come from a common stock, have shared much of the common history, but the people represented here are divided. About half of them belong to one group that never wanted to be a denomination but is now ready to call itself one. About half belong to another group of congregations or local churches that resist the idea of being seen as a denomination, though nonmembers classify this cluster as one.

Who are these people? They derive from a common and very American impulse from the early nineteenth century. Americans in the period of great revivals saw what looked to them to be almost too much "free enterprise" in religion. New ferments and new move-

ments were popping up every day in this society, the first that really granted religious freedom to all and that permitted free experimentation in religion. Where was the true Church of Christ in all this competitive mixture? Who were the Disciples of Christ, lost in the maze of contending Presbyterians and Moravians and Episcopalians and Mennonites? Sincerely troubled people decided to do something about the situation. They did not stop participating in revivals; they simply said that they wanted to stop caring about creeds and dogmas, organizations and institutions. Somewhere in the American dream was the sense that people could start all over again. The Church of Jesus Christ, obscured by Catholic and pluralist Protestant history, was waiting to be rediscovered, restored, reestablished in its pristine and pure character.

The people who shared this vision—Alexander Campbell and his father Thomas, Presbyterians of a sort from Scotland; Walter Scott; Barton Stone; there were others, and they were impressively determined people all—at times teamed and at times worked rather independently toward similar goals. They dreamed of Christian unity. Some called themselves Disciples of Christ or simply Christian or members of the Church of Christ. Where the Bible spoke, they would speak; where it was silent, they were silent. They believed the Bible described baptism by immersion only, and they followed this description. They believed that a Lord's Supper or communion should occur weekly, so they celebrated it. Some saw no command or permission for instrumental music, and many banned the organ from churches. None of them wanted to be denominationalized. But in the American environment there is no space between denominations; they had to be seen as denominations.

Through the years a group as free spirited and independent as this cluster inevitably developed internal tensions and competing directions. To oversimplify greatly, about half of the descendants of these visionaries and planners went one way into what today is called the Christian Church (Disciples of Christ). Today it is considered to be a mainline religious group, and it suffers some of the decline or "life in a holding pattern" that such accommodated groups do. It now recognizes the need for organization beyond the local level. The theological schools in this tradition are sophisticated; the church participates in ecumenical endeavors and is at ease with other Christians. About 1.3 million people are members.

The other half is encompassed in what is called the Christian Churches and Churches of Christ, who listed 0.9 million members in 1971 but by 1974 numbered 1,034,047 members in over five thousand strenuously autonomous local congregations. They are not to be confused with the more fundamentalistic and aggressive Churches of Christ, which did not participate in this study, a cluster of congregations that includes over 1.5

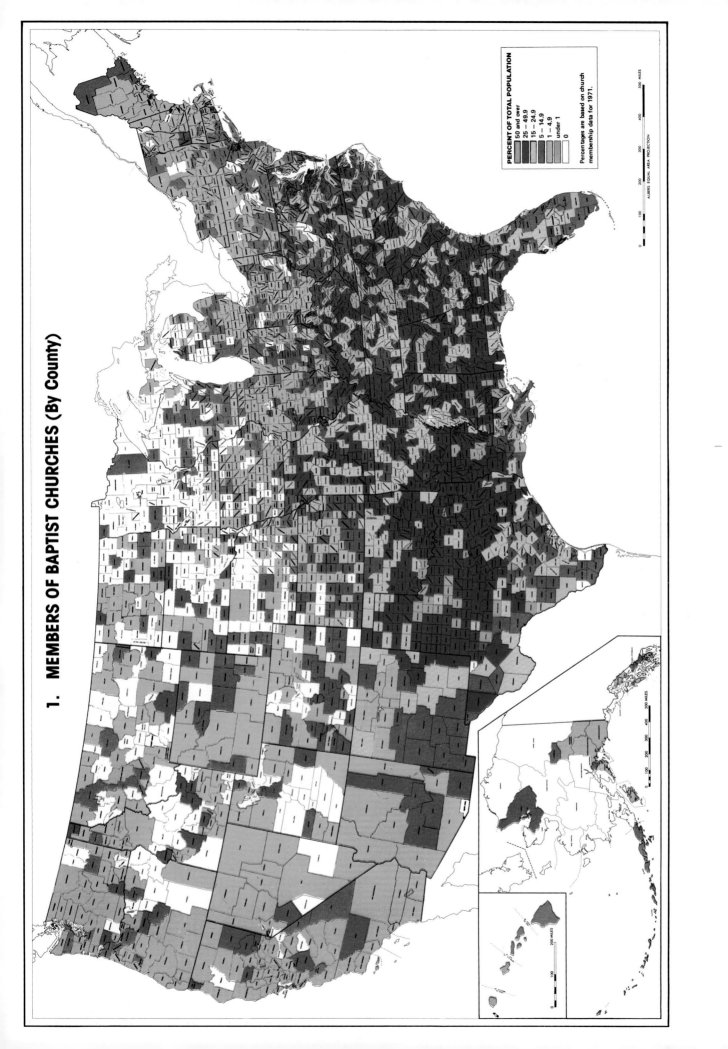

1. MEMBERS OF BAPTIST CHURCHES (By County)

PERCENT OF TOTAL POPULATION

50 and over
25 – 49.9
15 – 24.9
5 – 14.9
1 – 4.9
under 1
0

Percentages are based on church membership data for 1971.

ALBERS EQUAL AREA PROJECTION

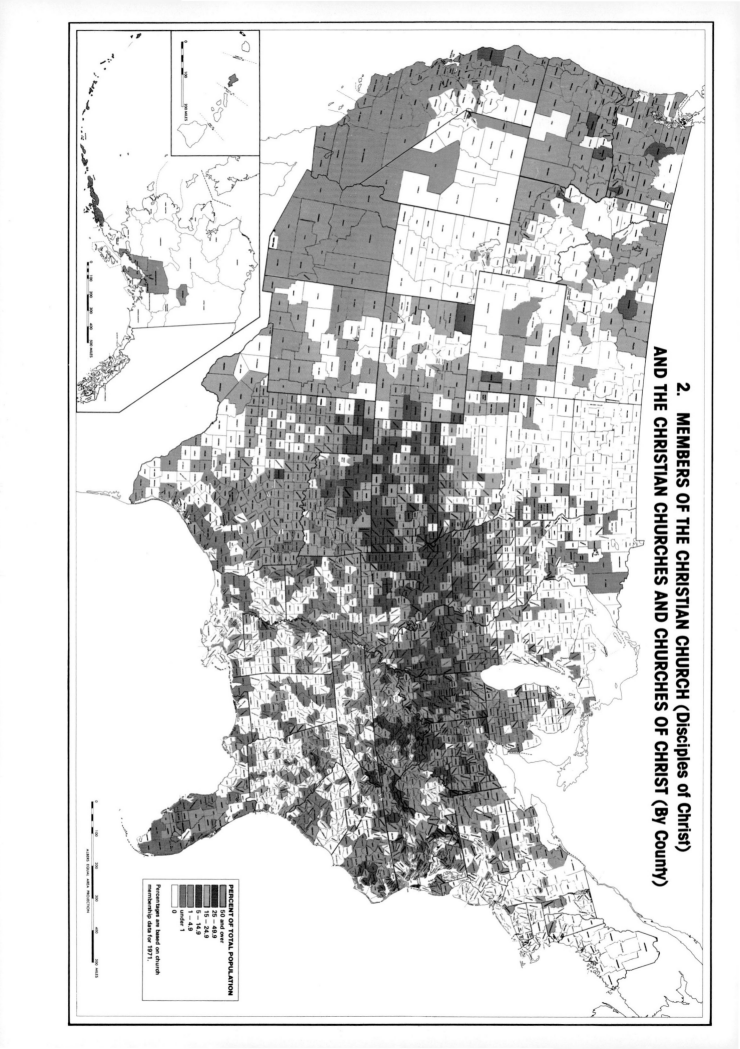

2. MEMBERS OF THE CHRISTIAN CHURCH (Disciples of Christ) AND THE CHRISTIAN CHURCHES AND CHURCHES OF CHRIST (By County)

PERCENT OF TOTAL POPULATION

50 and over
25 — 49.9
15 — 24.9
5 — 14.9
1 — 4.9
under 1
0

Percentages are based on church
membership data for 1971.

ALBERS EQUAL AREA PROJECTION

0   100   200   300   400   500 MILES

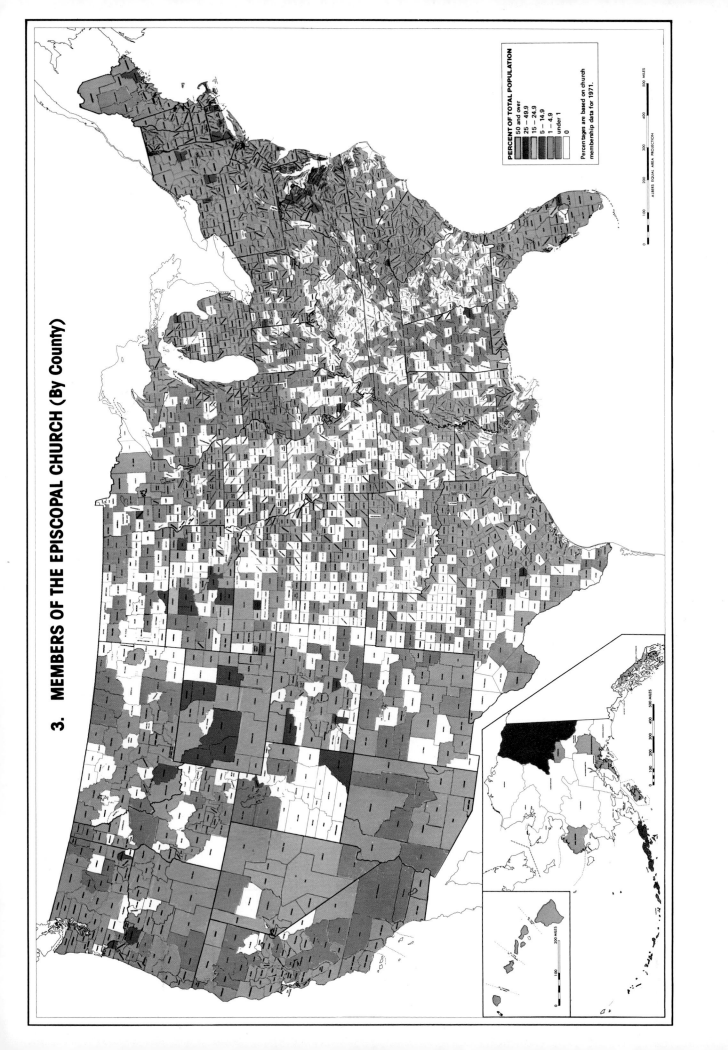

3. MEMBERS OF THE EPISCOPAL CHURCH (By County)

PERCENT OF TOTAL POPULATION

50 and over
25 — 49.9
15 — 24.9
5 — 14.9
1 — 4.9
under 1
0

Percentages are based on church membership data for 1971.

ALBERS EQUAL AREA PROJECTION

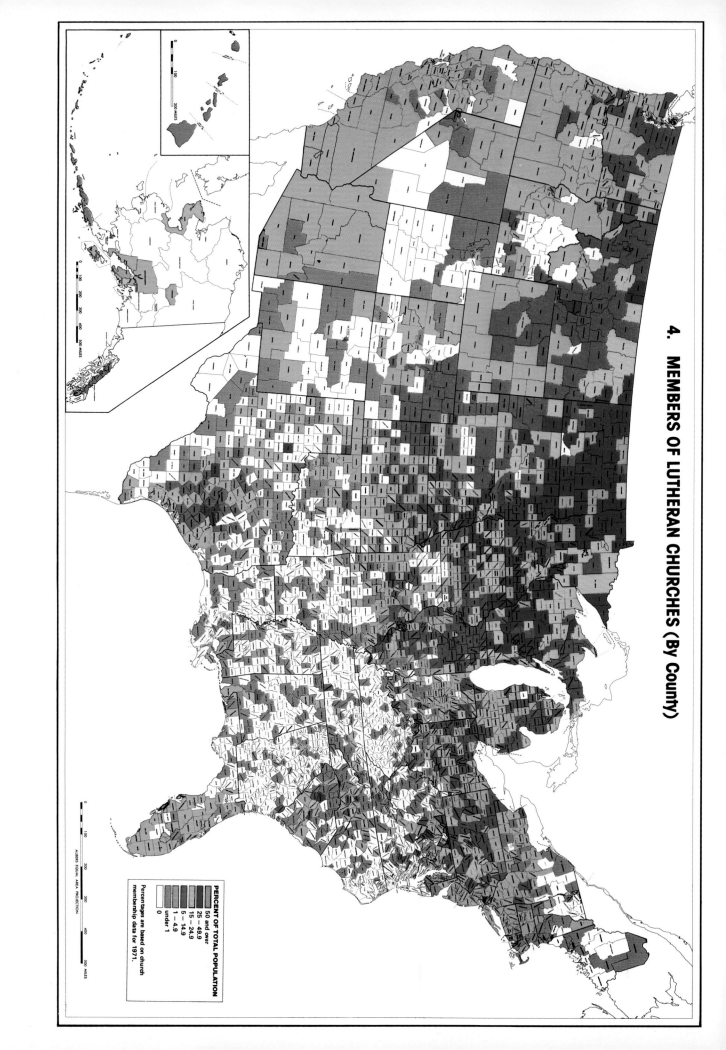

4. MEMBERS OF LUTHERAN CHURCHES (By County)

PERCENT OF TOTAL POPULATION

- 50 and over
- 25 — 49.9
- 15 — 24.9
- 5 — 14.9
- 1 — 4.9
- under 1
- 0

Percentages are based on church membership data for 1971.

ALBERS EQUAL AREA PROJECTION

0   100   200   300   400   500 MILES

5. MEMBERS OF METHODIST CHURCHES (By County)

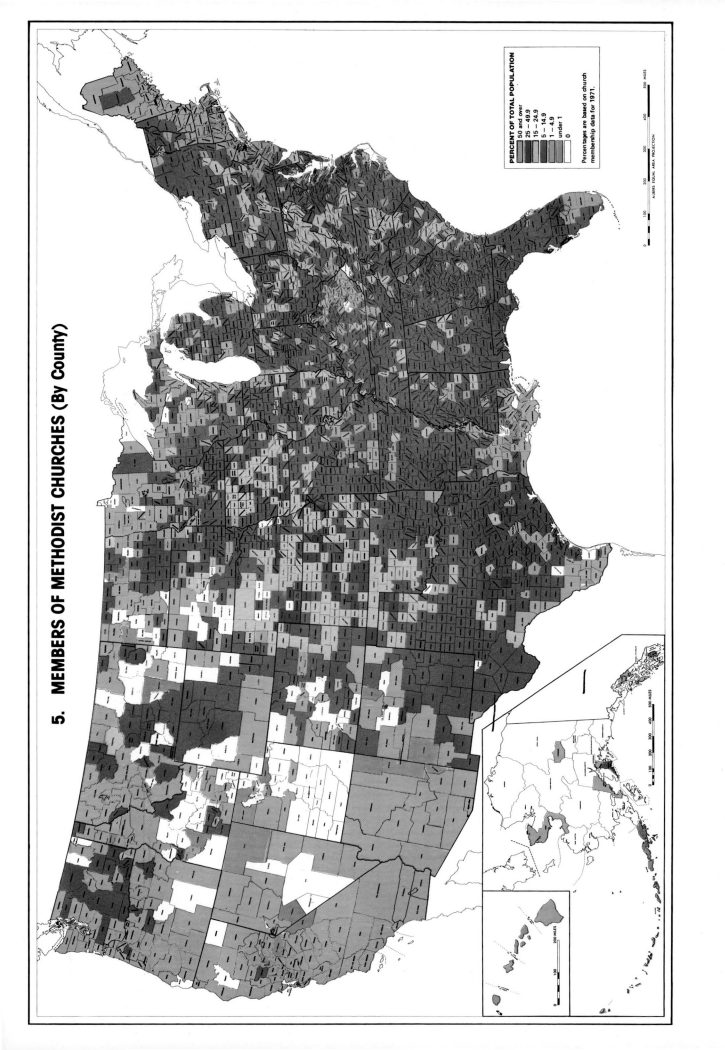

PERCENT OF TOTAL POPULATION

50 and over
25 – 49.9
15 – 24.9
5 – 14.9
1 – 4.9
under 1
0

Percentages are based on church membership data for 1971.

ALBERS EQUAL AREA PROJECTION

0   100   200   300   400   500 MILES

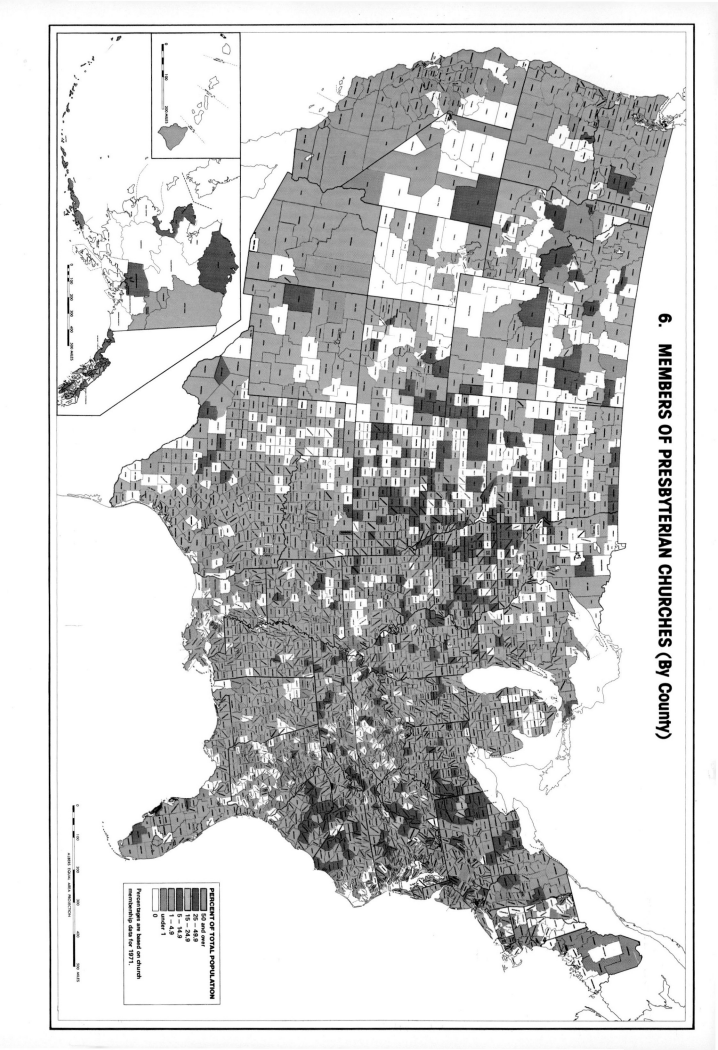

6. MEMBERS OF PRESBYTERIAN CHURCHES (By County)

PERCENT OF TOTAL POPULATION

50 and over
25 — 49.9
15 — 24.9
5 — 14.9
1 — 4.9
under 1
0

Percentages are based on church
membership data for 1971.

ALBERS EQUAL AREA PROJECTION

0   100   200   300   400   500 MILES

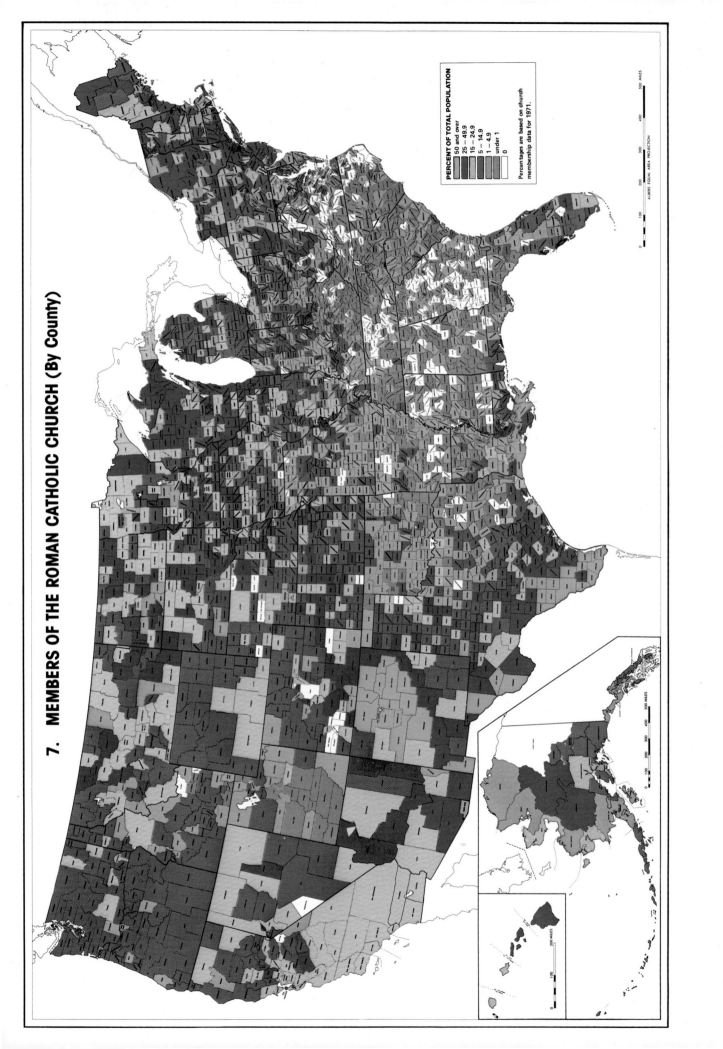

7. MEMBERS OF THE ROMAN CATHOLIC CHURCH (By County)

PERCENT OF TOTAL POPULATION

50 and over
25 — 49.9
15 — 24.9
5 — 14.9
1 — 4.9
under 1
0

Percentages are based on church
membership data for 1971.

ALBERS EQUAL AREA PROJECTION

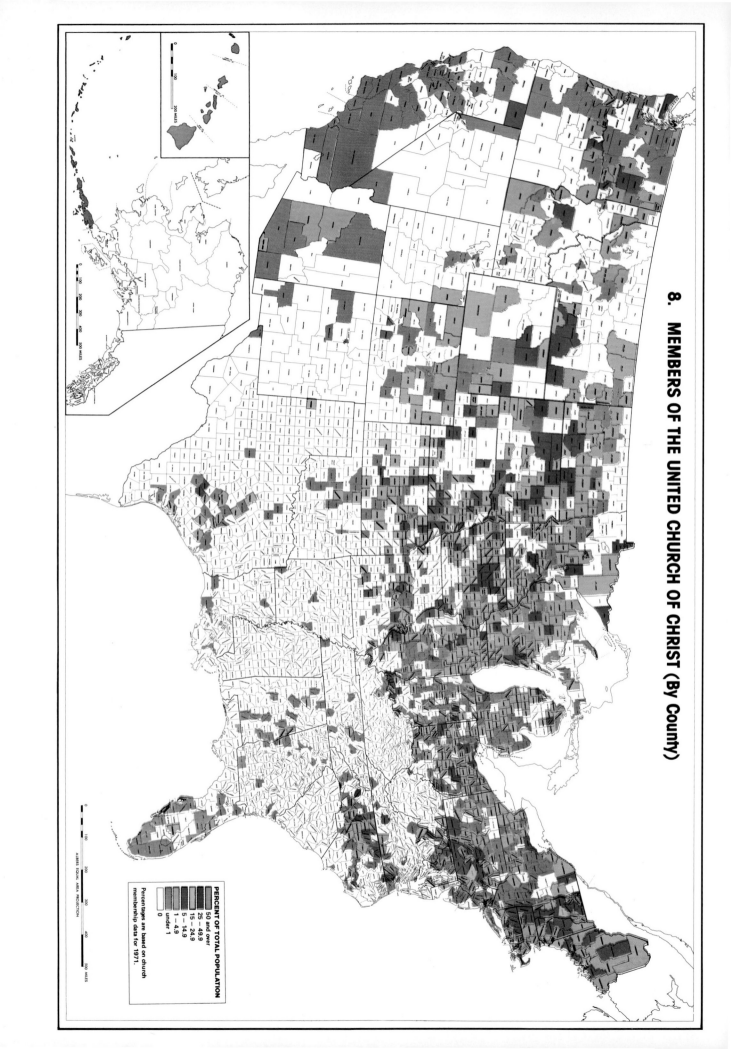

8. MEMBERS OF THE UNITED CHURCH OF CHRIST (By County)

PERCENT OF TOTAL POPULATION

50 and over
25 — 49.9
15 — 24.9
5 — 14.9
1 — 4.9
under 1
0

Percentages are based on church membership data for 1971.

ALBERS EQUAL AREA PROJECTION

0   100   200   300   400   500 MILES

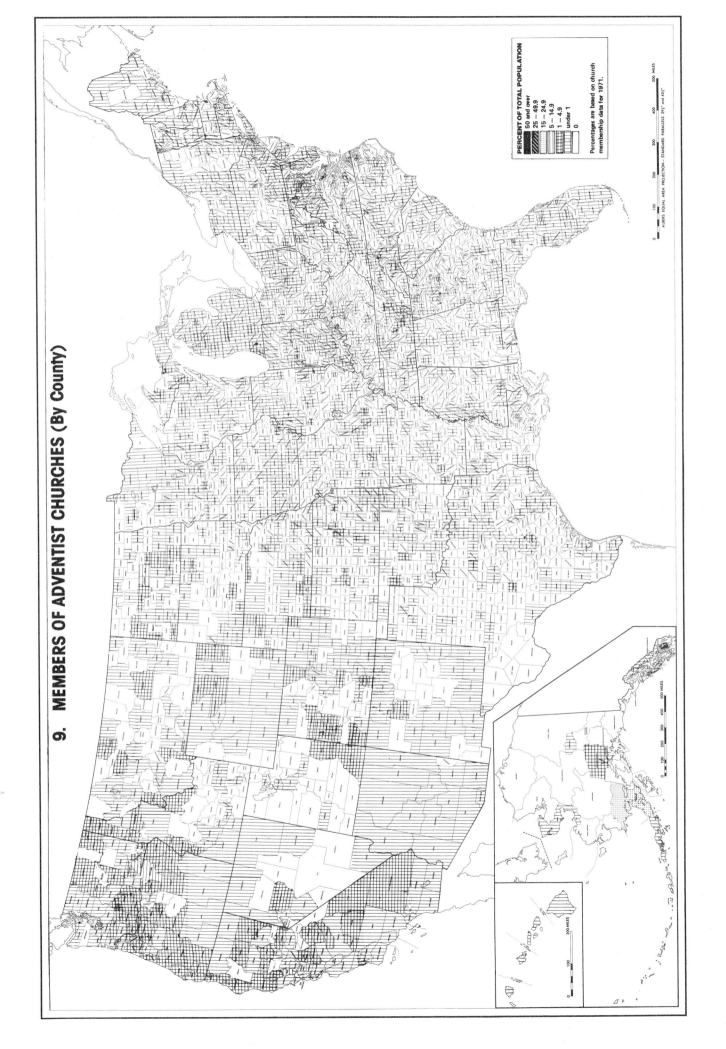

9. MEMBERS OF ADVENTIST CHURCHES (By County)

PERCENT OF TOTAL POPULATION

50 and over
25 – 49.9
15 – 24.9
5 – 14.9
1 – 4.9
under 1
0

Percentages are based on church membership data for 1971.

ALBERS EQUAL AREA PROJECTION · STANDARD PARALLELS 29½° and 45½°

0   100   200   300   400   500 MILES

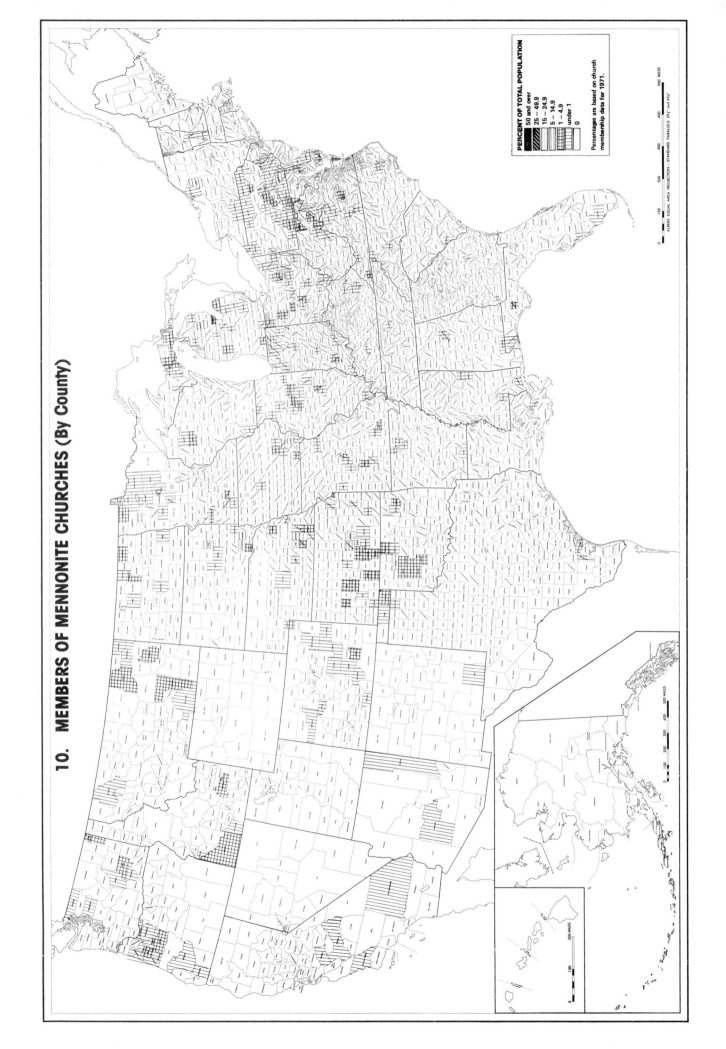

10. MEMBERS OF MENNONITE CHURCHES (By County)

PERCENT OF TOTAL POPULATION

- 50 and over
- 25 – 49.9
- 15 – 24.9
- 5 – 14.9
- 1 – 4.9
- under 1
- 0

Percentages are based on church membership data for 1971.

ALBERS EQUAL AREA PROJECTION – STANDARD PARALLELS 29½° and 45½°

11. MEMBERS OF MORAVIAN CHURCHES (By County)

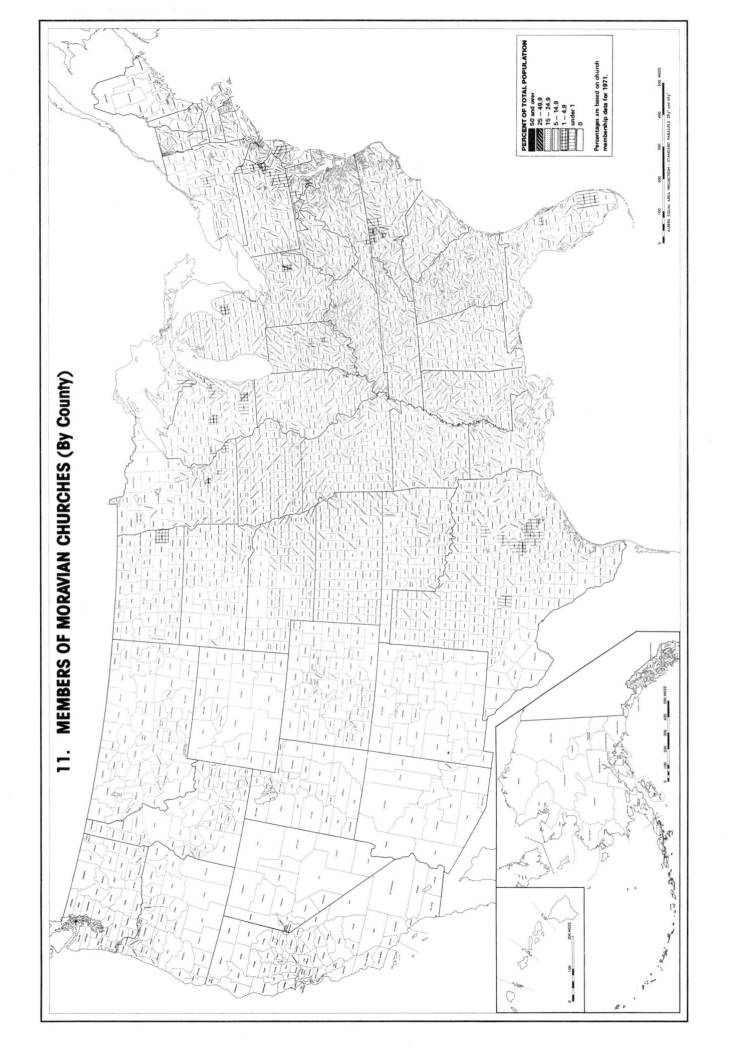

PERCENT OF TOTAL POPULATION

50 and over
25 — 49.9
15 — 24.9
5 — 14.9
1 — 4.9
under 1
0

Percentages are based on church membership data for 1971.

ALBERS EQUAL AREA PROJECTION – STANDARD PARALLELS 29½° and 45½°

0   100   200   300   400   500 MILES

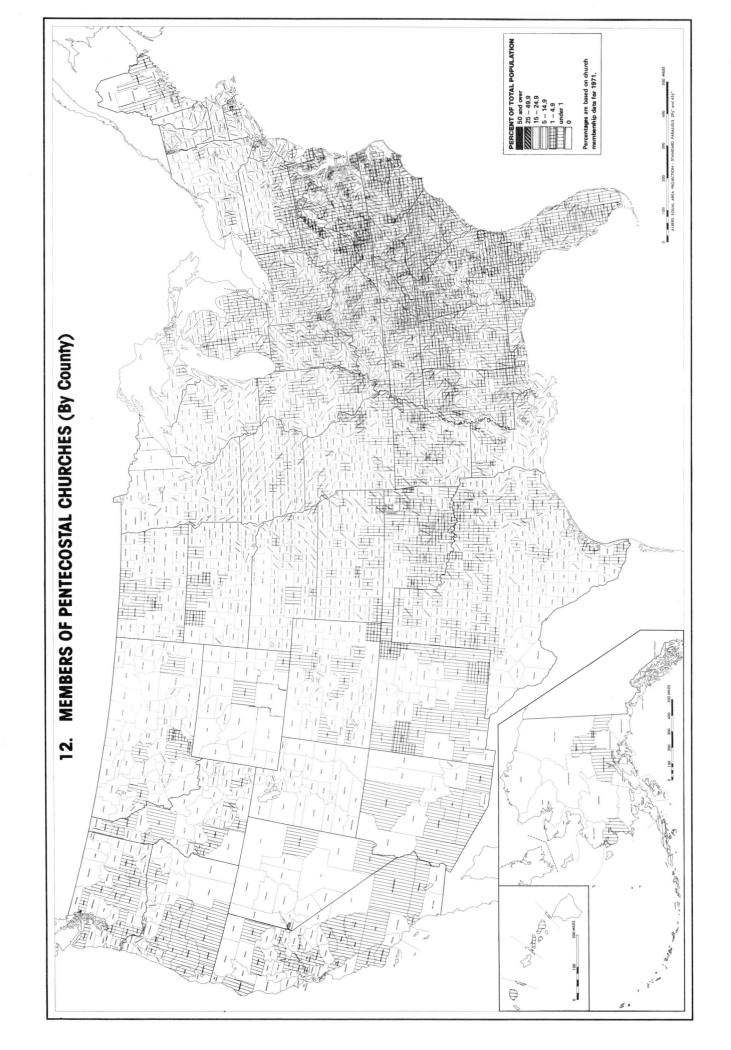

12. MEMBERS OF PENTECOSTAL CHURCHES (By County)

PERCENT OF TOTAL POPULATION

- 50 and over
- 25 – 49.9
- 15 – 24.9
- 5 – 14.9
- 1 – 4.9
- under 1
- 0

Percentages are based on church membership data for 1971.

0   100   200   300   400   500 MILES

ALBERS EQUAL AREA PROJECTION – STANDARD PARALLELS 29½° and 45½°

0   100   200 MILES

0   100   200   300   400   500 MILES

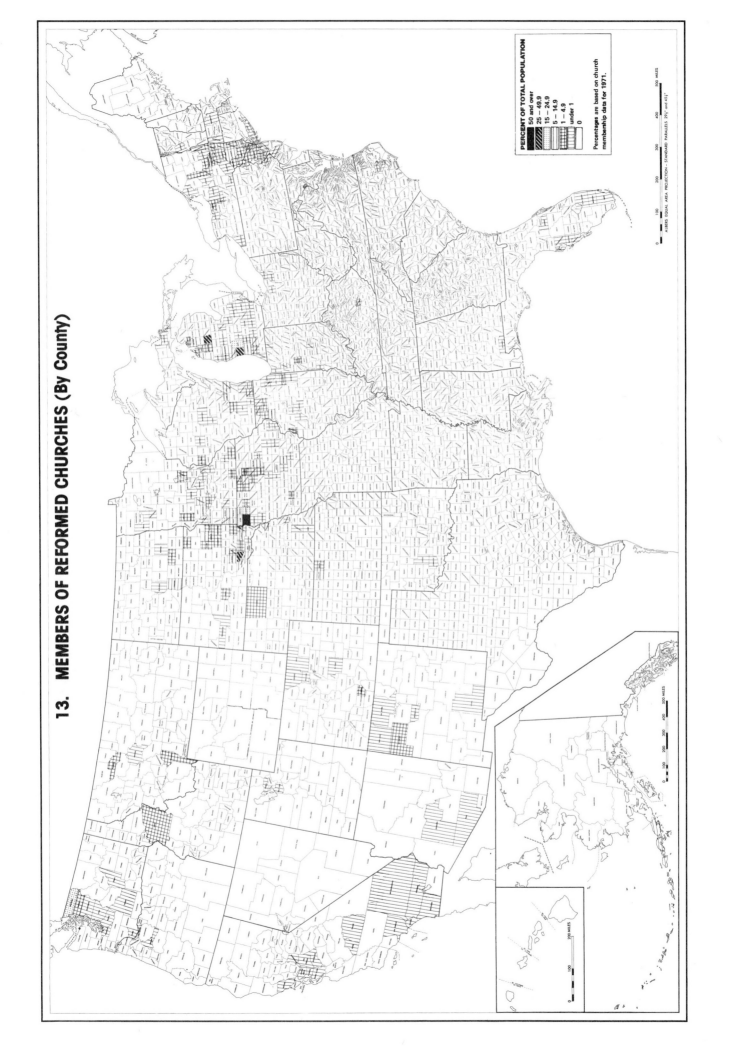

13. MEMBERS OF REFORMED CHURCHES (By County)

PERCENT OF TOTAL POPULATION

50 and over
25 — 49.9
15 — 24.9
5 — 14.9
1 — 4.9
under 1
0

Percentages are based on church membership data for 1971.

ALBERS EQUAL AREA PROJECTION — STANDARD PARALLELS 29½° and 45½°

0   100   200   300   400   500 MILES

million members and whose greatest strength is in Oklahoma and Texas. This latter group has no general organization at all beyond local congregations, though numbers of periodicals appear in its name.

In the Disciples of Christ, the Christian Churches and Churches of Christ, and finally, the Churches of Christ, for all their theological differences, the ideal of congregational independence is cherished. It is the third group, not mapped here, that keeps most to itself and shuns most kinds of relations with other Christian groups or movements. The Disciples of Christ, more at home in the less fast growing parts of the country, are themselves growing less rapidly than the other two.

MAP 3. EPISCOPALIANS

The 2,917,165 (1973) members of The Episcopal Church seem to be everywhere, yet they can lord it over others almost nowhere. A glance at the map finds them to be representatives of what looks like a truly national body. Few other Protestant churches seem to have even a thin spread of members in so many counties and in so many regions. In most northeastern and West Coast counties Episcopalians have up to 5 percent of the population, and in what would appear to be about half the counties between the Appalachians and the Rockies, both North and South, they have under 1 percent but are a recognized presence. They are a church neither of the North nor of the South alone.

At the beginning of the seventeenth century, one might have predicted that America was to become an Episcopal nation. At the end of the eighteenth century, there would have been good reasons to believe that there would be little or no Episcopalianism in America at all. When colonization began, most of the first migrants were from England, where a century earlier the established church had become Protestant and was Episcopal. The capital, the ventures, the religious power—all were in the hands of the overwhelming Episcopal majority in England. True, Episcopalians did lead in populating the southern colonies of Virginia, Maryland, the Carolinas, and eventually Georgia. But in New England the Puritan minority, which had more motivation to leave England and make a new planting, came to dominance. Episcopalians did not intrude in New England until after 1701, when a Society for the Propagation of the Gospel organized converting efforts, or after 1722, when some celebrated conversions to the Episcopal communion began to set a trend. By 1750 congregations of this communion dotted the entire coast, to make up the second largest (in number of congregations) church in the colonies.

By 1780, however, the church's relative position had changed, and now there were not only more Congregational churches but also more Presbyterians and more Baptists; taken together, even the churches of German origin (Lutheran and Reformed) already outnumbered the Episcopal outposts. What had happened? The answer is fairly simple: The Anglican churches had languished through much of the colonial period. The southern parishes were often strung out as long, narrow ribbons along the rivers where plantations prospered. This was not a pattern conducive to fellowship of the kind New England village Congregationalists knew. The church was often laggard and drowsy, far beyond the range of care of its presiding bishop, who was in London. The American parishes were not attractive to good clerical talent.

Most of all, the Anglican clerics had sworn loyalty to the King of England, and many of them were thus Loyalist in the American Revolution. They returned to England or drifted off into silence. At the end of the war, many felt that the church could not revive. It happens, however, that sufficient strength had developed in New England, New York, Pennsylvania, and New Jersey to supplement the southern style. (Northern laity, being more recent converts in many cases, actually were more frequently Tory than were their southern counterparts; the majority of the signers of the Declaration of Independence were Episcopalian laity.) The South was swept by Baptist–Methodist revivals. Only one or two Episcopal clerics even tried to adopt the revivalist style. Where the Anglican churches had been established and had had a monopoly, as in Virginia, few counties today have more than 1 percent or, in some cases, 5 percent of the population on Episcopal church rolls.

Despite their revolutionary-era doldrums and setbacks, the Episcopalians did recover their sense of churchly integrity. The presence of domestic bishops in the nineteenth century assured new direction for the church. In many places Episcopalians represented local elites of wealth, education, and influence. They established fine colleges and set the cultural terms for smaller communities. Some of them supported missions to Indians; in fact, some western counties where Episcopalians are fairly strong today were the scene of such missions.

The result of all the vicissitudes and moderate triumphs of the old Episcopal majority-turned-minority has been a curious phenomenon. In some respects the old Loyalist church became the national church of the successful revolutionaries. Thus the National Cathedral in Washington, D.C., is Episcopal, yet it is the site of the burial of many non-Episcopal high officials in both military and civilian circles. To the nation at large, such a burial setting is not sectarian or denominational but national.

Episcopalians, because they are securely located in the nation's memory and have been identified with so many of its great events, take on the responsibility of interpreting the culture and serving as experimenters in it. They seem to be more "typically American" than the rapidly growing conservative churches. Yet they are not able to summon large numbers of people anywhere and have become a minority church in most American communities.

The Episcopal Church has also not been exempt from the difficulties that afflict most denominations in the 1970s. In protest against a decision by the Episcopalians to ordain women and against a revision of the Book of Common Prayer, a small group of congregations split off to form the Anglican Church of North America in 1977. While the worldwide Anglican communion refused to recognize this body, its leaders saw themselves as the true perpetuators of the Episcopal tradition.

MAP 4. LUTHERANS

The Lutherans, like the Baptists and to a lesser extent the Methodists, have a kind of empire, a scene of Lutherandom, but they have not known quite what to do with it for the public presence. The map shows them to be solidly represented all across the North, except for a bit of the extreme Northeast and some counties in or near Idaho. Among Protestants they share with the Baptists alone (and in the case of a single Iowa county, with the Reformed!) a set of counties where more than 50 percent of the population belong to their churches. These occur chiefly in Iowa, Minnesota, and the Dakotas, but a stray county or two in Texas and Nebraska add to strength in the Lutheran dispersion. The entire upper Midwest has a generous number of counties in which 25-50 percent of the people are Lutheran.

Locally their cultural stamp tends to be fairly strong. They have built a number of excellent colleges, have led in dotting the landscape with first-rate contemporary church architectural achievements, and have many healthy congregations. But even where they are strong, they tend to be underrepresented in politics and other public spheres. A traditional passivity about affairs of state or, in more positive terms, a theology that expects Christians to act as citizens without expecting them to transform the world in Christ's picture of the Kingdom of God, has made them seem apolitical and ineffective in public life.

Lutherans, in other words, are very numerous; their three main bodies number between 2.5 and 3 million members each, and with all the satellites and schismatic Lutheran groups accounted for, their numbers approach the 10 million range. But they are not well known, despite those numbers. A survey taken not many years ago found that Lutheranism had a very indistinct image in the mind of non-Lutheran America. It had few enemies and many friends, but these were vague friends who did not know much of what Lutherans have been about.

In addition to their public passivity, these loyal church members suffered another handicap: their eth-nic differences and linguistic distances from each other and from the rest of English-speaking America. A great mass of Lutherans came with the continental Catholics around the middle of the nineteenth century. They came as Swedes and Danes, Norwegians and Finns, and most of all as Germans. They did not know each other as Europeans and mistrusted each other as Americans. They had had no common experience. At the beginning of the twentieth century, approximately sixty church bodies divided the Lutheran scene. Meanwhile, they were often regarded as peculiar for their reluctance to learn the English language and to expose themselves to the forces of American assimilation. It should be added, however, that the mistrust and isolation contributed considerably to group solidarity within the individual Lutheran bodies. They were able to hold the loyalty of their members as their clerical leaders debated endlessly and furiously about minute points of doctrine. Intermarriage between members of Lutheran synods was rare and was even rarer between Lutherans and other Americans.

This situation began to change around World War I, when the German half was embarrassed by its loyalty to German language and manners while the nation was at war with Germany. In characteristic Lutheran style, the members were very loyal to "the powers that be," the American government and military. But their history made them objects of suspicion. The younger generation, wanting to overcome the liabilities of such a position and being restless anyhow about seeming so different, made sudden moves to change the language and the styles and to Americanize. The upper Midwest Lutherans, many of whom had come up the Mississippi from their Atlantic-crossing ships, saw their churches grow very rapidly, especially after the Second World War. They verge on mainline status and have tended to see a stabilization of their growth, although, especially in the case of the Missouri Synod, they have not seen a cessation of doctrinal argument and schismatic tendency.

We have been speaking chiefly here about what is really the second wave of Lutherans, who made up much of Lutherandom in the upper Midwest. We have focused there at the expense of the equally important first wave, the immigrants who reached the middle colonies by the middle of the eighteenth century. The Lutheran patriarch, Henry Melchior Muhlenberg, helped his fellow Pennsylvanians overcome the hostility of English-speaking neighbors, from Benjamin Franklin on down. The Muhlenberg people were pietist, missionary minded. They came on a scene where the earliest Lutherans, many of them of Swedish descent, had already turned Episcopalian, and they developed congregations with loyal members in Pennsylvania and New York in the North and Maryland and Virginia in the South. From those bases they spread rapidly. Many of them cast their lot with non-Lutheran evangelicals and were beginning to blend into the American environment with Methodists and Presbyterians and others. But even as they debated the virtues and vices of Americanization, they were matched by the new millions who settled the West. The newer arrivals tended to be doctrinally more strict and liturgically more traditional.

The Lutherans have never successfully made their way in most of the South. There is a band of them in western Virginia and the Carolinas and in much of Florida, but Baptist territory has not been congenial to the Lutheran presence. So it remains a strong, increasingly adaptive church in the American North, its future marred by a chronic question about its identity and the acute embarrassment or trauma of internal battles within its 3 million-member Missouri Synod, a national, though largely northern, group despite its provincial sounding name. These internal disputes led in 1977 to the formation by former Missouri Synod "moderates" of a new 100,000-member Association of Evangelical Lutheran Churches, which made moves to link up with the Lutheran Church in America and the American Lutheran Church. AELC strength is chiefly in the states surrounding the Great Lakes.

MAP 5. METHODISTS

If any religious body should be tied to the American success story, it is Methodism. A late comer to the colonies, the Methodist Church was only being formed in England during the half century before American independence. It organized America in 1784, having suffered setbacks after its earliest settlements because of the identification of some of its leaders with the British cause during the War for Independence. Yet from that frail base this church, which had set out under its founder simply to warm up and revive the Anglican church, spread with miraculous speed throughout the nineteenth century and today remains the second-largest Protestant group in America. If the black Methodists are added to the largely white churches represented on this map, and if the same addition occurs in the case of Baptists, the two still retain their relative position as dominant Protestants.

Today's Methodists do not have an empire as secure as that of the Baptists. They have no solid mid-South as Baptists have a solid South. In most counties of their greatest strength, they have between 25 and 50 percent of the church members, while Baptists characteristically have more than 50 percent where they are represented significantly throughout the South.

Nor do the Methodists make as strenuous efforts as they once did or as Baptists now do to envelop their members with their church as the approach to a total way of life. Methodists today tend to lead a more exposed, pluralist, rough-and-tumble existence in the midst of the American mix than do the Baptists of the South. But enough momentum remains after the nineteenth-century successes to assure Methodism an enduring and vital place in American religion. If there are some declines in the 1970s, these result in part from the exposure to the environment and the loss of some traditional Methodist resources and reserves of power. In short, they have joined the mainline and suffer as a result of the vulnerability that goes with such environmental contacts. They take on burdens of cultural interpretation and engagement that more sectarian bodies do not risk, and there is therefore some slippage from the membership roles.

How do we account for the fact that Methodism shows up on our map more than any other body? Methodists have the advantage of being four times as numerous as the Episcopalians, who make a widespread but very thin showing. Only the Presbyterians come close, but they are only a third as numerous and have fewer areas of real population density. The Methodists win the Protestant prizes, failing to appear with even 1 percent only in the most sparsely settled counties of Latter-Day Saints territory and a sprinkling of counties along the Dakotas–Montana line and elsewhere in the Northwest. All but a dozen counties east of the Mississippi have at least that minimal representation of 1 percent or more.

The map shows the strength of the Methodist corridor that stretches from the middle states on the East Coast all the way to the Rockies. It happens that when the Second Great Awakening, the event that determined the Protestant map as nothing since has done, broke out, Methodism was poised to take advantage of the opening. The older colonial churches were maladroit, or reluctant to exploit the frontier situation, and tended to stay settled in the East. But Methodists poured through mountain passes, down to Kentucky and Tennessee, where the familiar camp meeting and other revivals helped spread Christianity.

They developed a style of ministry that helped greatly in the churching of America. They used circuit riders and other clerics who were mobile, ready to go where their superintendents and bishops would send them. These were joined by lay preachers and evangelists. Thus a centralized polity made for great efficiency; while their theology looked *democratic*, to use the term that opponents of their polity used to explain their charm among a democracy-minded Western populace. A class meeting system and an efficient means of exercising church discipline provided order for those who had been converted through attractive emotional preaching.

In the second half of the nineteenth century, Methodism continued its earlier patterns of growth while knowing new successes in urban and industrial America. Its informal worship appealed to workers who were put off by what seemed stodgy or forbidding styles of the Episcopalians or Congregationalists. The Methodists knew how to use a kind of bureaucratic system to send missionaries west and an appeal to the heart for recruits to go or for money to support them.

By 1908, when the old Federal Council of Churches was formed, both it and the Methodist Church of the North were ready with social creeds, as Methodism transformed its reformist energies to the Social Gospel and the task of Christianizing the social order, along with liberal Baptists and others. So it became known anew in the public sphere. It has the assets of familiarity, belonging so firmly as it does to the mainline. It has the liabilities that go with that familiarity: a taken-for-grantedness on the part of outsiders and some sense of loss of mission within. But to draw the map of American religion leaving out Methodism would be to leave a void of influence that goes far beyond the membership of Methodism, another manifestly national church that in the twentieth century overcame its major North-South schism.

MAP 6. PRESBYTERIANS

There are two large Presbyterian bodies in the United States. The United Presbyterian Church in the United States of America numbered 2,808,942 adherents in 1973; the Presbyterian Church in the United States, often identified with the South, had 906,359. There is a smaller Presbyterian Church in America, a recent split off the latter, with 41,232 members, and a Cumberland Presbyterian Church with 94,395 members in 1973. But to most Americans it is the first two of these groups that signify Presbyterians in their community. In 1837 the Presbyterians experienced a schism that was exacerbated by North–South hostilities through and beyond the Civil War. In our own time tentative steps are being taken toward reunion.

The Presbyterians rank with the United Church of Christ and the Episcopalians as representatives of the older establishment at the heart of what has come to be called the mainline of churches. Along with those denominations, Presbyterianism has been central to much of the main story of American Protestantism, the home of many theological debates, educational endeavors, and activities that had an import far beyond the confines of the denomination. While the social classes of members vary greatly, in public image Presbyterianism often represents a more or less elite element in the population.

Arriving later than did the Congregationalists or Episcopalians, the Presbyterians began to trickle into the colonies in the eighteenth century. They began on Long Island and in the Pennsylvania–New Jersey sector of the middle colonies. Before long they linked up with

New England churches that had turned Presbyterian in polity; that is, they were churches that did not insist on complete congregational autonomy. A split over polity, doctrine, and revivalist attitudes kept Presbyterians apart from 1741 to 1758, but they were subsequently well poised to be "all things to all people," and they prospered after the Revolution. They had worked their way into Virginia and other southern colonies where, as a dissenting church, they helped bring about the separation of church and state.

When in 1801 they linked up in a Plan of Union with Congregationalists, it was the Presbyterians who were more at home with revivalist styles and who profited more from the new fervent and mobile approaches to churching America. (By 1837 the Plan of Union was abandoned just as Presbyterianism was dividing.) Like Episcopalianism and Congregationalism, Presbyterianism was slowed down on the frontier by its adherence to the ideal of a learned ministry. But it compensated for this setback by developing more efficient means for spreading that ministry. The Presbyterians opened numerous colleges and seminaries and participated in what has been called an Errand of Mercy, made up of various missionary, educational, and reformist societies.

In all these respects the Presbyterians seemed to be especially adaptive to the western environment. They had both revivalism and learning, settled pastoral care and mobile ministries, access to elites and some successes among the southern poor. Missions to American Indians and carefully plotted church extension through the West helped Presbyterians move there. The map reveals how relatively successful they were. They are at least sparsely represented almost everywhere. They seem to have run out of energy in the lightly populated western Great Plains and some of the Rocky Mountain or desert counties. But they are a thoroughly southern and northern church, with a better planting in California and the Northwest than most churches knew.

For those who would seek "Presbyteriandom," however, a place where members of this church could exercise power by weight of numbers, the search will be long. In only one or two counties east of the Mississippi are there more Presbyterians than members of any other church. When one comes to a rare western county with a Presbyterian majority, the statistics are embarrassing. Thus in Park County, Colorado, the Presbyterian majority of thirty-three members in one church can lord it over the five members of the only other reported congregation, the Seventh-day Adventist church. In Treasure County, Montana, 190 Presbyterian members outnumber the 150 Roman Catholics. South Dakota's Jackson County they share with four other church bodies, but the Presbyterian majority is only 375 strong. The Southern Baptists would yawn in the face of such small numbers.

We stress this not to have fun with the Presbyterians

but to underscore once again the fundamental fact about the heirs of the bigger colonial churches. Americans think of them as typical, established, elite, powerful. They are busy with theology, activism, public affairs, works of charity, and efforts at social change. But they must do this from a vulnerable base, for they are outnumbered virtually everywhere and cannot set the terms for their local culture, nor can they protect their members by weight of numbers. It is fair to speak of Presbyterians as a successful national church that has experienced internal tensions in recent years.

MAP 7. ROMAN CATHOLICS

The Roman Catholics, from some points of view, are among the most "neat" denominations with which to deal on the map, despite their size and apparent sprawl. The reasons are twofold. First, they are organized under the central authority of a hierarchy that culminates with the Pope. This means that there are not important schismatic groups existing under the Catholic name. If the word *Catholic* appears in the name of a few other churches—as in the case of the Polish National Catholic Church of America, the absence of the adjective *Roman* helps everyone to keep the lines clear and to avoid confusion. Secondly, attempts are made to register all active Catholics, so the method of bookkeeping, one might say, is more accurate than that of some other churches. This second asset is compromised, however, by the fact that many rather inert and lapsed Catholics do remain on the rolls, so one might also say that the standards of active membership are lower than those of at least the more strict Protestant groups.

Catholics seem to be everywhere. As well they might be, given the fact that they are by far the largest single denomination in the United States. In 1973 the Roman Catholic Church reported 48,465,438 members. In the North, from Maine to Seattle, there are hardly more than a dozen counties where there are almost no Catholics. The Baptist solid South and the Methodist strip in the "southern North" are the two areas where there are most counties with fewest Catholics. On the other hand, despite the church's great size, there are not many counties in which the majority of the population is Catholic. Most of such counties are in the very lightly populated Southwest and southern Texas, where the Spanish-speaking church is strong, and in the Delta country of Louisiana. In the rest of the nation the great exception is in the very heavily populated state of Massachusetts. It is more than slightly ironic that Massachusetts, settled by some of the strongest minded Protestant pioneers in the "land where our fathers died," turned out to be the Catholic stronghold. The Northeast and the Great Lakes states do show scores of counties in which 25–50 percent of the people are Catholic.

The Catholics came late to the United States and proceeded from a very small base at the time of the birth of the nation. True, Spanish Catholics discovered and first settled the Caribbean and reached the extreme southeast and southwest of what was to become the United States. And French Catholics early dominated in the northeast, though in the end they were centered in Canada and not the United States. But in the thirteen colonies by 1776, there were only 20,000 to 30,000 Catholics in a population of several million.

During the years of settlement of the thirteen colonies, the predominating empires of northwest Europe were in the best position to colonize. This meant that it was Protestant nations, England most of all but also the Netherlands, for a time Sweden, and eventually the Scotch–Irish people of the British empire, who came to the new land. They were sometimes refugees from European Catholic areas. They had long memories of Reformation-era persecutions by Catholics. (They had shorter memories of their own acts of persecution against Catholics where they themselves had the power.) These immigrants wanted to set up their own Protestant civilizations, so they were hostile to Catholics and tried to exclude them or harass them when they came. A map of 1776 would have shown significant Roman Catholic concentrations only in Maryland and Pennsylvania.

So matters remained until the second third of the nineteenth century. From then on the Protestant monopoly in America was broken, but not without a century of struggle by Catholics to establish themselves as a rightful presence in the American mixture. They were often discriminated against on ethnic grounds; the Irish and the southern and eastern Europeans were particularly despised. But even when the Catholics came from acceptable stock, for instance, German, nativist groups still ranged themselves and raged against them. They feared that Catholics would have to demonstrate fealty to antidemocratic forces, notably the papacy, which in the *Syllabus of Errors* in 1864 condemned many of the features of democracy cherished by Protestants in America.

Drastic and sudden population growth in northwest Europe with the rise of the industrial revolution made it impossible for Europe to sustain all the Catholic mouths to feed. Dreadful famines in Ireland in the late 1840s added to the motivation to migrate. The American form of government did assure freedoms that were often lacking to Catholics in Europe. The attractions were strong, and they won out over the harassments and privations. The Catholics came by the millions and propagated themselves more rapidly than did the Protestants, while their missionaries also gained significant numbers of converts—chiefly from the lapsed-Catholic heirs of European churchdom.

The map shows important percentages of Catholics in rural America, but their true importance has come because of their urban dominance. America was becoming citified during the very decades of Catholic arrival, and a kind of Catholic urban empire met and challenged the old Protestant rural one. Concerned Protestants late in the nineteenth century worried equally about the growth of cities and the growth of Catholicism. The invention of the parochial school in the face of semi-Protestantized public schools and as an instrument for keeping urban Catholics together greatly aided in the spread of the Roman Catholic Church, especially in the cities.

The Catholics concentrate in the northeastern and in the Great Lakes states because those were the areas of greatest population growth in the industrial era. The cities needed the muscle that Catholics could provide. Catholics built the cities, huddled in them, prospered there, and moved after World War II into the suburban areas. While the immigrant ships brought plenty of "warm bodies," often overlooked has been the role of priests and missioners who carried on work comparable to that of Protestant revivalists. Someone had to inspire, create enthusiasm among, and encourage cooperative efforts from the relaxed and sometimes sullen Catholics who arrived. These priests were artists at building both morale and church edifices throughout the North.

The South has not been the scene of much Catholic dominance, in part because of its later urbanization and in part because revivalists had worked so successfully with the old-stock whites, making them Baptists and Methodists. But Catholics did arrive with the great twentieth-century migrants to the currently most populated state, California, where they dominate even though percentages of the total population of most counties are not too high.

Catholics have long worried about several hundred "priestless counties," although with the decline in priestly vocations whether much can be done about priesting them all is a question. Fifty years after the immigration laws were changed to inhibit the growth of peoples from whom Catholics derived their members, and in the face of troubles resulting from churchly upsets after the Second Vatican Council (1962–1965), Catholic growth has slowed. It is quite likely that in the years ahead, as northern industries move south, slightly higher Catholic percentages will show in the South, while the church tends, at best, to hold its own in areas of existing strength.

MAP 8. UNITED CHURCH OF CHRIST

The merger of the Evangelical and Reformed Church with the Congregational Christian churches in 1957 produced the United Church of Christ—and also produced a problem for interpreters of maps of religious America. It is difficult to sort out with any precision just how many Evangelical and Reformed and how many Congregational Christian members made up U.C.C. strength in any particular county. Had we a map from 1957, however, it is likely that the Evangelical and Reformed would have shown their greatest strengths in the Midwest, in Illinois and Wisconsin and Missouri, while the Congregationalists would be stronger elsewhere.

Strange it is that on the inclusive map of religious groups in America, the United Church of Christ shows up hardly at all. It had a near monopoly in New England when the nation was born, its 749 congregations–the largest cluster in America, with no other body having more than 500–gathered in the North. Congregationalism was almost unrepresented outside of New England; one congregation on the New York mainland, four on Long Island, two in New Jersey, and four lonely outposts in South Carolina represented the entire extent of the diaspora. But where they were strong, they were very strong. It was not implausible for Yale University President Ezra Stiles in 1783 to picture an American religious future divided almost equally among Congregationalists, Presbyterians, and Episcopalians.

Nineteenth-century events were to deny the fulfilment of that prophesy. The heirs of the Puritans, many of them agents of the First Great Awakening in the second third of the eighteenth century, failed to follow up by participating on a large scale in the Second Great Awakening and other nineteenth-century revivals. Congregationalism was torn over the Unitarian controversy. It had come to rely on an educated and not always mobile ministry. The emotional theology of the newer revivalists struck many Congregationalists as crude.

This is not to say that Congregationalism had no interest in propagating itself and its version of Christianity. But it chose the path of quiet civility. In 1801 in a Plan of Union, it agreed to cooperate with Presbyterians, but the Presbyterians were to prosper more than did Congregationalists in the West. The westward movement of Congregationalism occurred very gradually, as members moved first into New York and then, step by step, through Ohio, Illinois, and into Iowa. They often planted what became excellent colleges and centers of learning or culture. But they were relatively overwhelmed by the fervent revivalists and the continental immigrants. The South Carolina congregations of the eighteenth century had been isolated, and they had few heirs. The United Church of Christ is a rare and lonely presence anywhere in the South. The rural and small-town upper Midwest and New England continue to have a generous sprinkling of United Church of Christ congregations, but most of them occur in counties where the proportion of U.C.C. members to the whole population remains under 5 percent.

The Evangelical and Reformed congregations resulted from mid-nineteenth-century immigrations, most of them from Germany. These movements of people paralleled Lutheran migrations. Indeed, many of the newer evangelicals had been united with Lutherans in the Prussian state·church after 1817, but the two groups chose to part when they reached the American shores. The overlapping of their populations with that of Congregational Christians in the Midwest helped make plausible the merger of 1957. Still, theirs was the first and remains the only significant and sizable American merger that transgressed and transcended ethnic (English-German) and traditional boundaries.

What is the significance of minority status everywhere for a sizable church? Because of its long lineage, its bond with American environments, its shaping role in national events, the United Church of Christ is well known and represented throughout the North. At the same time, nowhere can it summon majorities or even sizable minorities. It is difficult for such a group, even were it minded to do so, to "throw its weight around" or to create a cultural style for nonmembers. In this respect it differs drastically from the Baptist, Lutheran, and Roman Catholic representations around the nation.

MAP 9. ADVENTISTS

This chapter is not an essay on church growth so much as a historical accounting that sets out to say who is where, why, and with what strength. The *who*, in this case, is largely the Seventh-day Adventists, since the Advent Christian Church claims only 30,000 people, and one or two other churches are infinitesimally small. Part of an international movement that developed toward the middle of the nineteenth century, Adventists hold a belief centered in *premillennialism*, a vision of a future in which Christ would return and inaugurate a thousand-year rule. Certain behavioral corollaries of Adventist teaching have made Adventists highly visible: they worship on Saturday, not Sunday, they are vegetarians, and they reject alcohol and tobacco. They are generally classified with the conservative evangelicals.

The group began in upper New York state, in what came to be called the burned-over district, because so many revivals had been held there. The original leader, William Miller (after whom they were first called Millerites), made the mistake of setting exact dates for Christ's Second Coming, and his failure led to setbacks. Modern Adventism dates just as plausibly from the prophecies of Ellen G. White a third of a century later.

The concern for health led Adventists to build excellent sanitaria—Battle Creek (Michigan), Takoma Park (Maryland), and Loma Linda (California) are located at three Adventist population centers—and these became foci for further growth. Publicity put out by the Adventists always tends to concentrate on the church body's educational, healing, and evangelistic ministries. It is truly international in outlook and scope.

By the nature of its missionary outreach, Adventism is not and probably will not be soon concentrated in particular areas. The map shows more areas "under 1 percent" unsupplemented by other shadings on more parts of the map than is the case with the other groups included here. Apart from the medical-educational centers there seems to be no area that is "Adventist soil," but members of this church can be found at all national compass points.

Almost nowhere are more than 5 percent of the people in any American county members of Adventist churches—the single exception being two on the Washington–Oregon line. Even the historic centers of strength like Calhoun County, Michigan, with its familiar Adventist site of Battle Creek, lists only about 1700 members. The county in which Takoma Park, Maryland, lies—another Adventist sanitarium center—claims only 9000 members, despite generally high suburban Washington population bases. There are more Adventists, about 27,000 of them, in Los Angeles County, California, especially around Loma Linda, where they operate a university with a medical school. But 27,000 people can be overwhelmed in congested Los Angeles County.

If Adventists have few strong bases, they are not inhibited. The map shows that they have 1 percent, or sometimes up to 5 percent, of the people "almost everywhere," and, a fervently evangelistic group, they are growing very rapidly. On any scale or graph of recent church growth, they are among the leaders. In 1940 they claimed 176,000 members, a number that had grown to 237,000 a decade later; 318,000 by 1960; and 420,000 in 1970. In 1973 they listed 464,267 members, a probably reliable figure since Adventist standards are high, discipline is efficient, and record keeping is accurate. If present trends continue, we can picture a future map on which at least in some counties this later starting but aggressive cluster of church bodies will have a higher percentage of the population.

MAP 10. MENNONITES

The Mennonite churches are not well known in urban America, though their peace witness is recognized and the very conservative groups to the right of the Mennonites, the Amish, are familiar in American folklore and are favorite subjects for photographers who hurry past their buggies and their settlements in rural America. It is quite difficult to conceive of the mainline Mennonites ever growing very large; from the sixteenth century they have existed as a witness against the officially established faiths and have perpetuated high standards of church membership. Just as the standards tend to be forbiddingly high, it must also be said that most unchurched Americans are simply not in range of the locales or the styles of the Mennonites.

The Mennonites are also by definition a divided

group. Whenever high standards are preserved after several centuries, and because different migrations reached America from different places at different times, the definitions of church life become quite narrow. Whoever consults any kind of yearbook of American churches will find a half dozen tiny Mennonite churches: Beachy Amish Mennonite Churches, Church of God in Christ (Mennonite), Conference of the Evangelical Mennonite Church, Conservative Mennonite Conference, Evangelical Mennonite Brethren, Hutterian Brethren, Old Order Mennonite Church, Reformed Mennonite Church, and the like. They all number up to only 6000 or 7000 members each in a cluster of tiny congregations—usually geographically isolated from others. The Old Order Amish Mennonite Church did report almost 15,000 members in 1972.

That leaves two larger groups. The General Conference Mennonite Church numbered 36,483 in 1973; they are often thought of as relatively liberal and least traditionalist. But the larger by far is the Mennonite Church, with 90,367 members in 1973. With almost 1000 congregations, the Mennonite Church comes nearest to having a national representation. Hardly less congregational than the General Conference Mennonite Church, it is more ready to adhere formally to sixteenth-century Mennonite standards of belief. The members can trace American roots as far back as 1683.

The stronghold of the Mennonite Church members is in northern Indiana, around Goshen and Elkhart, where they have a college and seminary and whence some of their publishing ventures issue; but Scottdale, Pennsylvania, remains the main center for book and magazine production. The General Conference people, on the other hand, are more associated with Kansas, where they operate Bethel College at Newton, the town that is also their central office.

The map shows Mennonite strength to be most visible in southern Kansas, southeast Nebraska, and southeast South Dakota, where low populations make it easier for them to have a higher percentage of the total than in Pennsylvania, Ohio, and Indiana, where they have substantial numbers but are overwhelmed by the numbers of people around them. How did Mennonites get to where they are? Historically, they have been "on the run," victims of persecution by established Protestants ever since their "radical Reformation" in Europe.

In the United States they were, of course, free from most kinds of persecution—some Hutterian groups and other extreme pacifists have suffered some in war times—and chose their sites in part with reference to the quality of farmland and the potential for remaining some distance from strangers who might lead them to compromise their style of living. Few made their way into the South and there are not many centers in the West, though the Northwest has counties where up to 5 percent of the people are Mennonite.

MAP 11. MORAVIANS

Moravian bodies are among the smallest to be charted. The Moravian Church in America, Northern Province numbered only 33,321 members in 1973, while the Moravian Church in America, Southern Province had 22,411 members. Taken together, therefore, they stand no chance of being represented by as much as 5 percent of the population in any county. Yet it is important to have some small churches represented, for they help make up an important element in American religious life.

The Moravians are an exceptionally familial church body. For example, in 1952 The Moravian Church in America published a *Moravian Travel Guide*, which was designed to "fit handily into the pocket of your coat or the glove compartment of your car." The idea was clear: wherever a Moravian would travel, if other Moravians were to be found, he or she would be welcome among them. (The Moravians being a friendly people, one might add that non-Moravians could also be assured of hospitality in what the book calls Moraviandom.) Brief historical sketches of the various congregations were highlighted in the *Guide*.

The Moravians derived from the pre-Reformation Bohemian Brethren who took new impetus from the energies of the pietist Lutheran German Count Ludwig von Zinzendorf after 1722. Known for their pietism, missionary spirit, and pacific temperament and tendency, the Moravians came to the New World in the middle of the eighteenth century. More than half of the world's Moravians live in the United States and Canada. Their great pioneer, von Zinzendorf, himself came to the states to help propagate this form of Protestantism. He was a frequent visitor to New York City, where several tiny churches exist in numbers too small to show up on the map and as exceptions to the generally rural situation of Moravians.

The major concentration in the East is in eastern Pennsylvania, the true site of Moraviandom. Disciples of early leader Peter Boehler settled in 1740 around Nazareth, on soil that was obtained from the great evangelist George Whitefield. Even better known is the settlement at Bethlehem, where there are numerous Moravian shrines and where a well-known Christmas observance has done almost as much to put the city on the map as has its importance as a steel city. Headquarters of the Northern Province are here.

Eleven years after von Zinzendorf helped Bethlehemites start, Bishop Augustus Spangenberg, the other well-known Moravian leader, initiated a colony in North Carolina in the area where the cities of Winston and Salem, now combined as Winston-Salem, prosper. Salem is to the Southern Province what Bethlehem is to the Northern, and its historic sites regularly attract non-Moravians. There are areas of strength in Texas, but otherwise only four or five counties west of the Mississippi—in Minnesota and North Dakota—contain even the minimal number of Moravians that would warrant them a place on the map. One county in Ohio, one in Michigan, and two in Wisconsin are more than 1 percent Moravian, while central and northeast Wisconsin include a sprinkling of Moravians. All these arrived as the result of later immigrations from Europe and of missionary activity, some of which had been directed first to American Indians, for whom Moravians often expressed a genteel regard and among whom they worked selflessly.

MAP 12. PENTECOSTAL CHURCHES

The Pentecostalists share with Adventists the fastest growing status on a percentage basis of all the groups described in this book. But whereas Adventists appear in counties all over the map, the Pentecostalists tend still to be a largely southern and even southeastern movement. (Were black Pentecostalists to be included, the picture might be somewhat different. One black denomination of this type, the Church of God in Christ, now lists 2.5 million members, and many of these are in the urban North). Nowhere do Pentecostalists dominate; only in four or five far-southeastern counties do they reach 5 percent of the population. In the Northeast and the upper Midwest and Rocky Mountain states they are almost unrepresented.

Some years from now the map may very well show more dispersion. A sample of Pentecostal bodies will show why. From 1940 to 1970 the Church of God of Cleveland, Tennessee, grew 332 percent from 63,000 to 272,000. The 1973 yearbooks list 313,332 members in this "Number 1" growing group. (The Assemblies of God, not represented on this map because they did not participate in the data gathering, were second nationally, with 224 percent growth over thirty years to their 1973 figure of 1,117,116.)

Modern Pentecostalism is a twentieth-century movement. For those who like their church history neat, it might be noted that at a revival healing service in Topeka, Kansas, on the last night of the old century, a Miss Agnes Ozman experienced the gift of speaking in tongues—a distinguishing Pentecostal mark—and the next day a group of students among whom she worked decided to prolong the revival and perpetuate its practices. Kansas did not become a Pentecostal center. Six years later on Azusa Street in Los Angeles there was a fresh spurt of tongue-speaking evangelism, and southern California has since come to play host to thousands of Pentecostals. However, the population there is so dense that small but growing groups have little opportunity to show up impressively on the maps.

The fertile soil for Pentecostalism was originally among the poor whites of Appalachia, for in its earlier forms it was clearly a typical "religion for the dispossessed." Little premium was placed on a learned ministry or on education for members. Sharing much with other conservative evangelicals but being less reliant than many of them on rigid doctrinal formulations and more attuned to spontaneous spiritual expression, the Pentecostals attracted many of the outcast, unlearned, and what the rest of society regarded as marginal citizens.

Around the world Pentecostalism is one of the fastest growing forms of Christianity, particularly in the southern hemisphere. Growth in North America is also rapid, especially since the movement has gained new respectability, thanks to the movement of historic denominations of this stripe toward the middle class. There they have been joined, a bit uneasily, by some "pentecostal" or "charismatic" members of mainline churches. There have also been urban and suburban moves, as Pentecostalism has been shedding its old negative images: "hillybilly," "snakehandling," "holy-rolling." None of these well describe the new buoyant and aggressive Pentecostalists' styles.

A work by John Thomas Nichol, *The Pentecostals*, (New York: Harper & Row, 1966) typically tries to account for and classify the scores of emerging Pentecostal denominations. But in a period of ferment there is normally considerable fragmentation, and it is difficult to keep track of the changing names, statuses, and locales of Pentecostalism. For this reason there is no easy way of relating the map to the experience of other Americans. More and more the Pentecostalists are becoming visible, even if they are very far from being able to develop Pentecostaldom or from having an empire. Expect a map in a decade or two that will show more northern counties suggesting at least traces of members from these denominations. They have too many energies and plans to remain confined to the South and Southeast.

MAP 13. REFORMED CHURCHES

Over half a million American Protestants are members of two Reformed bodies of Dutch extraction. Most of the German Reformed have merged into what was the Evangelical and Reformed Church, which merged again into the United Church of Christ. This means that when one hears the word *Reformed* today it is almost always in connection with people who migrated from the Netherlands. The larger number of them are in the Reformed Church in America; in 1973, 360,746 members were reported. The later migrations produced the Christian Reformed Church, which in 1973 had 210,000 adherents.

It is not unfair to the two major Reformed bodies to stress the ethnic tie—unless we also forget that most religious groups in America are still marked, after three or four centuries, by ethnic characteristics. It is impossible to tell the story of American Lutheran divisions and reunions without reference to the European origins of the various German or Scandinavian groups. Mainline Protestantism, which had never "looked ethnic" is being interpreted increasingly on racial and ethnic grounds. Its history is being retold over against that of Judaism, black Protestantism, and Roman Catholicism. In the retelling, racial preferences and prejudices emerge as factors in Protestant definition.

So with the Reformed. As the years pass, because of expansive efforts in post-World War II and especially suburban America, the Reformed churches each year lose more of their Dutch reminiscence. The assimilating processes in America are strong. But for decades to come it will not be hard to see ties between Dutch past and Reformed present in America. One might almost say that the reason the two churches are not larger is simply that there was a small population base to begin with in Holland; there was too small a cohort from which to draw many migrants.

These immigrants came essentially in two waves, and it is these two waves that determined the character of the two Reformed bodies. The first was colonial. It must be remembered that the Netherlands was a budding empire early in the seventeenth century, competing against Catholic Spain and Portugal and ready to hold its own relative to France and, most of all, England. The story of Dutch ventures in early America are familiar to those who know anything about colonial settlement, particularly because of early successes at New Netherlands and in the New Amsterdam that became America's greatest city. The colonizers were largely commercial venturers, not motivated chiefly by religion. Indeed, many of them did what they could to keep the churches at a little distance.

The clergy did arrive, to care for those who had come across and for their children. A century was to pass, however, before the Dutch began to spread their Reformed faith on any large scale. In 1700 there were only 26 Dutch Reformed churches in America, while in 1780 there were 127. Between these two events there had occurred the First Great Awakening. Its first major revivalist was himself Dutch Reformed, Theodore Jacobus Freylinghuysen. He had moved with others into the Raritan Valley in New Jersey, after the New York

settlement became less attractive. In this valley the Dutch were to found what has become Rutgers University and the oldest Protestant seminary in America at New Brunswick. Freylinghuysen had particular success with revivalist measures that led to warmed hearts, vital congregational life, and a missionary impulse. A map of church locations in 1750, a quarter of a century after his first efforts, shows congregations all the way up the Hudson in New York and throughout northern New Jersey, but that was that—except for a congregation or so in Pennsylvania, where the German Reformed were strong. Not a single Reformed church of any sort was in New England in this period.

Today's map shows that New England never was penetrated on any great scale. The entire South is almost untouched, except for traces in Florida and a county in Kentucky. The strength of the eastern Dutch Reformed churches remains in New York and New Jersey. But even as their members moved west and as they gained new adherents from the non-Dutch, something happened to alter the map.

A new wave of Reformed Christians migrated from the Netherlands. (The parallels to Lutheranism's two-wave movement are impressive.) The nineteenth-century settlers tended to be more conservative, seceders from the theologically liberal and somewhat more lax established church in Holland. Michigan was beckoning, and most of them settled in the western part of that state, where Grand Rapids and Holland became centers of education and parish strength. Efforts to merge with the older arrivals failed, and the two remain apart to this day.

The nineteenth century later comers moved west from Michigan and were joined by newer settlers. Some made it to California. A significant settlement went to Washington state; the northwest corner of the map, for instance, finds Reformed strength running as high as 13.8 percent in Whatcom county. But on the way to the West Coast some also "dropped out" or found Iowa attractive, and the most heavily Reformed counties in America are in Northwest Iowa, where further educational centers were established. Pella, Iowa, and Orange City, Iowa, join Grand Rapids and Holland—and older New Brunswick—as pulses and centers of Reformed church life in America.

8

Interpreting American Pluralism

MARTIN E. MARTY

THE CHARACTER OF AMERICAN PLURALISM

Americans like to speak of their religious settlement as one of pluralism, marked by tolerance. *Pluralism* is a rather recently applied term, necessitated by the presence of hundreds of competing religious groups and the freedom of citizens to have no religion at all.[1] As long as Protestantism dominated the religious landscape, the choice of a term like pluralism could be postponed. Citizens spoke of *religious freedom* and *the separation of church and state*. But they knew that by weight of numbers and history, Protestantism long had a kind of privileged position and that other groups looked more or less like dissent. In the twentieth century, after the great migrations from continental Europe, Catholic Ireland, and Asia, it was no longer plausible to think in terms of a Protestant empire containing little islands of religious alternatives.[2]

Pluralism, in colloquial language, means "any number can play." They can play on equal terms. There should be no governmental encouragement of one religious group over another, no governmental inhibition of one group at the expense of another. This legal resolution is supposed to have a corollary in the outlook of the citizens. While they are all free to pursue their own vision, to be religious or not or to be religious in a particular way, they are expected to honor other choices by other people, whether they have sympathies with other people or not. The Supreme Court expects the government to be "wholesomely neutral" with regard to religion, and citizens are to be wholesome, whether neutral or not.[3]

The boundaries of religious pluralism are, and of necessity must be, very broad and loosely defined. Constitutional guarantees of free speech and assembly and, most of all, of religious freedom, assure that the corral in which American religionists can graze is very large and the fences are very low. The courts do not want to get into the game of determining the truth or falsehood of doctrines, refuse to arbitrate between religious groups in questions of opinion, and are careful about intervening in the case of religious matters that might offend large sectors of the public.[4] Quite obviously, a religious group that advocated infant sacrifice or some other similar time-sanctioned religious practices would be prohibited from acting upon them. But it is more difficult for courts to take a stand when there has been the charge of a spiritual kidnapping and the brainwashing of a young person by a cult.

The law does not like to interfere with Christian Scientists' views of medicine and health, but it cannot protect them from fluoridation of water even if the Christian Scientists find this medicinal practice abhorrent. The terms of common civil life force them to have to share in a practice they cannot applaud. Jehovah's Witnesses, because of their own reading of certain biblical passages, reject blood transfusions. Yet there are many instances in which the government intervenes and forces blood transfusion upon an objecting member of a Jehovah's Witness family. Some religious sects and cults insist on bringing up children in their own schools, many of them educationally substandard and ill equipped to prepare children for life in a pluralistic society. But members of the groups are not interested in such preparation. They picture a future in which the child grows to adulthood protected from the erosions of pluralism. Only in extreme cases does the civil court interfere to force a broader education on the child. It is difficult for the taxing agencies to begin to determine where the boundaries of legitimacy exist in the matter of tax exemption for religious groups. "Diploma mills" can boldly and frankly merchandise theological degrees and ordination credentials and on the basis of these allow for tax exemption of enterprises presided over by ministers who buy these diplomas. The courts are bewildered as to how to prosecute when these practices violate standards of public approval and decency.

If American pluralism has forced citizens to be tolerant, it should be remembered that such religious tolerance is a rare and tardy aspect of interreligious life in human history. In prehistoric religion there are examples of different religious groups coexisting; even American Indian life shows some side-by-side, cheek-by-jowl native American cultures that seemed to coexist in a kind of urban pluralist setting for decades if not centuries.[5] But normally in remote pasts all the people in an area shared a single religious outlook, a single symbol system, one that was ordinarily supported by state and sword. Such policies often grew out of accident and ignorance. People simply were too far from alternatives to be attracted to them or repulsed by them.

When different religious groups came into each others' spheres of influence, all the problems associated with today's terms *pluralism* and *tolerance* began to come into play. Since most religions have a universalistic outlook, the claim that theirs is a truth for all people, it may seem strange that they cannot be simply tolerant. But the obverse of this universalistic outlook is a kind of exclusivism that marks most religions.[6] Even those that claim to be most sympathetic—one thinks of Hinduism or the "publick religion" of the American Founding Fathers—turn out to have an exclusivist tinge. Not everyone shares the outlook of the Hindus or the civil religionists. In turn, holders of these faiths begin by suggesting that they can embrace all the particular religions on their territory. When they meet with resistance by others, their advocates and articulators often reveal the limits of their own tolerance and sympathy.

Exclusivism seems to "go with the territory" in religion, unless people take pains to do something about it. Religions are born when a cluster of people share a certain vision, experience, or revelation. They almost inevitably seek out other people who have or can gain the same vision, and in order to reinforce themselves and to protect values for transmission, they huddle together. In the process they turn their backs on the larger world. The faiths that came to majority in America were of this type. Judaism, according to the Hebrew scriptures, was supposed to be a "light to the nations."

The prophet Amos was not alone when he reminded the children of Israel that God was active also in Egypt and among other peoples. But the "light to the nations" idea was paralleled by the concept of chosenness. Chosenness may be stressed for the sake of a vocation for others, but it is also easy to think of chosenness as a license for privilege, a claim of uniqueness over all other claims.

Christianity, daughter of Judaism, kept this ambiguity. The early Christians believed that Christ died for all people, that his meaning was of cosmic significance and value. Yet they also asserted that because there was "none other name under heaven given among men" whereby they might be saved, adherents were false teachers and practitioners. This outlook inspired the Crusades, in which Christians assumed the military right to wrest sacred shrines from the infidel. It also permitted the practice of forcing Jews into ghettos, where they could not taint Christians, and of forcing dissenters who were themselves Christian into exile or to the gallows.[7]

Because America's majority has been Christian, it might be said that America's problem with pluralism began around A.D. 313, the symbolic date for the birth of "Constantinianism." Until that time the Christian church was one of hundreds of sects that shared life under the Roman sun, the sometime beneficiary of Roman pluralism and sometime victim of the limits of Roman tolerance. But with Constantine's conversion came a cluster of documents that authorized a new policy. Now Christianity would have support of law. Within decades the once persecuted Christians were doing the persecuting themselves.[8] The old Roman deities were proscribed, and Christians began to carry on mission to the outer limits of their new empires, east and west. In the Middle Ages whenever a new sect might appear, it had to take refuge in remote valleys, or far from the centers of power and civilization where its adherents would know little security.

The Protestant Reformation, an event that had much to do with the founding and settling of America, is often looked back to as the moment when modern pluralism and its corollary tolerances were born. Not so.[9] The mainline Reformers carried over the practices of a millennium and more. *Cuius regio eius religio* was the norm and standard. Whoever ruled or "owned" the region determined its religion, its sole and exclusive faith. Northern Europe turned Protestant–Lutheran, Anglican, Presbyterian, Reformed—and this Protestantism was established by law in territory after territory. Germany became a patchwork of literally hundreds of such territories for centuries more. Religion remained established by law. Protestants persecuted their own radicals as much as Catholics ever persecuted Protestants. Mennonites, Quakers, Anabaptists had to go into hiding or later escape to America.

In the long discredited mythic picture, America was

born as a haven of pluralism and tolerance. It is always difficult to picture how life was lived before a certain epochal shift occurred. Latter-day Americans so took for granted the achievements won over centuries that they were not able to keep in mind a clear picture of how this development occurred. It is not true that the founders of North America came to assure religious freedom for persecuted Europeans. Almost all of them came to find it for themselves.

No one is likely to understand the complications of American pluralism without some sense of how it did come about. A combination of factors, including the fate of declining European empires, coincidence, practical necessity, the ideology of some religious groups, and some Enlightenment statesmen, conspired to bring in a new day. Each step toward pluralism was hard won. A broadbrush history of the course people took toward the American resolution is helpful at this point.

The Europe that discovered America was not ready for pluralism; if anything, it was moving *away* from the measures of tolerance that had begun to develop in some parts of Europe. The Spanish discoverers came across to America in the very year that Ferdinand and Isabella defeated the Moors (Muslims) and boxed them in in Spain, and as Columbus left for the New World, the monarchs of Aragon and Castile expelled hundreds of thousands of Jews from Spain. In order to have an empire it was thought necessary to have a completely homogeneous religious pattern on the home front. Spain was not especially villainous in this respect. Portugal, which dominated parts of South America, moved by the same impulses. Their powerful French rival spent the century of discovery trying to learn how Catholics and Protestants could live together in France before they could even dream of living together with Spaniards at all. When the first French Protestant refugees set up a little colony not far from where Spanish Catholics made the first successful and permanent settlement on American soil, they were massacred. Such was the inherited Christian pattern.

The Dutch in New Amsterdam were not much different, though necessity forced them to act differently. Old Amsterdam was one of the more tolerant cities of that day's Christendom. Jews had more freedom there than in most places, Catholics and Protestants at times coexisted, and numerous sects found their way to the lowlands. One would have thought that since the Dutch were attempting to establish a trade outpost more than a colony, religious diversity would not have represented a problem. Still, the early governors, who happened to welcome Jews because of their merchandizing and trade expertise, worried about and tried to prohibit Lutherans and Catholics from settling.

England settled America decades before the Glorious Revolution of 1688 helped spread the idea of tolerance. So the Virginia colonists came expecting everyone to be Episcopalian and soon developed laws limiting freedom of expression. Best known were the Puritan Separatists at Plymouth Colony, the Puritans themselves at Massachusetts Bay, and then New Haven and the Connecticut settlements. They made no secret that they were not going to be tolerant or welcome pluralism. They would hang a Quaker, banish an Antinomian, eject anyone who made a point of rejecting their concept of the covenant that bound them together. They could never comprehend Rogue's Island, or Rhode Island, the "latrina of New England," which was built on some newfangled Baptists' ideas of relative tolerance; Pennsylvania, where Quaker William Penn allowed for diversity; or the Calverts' Maryland, founded by the English Catholic minority that had to grant and did grant relatively broad religious freedoms.

By the time of independence, a privileged or established church existed in nine of the thirteen colonies. But the pioneer revival called the First Great Awakening of the 1730s and 1740s had forced Americans to see religion in a new way. Itinerant and circuit-riding evangelists with their new messages of grace rode into American towns to unsettle the settled clergy and the churches. People also became aware of religious diversity on an intercolonial basis. The colonies came together to fight a war of independence; how could these colonies continue to stay together with their competing establishments, yet how could they let themselves be pushed apart on religious, not political, grounds? In their midst were dissenting sects—Baptists everywhere, and Presbyterians moving into the South—who insisted that establishments fall and that people be free to support only their own churches, if they chose to support any at all.

On this scene came that remarkable generation of Enlightened founding fathers, people influenced by religious viewpoints that did encourage tolerance. They tended to believe that exclusivism was unnecessary and, indeed, wrong in religion. They rejected separate revelations, were critical of dogmas that divided, despised "priestcraft" when it guarded competing and jealous separate faiths and churches. They believed in God, in rewards and punishments, in morality and good living, and in the possibility that where the churches' mission and messages overlapped they could contribute to the common good.[10]

Given their problem of forming one nation out of several religious establishments, the pestering of freedom-seeking dissent groups, and the universalist outlook of the Washingtons, Jeffersons, Madisons, and Franklins, the citizens of the new United States pioneered in encouraging diversity. Madison saw security in "the multiplicity of sects" in America. Jefferson did not care whether his neighbors believed in one god or twenty gods, so long as they kept the civil peace. Franklin admired all the sects insofar as they contributed to "publick religion" and morality, and disdained or over-looked their importance insofar as they dwelt on private teachings. Natural law and natural reason were to prevail. As a result of these problems and circumstances, the First Amendment to the Constitution prevented Congress from effecting the establishment of religion or prohibiting the free exercise thereof. In this spirit the state constitutions forbade such establishment by the year 1833, and the new pattern was firmly rooted.

Disestablishment by law did not mean loss of dominance by already dominant groups and did not prevent a kind of reestablishment of religion in the mores, ethos, or customs. For a hundred years and more, Americans made little of pluralism. Catholics by the millions, continental Protestants, and later Eastern Orthodox and Jewish peoples experienced prejudice and suffered disabilities from citizens despite the law's protection.[11]

By the twentieth century thoughtful people sought new formulas to assure freedom for the free. Taking refuge behind Thomas Jefferson's "wall of separation between church and state," some of them searched for a new metaphor. Playwright Israel Zangwill came up with one: America was a *melting pot*.[12] Ecumenically minded thoughtful people tried to carry out the implications of this image. They stressed the way American life forced assimilation of groups, eroded and corroded the boundaries and edges of religious organizations, encouraged adaptation and accommodation by the exclusivists. The melting pot image helped new groups make their way into American life. It did not help them keep their identities when they had been in the nation for a while.

In the middle of the twentieth century, several new claims were being put forward for determining life within a pluralist society. Only a few imported poet T.S. Eliot's or Christopher Dawson's revived ideas of a Christian culture or society as normative, though many folk religionists still did seek a "Christian culture" that at best would be hospitable to those who were not Christian. More favored something akin to Will Herberg's model. In his celebrated work of 1955, *Protestant, Catholic, Jew*, Herberg said that what really dominated was a single civic faith, a religion of the American Way of Life. This single faith was appropriated and nurtured in three clusters of identity called Protestant, Catholic, or Jewish.

While Herberg's ink was still drying, two counter-trends began to develop. On the one hand a group of social analysts and scholars, among them Robin Williams, J. Paul Williams, Sidney E. Mead, and Robert Bellah, began to worry about the competition of denominations and the failure of anyone to generate a common set of symbols or values to be transmitted across denominations, regions, and generations. One heard of the renewed necessity for Benjamin Franklin's publick religion, now called a common faith, the reli-

gion of the republic, and civil religion. These claims took up again the Enlightenment's long neglected religious proposals and advocated the highest possible levels of consensus among Americans. These inclusive approaches displayed a common spirit in the prospering interfaith and "brotherhood" groups or, on more narrow grounds, Christian ecumenism.[13]

An equally strong and more popularly received counterforce came in the 1960s with the assertions of new particularities, all of which complicated the picture of pluralism. Various ethnic and racial groups were linked with religious claims. Black Muslims wanted to be cut out of pluralism entirely, asking as they did for a couple of the states all to themselves. Black power, youth power, sisterhood power, and Chicano power, were voiced or unvoiced claims arguing that only in one's own group could one find identity and meaning, and that the blur of pluralism would lead to chaos, anarchy, or anomie.[14]

In the course of the 1960s two differing concepts of pluralism emerged. British social philosopher Ernest Gellner defines the one as "the specific view that freedom and social health are best ensured by dispersing power, by avoiding its excessive concentration." This was the idea of James Madison's multiplicity of sects. The other view was that any and all philosophic and religious views were equally true. Gellner, of course, approved the former, as all democrats must. The latter he and many others abhorred, because it removed all seriousness from philosophical, moral, and religious quests.[15] Roman Catholics call this attitude *indifferentism*: "After all, we're all in different boats heading for the same shore." "After all, it does not make any difference what you believe, so long as you believe." It was against these affirmations that the new particularisms emerged at the beginning of the last third of the twentieth century. Two families of these particularities deserve more careful attention than they have yet received.

The first force has been the impact of world religions, particularly of non-Western and nonbiblical faiths, on the American outlook. From 1492 until the late twentieth century, biblical religion had the privileged position and, for a long time, a monopoly. Some Americans coined the idea of a Judeo-Christian tradition to embody this. The colonizers invoked biblical mandates to legitimate the act of their taking the land from the Indians. They used the Bible's images to establish their covenant and their mission. "We are as a city set upon a hill." We are "God's New Israel," his remnant, his exiled people in their exodus. The keepers of the covenant used the Old Testament to help them set up laws in the colonies. As a result they began to impose on the nation a particular biblical way of seeing manifest destiny in the world's future, for Americans were God's new chosen people.[16]

Few could deny that, when broadened to include most biblical faiths in America and when united with the civic faiths, this approach was capable of producing some good. The emancipation of slaves was a movement that had some roots in such biblical faith—though it must be said that support for slavery also came from biblicists. The biblical senses of mission inspired great humanitarian and charitable ventures, informed some attempts to enlarge human liberties, and helped move some people toward responsibility and even toward altruism. But it had another side. As Americans became more tolerant of internal diversity, they closed ranks against an outside world. They engaged in a worldwide "crusade against atheistic communism" often without taking pains to learn the varieties of alternatives to the American way, including the religious way.

As is often the case in national life, when citizens push a case too far, they have to come to terms with a reaction or counterforce. One came in the 1950s and 1960s as a result of numerous factors. Great increases in the ease of travel and communication brought a complicated world to the American living room. Middle-class people had been in military service all over the world, and many returned with a new appreciation of non-Jewish, non-Christian ways. More could now afford travel, or experience exchange with foreign students, and came to new appreciations of other religions. Those who went to college or university were exposed to religion courses that no longer began with a view that biblical faith was true and all other religions were idolatrous. Television and magazines brought positive images of "the family of man" into the home.

For a certain number of Americans, confrontation with these images was not threatening at all but attractive. Young people, seeking an identity of their own, often found their neighborhood synagogue or hometown church to be too blended into the environment to be satisfying. For a period in the 1960s, the churches were included with the military, the university, and the world of business, as power structures or establishments that deserved to be brought down, or at least rejected. Yet not all who rejected the establishment were ready for agnosticism or ready to ignore religion. They found new meaning in faiths that had few previous roots in the United States.[17]

Wherever psychically mobile people congregated—in California, on or near campuses, in communes, and the like—they found available religious sources of meaning that further tested and enlarged the conventional American pattern. Biblical faiths and the American covenant were then typed as being too pushy and productive, too grim and manipulative. All the alternatives were more liberating. But these alternatives also had a history. In their own parts of the world most of them represented another circle of exclusivism and prejudice. They simply did not appear to be hungry for

dominating or persecuting privileges in America because they were exotics, faiths of tiny minorities.

These options also had a past in America. In the middle of the nineteenth century, Ralph Waldo Emerson welcomed the Hindu presence and power. Theosophy, a kind of religion that wanted to be universal in its embrace, challenged biblical religions for a century. At the World's Parliament of Religions during the Chicago Columbian Exposition in 1893, Americans came to be familiar for the first time with some swamis and Zen masters. In the 1930s literary figures advocated "the perennial philosophy" of Oriental religion, and in the 1950s a set of intellectual "beatniks" took up Zen. But these were still the religions or philosophies of tiny and esoteric elites.

In the late 1960s the new flowering of non-Western religious groups occurred, and the groups acquired a new legitimacy. The "beautiful people" on late-night television spread the word of astrology and yoga. Members of the counterculture took up occult and metaphysical wisdom in "the Age of Aquarius." A live-and-let-live philosophy among the "flower children" was designed to counter the denominational competition of the existing faiths. Gentle and peaceful people practiced Oriental philosophy, or they transcendentally meditated. A new age of toleration was supposed to be at hand.

The Age of Aquarius did not last long, and the advertised occult explosion soon quieted. In their legacy were countless fairly well-established, small, and new religious centers and an approach to religion that gently suffused the conventional ones of the society. Many Christians and Jews came back to Jesus, meditation, charismatic renewal, and Hassidism, thanks to the mystical ways of these Eastern and occult faiths' advocates. But it was not likely that in the near future any of the new groups would become strong enough to show up on the denominational map. They were miscroscopic, mobile, and fluid themselves. Such groups generally come and go, changing names and descriptions, shamans and gurus, claims and aspirations. They gain converts by the hundreds or the thousands, attracting more attention than mainline religionists usually do. But their conversions are not abundant enough for them to challenge the more than two-score religious groups that have from 100,000 to 48,000,000 members each.

Along with the cresting of the new religions came the visibility of another phenomenon. Not all the new groups were gentle. Some of the more durable ones were hardline cults. They were accused of luring young people from the family circle, subjecting them to various techniques of psychological manipulation, fencing them in with rules and regulations, and maybe even separating them with physical distance from the larger society. These survivors ironically served not to broaden the range of tolerance but to limit and bring it to a test. Many "liberal" people, who thought they could accept any kind of religious alternative, found themselves rejecting these hardliners. At the same time, from the same liberal camp came some of the more notable defenses of the legal rights of these groups that test both the biblical and the civil religious consensuses.

While the new religions were forcing Americans to take a new look at their pluralism, the already mentioned ethnic and racial emphases prospered. These were groups that linked religion with various concepts of "peoplehood." Jews became more self-conscious about their distance from the Christian consensus when Israel was threatened and almost abandoned during the Six-Day War of 1967. Blacks reacted vigorously against white churches that offered integration at last, but grudgingly and on the lines of purely white models. American Indians had better credentials than most for complaining about how God's authority had been invoked for the preemption of their lands, and for offering natural and tribal alternatives to the highly programmatic American religious groups.[18] Ethnic Catholics took some new pride in their heritages; Hispanic Catholics, for instance, did not want to be submerged in a generalizing Catholic outlook. Ethnic religion, or a "new tribalism," was born.

The new ethnic and racial emphasis served to confuse the denominational picture. It became clear that Polish and Irish Catholics were separated by wide cultural chasms, that southern and northern Protestantism formed no single camp, that black and white Baptists had separate clusters of values and ways of belonging. What did it clarify to speak of southern Baptist without including the millions of southern blacks along with the whites—even though most of them led very different existences? If after some years it becomes clear that there will be new societal impulses toward consensus again, toward intergroup understanding, and away from tribalism and the assertions of value associated with competitive uniquenesses, it will take still more years to revise the map of American religious power as a result of the awakening of "peoplehoods."

What also deserves mention here is the effect these groups have on the perceptions of what is normative in American religion. Thus when a Protestant speaks of *the* American experience and does so by reference to Puritans and Anglicans, to Jonathan Edwards and Ralph Waldo Emerson, the Chicano speaks up: "Are they *my* history, in the Southwest? Am I less the American than the New Englanders?" Or when advocates of civil religion define the civic faith in the broadest possible terms and believe that thereby they are describing a faith acceptable to the millions as distinctively American, the heir of the black slave or the reservation Indian asks, "*Whose* civil religion is that? Where am I in the founding creed, the Declaration of Independence? Have my forebears been consulted in developing this 'common faith' for all?" So the ethnic groups, like the

new religions, have served further to make relative the old absolutes of American religion, to cast new light on old apparently normative groups.[19]

One final complication to the picture of pluralism must be mentioned. Throughout this book the accent tends to fall on social contexts and membership, attendance and religious movements, denominations and institutions. But alongside all these there is developing on a wider scale than before what sociologist Thomas Luckmann calls *invisible religion*.[20] He refers to the fact that in a consumer society that assures great freedom, including the freedom to be nonreligious or utterly selective, many people find meaning without belonging, religions without community. They pick and choose among the offerings of the bookstore, the television set, the magazine rack, the dormitory, and the promptings of the heart. They are free to be eclectic, taking this from science and that from Zen, this from remembered Catholicism and that from hoped-for therapy, to form what Margaret Mead in one speech called "a mishmash of all the religions ever known."

The invisible religion is invisible because it is private, personal, not regularly institutionalized, not monitored by priests or contained in organizations. As such it lacks specific social power. Nowhere can it be mapped. But personal religion is chosen by millions as an alternative to religionlessness or godlessness. They must be getting something out of it. If millions of people are attracted, there must be some impact even if they are not organized as a force. Invisible religion is strongest where there are no props or supports from family, neighborhood, and primary associations. When nothing in a religious outlook is confirmed by important nearby people, one has to go it alone, and do one's own selecting and revising of religious vision and thought. This "religion of the highrise apartment and the long weekend" is likely to grow and be an ever more confusing alternative to church membership than antireligion or mere secularity ever was.

Americans through the years have developed many ways of living with pluralism. Sometimes tolerance was affirmed only reluctantly and at other times embraced with ideological fervor. To a Father John Courtney Murray pluralism was against the will of God,[21] but it was the human condition and had to be lived with. To the monist, the one who believes in a single skein of meaning or, in religious terms, one God, pluralism may seem to be part of "the fall of man," a distraction from religious seriousness. As Murray has said, it will not cease to trouble the human city. Unless someone coerces a single faith, there will be many faiths. As long as people are free and religion moves by persuasion, they will move by many persuasions. Some will equate the resulting pluralism of many-ness with mere secularism. Not to make up one's mind about God as a nation, they would say, is to make up one's mind—against him. And

America, they argue, has done so. Others believe that God works through pluralism to assure that people can serve him in utter freedom without taking time-honored and treacherous actions against neighbors who serve him other ways, if at all.

The usual charge against pluralism is that it leaves people bewildered. America is rich in promise, but that promise is denied as long as so many separate clusters of meaning are in competition. The attack against pluralism generally comes from people who have ideologies to promote. These are usually universal and embracing in intent, but are actually held by few. Such attackers also enjoy reprinting the longest possible lists of denominations, and sects, and stressing as much as possible the discord among them. Their attack leaves citizens with a question: Since America does somehow remain a functioning society, despite the fact that not all in it give unreserved support to its civic and "publick" faiths, how do people bring some measure of coherence to the pattern? I shall argue that the bewilderment and the blur are reduced significantly at this time, in the eyes of many, by some of the accidents of the religious map. Regionalism and localism do some sorting for them, presenting them with relatively simplified landscapes. People do not confront 221 denominations and countless movements without perspective, naked, unprotected, and with equal impressionability. Almost everywhere their landscape helps them do some sorting, whether they look from within the spiritual corridors of mobile America or from the chambers of more settled American religious life. To this mapped perception I now turn.

THE LIMITS OF AMERICAN PLURALISM

It is misleading to think of American pluralism as nothing but a blur, a crazy-quilt of equally strong or weak religious groups in competition and interaction. With many urbanites, especially those gathered in centers of power or where people make their way through the crossroads of national life, the impression of such blurry interaction may be strong. But a study of individual perceptions suggests that an entirely different situation presents itself to most people.

We tend to view the world from our own place. Much can be made of the way mass media of communication violate the boundaries of life and change perceptions. Thus the television set, once it made its appearance in the recreation lounge of the convent or the monastery, brought about changes. It informed inhabitants of options that had been remote from their own and impressed them with the fact that not all saw the world as they did. But the television set, as William Stephenson pointed out, touches only certain dimensions of our lives.[22] Those dimensions have to do with fads and fashions, opinions and attitudes and notions. The profound elements of life, those that most in-

volve the ego, are those shaped by much more controlling and intimate sources. These include the womb, the nursery, the childhood home, teachers and pastors, nurses and playmates. The media represent "convergent selectivity," says Stephenson. We select a channel, a best-seller, a journal, and converge on it with other people who share some of our interests. Thus we may form a part of an ad hoc community with the other people who subscribe to a specialized magazine, one that beams itself, for example, at all the lefthanded sailors of yachts or owners of dachshunds in the United States. We may attend conventions with the people who make up that loose community and may devote ourselves with considerable passion to their interests. These interests will change perceptions and outlooks.

The areas of what Stephenson calls *social control*, however, can cancel out the signals from the other zone at almost any time. The subscriber or convention attender, let us say, happens to be a Jewish man. In the midst of the convention, Israel is attacked in the Yom Kippur war. He leaves the convention, turns his back on the interests of the *goyim* there, and quickly convokes his family. His son has already gone to Kennedy airport in his eagerness to get to Israel to participate in the Jews' struggle. His rabbi has a special message dealing with the question of Jewish survival and identity. All his childhood memories of Jewish school and religious training are suddenly summoned as a resource.

The lefthanded yachtsman reads his magazine faithfully. But then one evening he feels a lump near a lymph gland in his throat. He goes to a doctor and hears, "You have a malignant tumor." In the hospital he may now and then leaf through the magazines, twist television dials, and keep up old interests. But he also falls back on the fellowship of his local Catholic church. From the priest he expects words and ministrations that will help him come to terms with his destiny. He hopes that people he has known since catechism class days will surround him with prayer and sympathy. These people come from the area of social control and mean much more to him when it comes to those things that concern him ultimately.

For some people that synagogue or church will appear to be more intact than it is for others. For some it never was a reality. Others have moved into the religious "alumni associations," and think of the organizations as at best residual elements in their lives, irretrievable and hardly responsible for contributing to their current perspective. But for tens of millions of other Americans, the religious organization does contribute mightily to perspective and outlook. The Sunday church bulletin with its calendar determines many of the activities and boundaries of the week. The names in such a program represent "significant others" to such a person.

Where that local fellowship is gathered tells a great deal about the perspective. The task of mapping American religion illustrates just how effective many religious groups are in providing such perspectives. Take the example of Judaism. One third of the nation's Jews live in New York City, and one half of them are in a several county area of New York and New Jersey. Jewish interests will show up in voting patterns, in cultural concerns, in the language and customs of the day, in the appearance of the people one meets in the course of that day. These impressions will be especially intense in the case of the faithful Orthodox synagogue attendant, while there may be weaker signals in the lives of secularized Jews whose vocation and location take them into fields of interaction with un-Orthodox, non-Jewish, and even nonreligious or nondescriptly religious people.

The New York Jew has great difficulty picturing life on an Indian reservation, where the native American faiths live on. How can one imagine living so close to nature and tribe? How can one see religion determined by a sense of sacred places, Blue Lakes, Catholic churches in the pueblo? How can one show so little positive interest in the outside world—including, in some cases, the signals emitted from New York's newspapers or on a television system that may have strong Jewish influences? Similarly, the small-town Georgian has great difficulty picturing the life of the New York Jew. They live in different countries.

These senses of place have long histories. Picture a Chicano from the Southwest who lives his life on the soil of the United States. He goes to a public school, and learns the American rites. He is protected, to some meagre extent at least, by United States labor laws. He is a full citizen. Then he goes to the University of California and hears a professor tell him *the* story of American religion. This story begins in Jamestown, but soon shifts from Virginia to New England. He hears that his spiritual ancestors are Puritans and Pilgrim Protestants. That Jonathan Edwards had something to do with his life. That this tradition was then transformed and transmitted through other New Englanders like Ralph Waldo Emerson and the Transcendentalists. The professor may successfully convey a sense of the intellectual power and cultural impact of such figures from such places. But in many senses the Chicano will think of what he hears as a voice from a foreign country. His life has been full without reference to it, and he sees few ways in which this history explains him. Yet he has been told that it was *the* American experience, tradition, experiment, or spirit that was being outlined for him.

What is true in education and history shows up also in voting patterns. In 1976 something of this was seen in the presidential election campaign. It cannot be said that the votes followed the lines of evangelical versus nonevangelical religion, for both candidates were visible and vocal evangelicals. Nor can it be observed that religion was decisive in the campaign in most ways and places. Except for Texas, the entire West voted for the Republican candidate, but it is almost impossible to discern any special ethnic or religious issues that shaped

this Republican West against a more divided East. But there were at least two special dramas. The Democratic candidate was an expressive embodiment of Southern evangelicalism, Baptist style. What he took for granted in the patterns of thought and conduct in a region where to be "born again" is the norm, was incomprehensible and frightening to those who had different regional experiences. So it was that both candidates worked strenuously to capture the "ethnic vote," which translated out to northeastern Catholicism. The southern Democrat also had to reassure northeastern urban Jews that they had nothing to fear from a conservative evangelical. Few of them had ever met anyone of his kind.

Still another illustration can be taken from the realm of civil religion, a field that is also regionalized. A southern congressman may be prepared to support an amendment to the United States Constitution in his interest, promoting prayer in the public schools. His impulse may be sincere, not simply born of a desire to gain votes through a defense of pure Americanism. He is concerned with the question, "How shall we sing the Lord's song in a strange land?" or, as Princeton theologian Paul Ramsey put it, "How shall we sing the Lord's song in a pluralistic land?"[23] He may be concerned about what values he can transmit to a new generation. Or he may be concerned lest a new godlessness prevail, a secular philosophy that takes the place of religion. So he hopes that, with constitutional backing, the United States Supreme Court's decisions (*Engel v. Vitale; Abington School District v. Schempp*) can be countered and thwarted.

The issue reaches the House Judiciary Committee. The committee welcomes the testimony of a great variety of witnesses, many of whom are lay people, heads of million-member interest groups that want such an amendment. Then comes a parade of theologians and denominational figures. Certainly they will support the school prayer amendment! But, no, they raise questions. They find that the southern congressman comes from a district where everyone who is not Baptist is Methodist or a member of the Church of Christ or Pentecostal. Not a single parent or child in a specific classroom comes from a context outside conservative evangelicalism. Who would be offended if prayers are said there in the name of Christ? Jews would, in the cities. Well, every Baptist in his district knows that we share a common Bible with the Jews. Cannot the scripture be read? Then the witness asks: but what about nonbiblical religious people? What about Muslims? What about West Coast Asians? Or what will be the Scripture in Utah's schools, where the dominant majority is Mormon? Will it not be the Book of Mormon?

The voice is then heard from the Hollywood-based Project Prayer: "How dare the court take away school prayer from our school districts? What we have all observed and taken for granted, they now want to tear away from us!''[24] The critical witness persists in the House Judiciary Committee. How can something be taken away that Californians did not already have or use? He hauls out the maps and surveys to show that even the practice of praying, reading the Bible, or having devotions in school was regionalized and differed widely from area to area.

Richard Dierenfeld found that just before the Supreme Court decisions of 1962 and 1963 there were really four Americas, so far as such practices are concerned.[25] In all four regions over 98 percent of the school officials reported that ''the aims and objectives of the schools system include the teaching of moral values.'' The United States average was exactly 99.44 percent. When it came to the question of religion, of spiritual values, different patterns set in. In the East 74.39 percent said they taught such values; in the Midwest 77.21 percent did so; the figure for the South was 94.32 percent; and in Hollywood Prayer Group country it was only 68.86 percent.

Regionalism showed up even more so far as Bible reading in the schools in 1962–63 was concerned. No wonder the southern congressman brought unique perspectives. It occurred in 76.84 percent of the southern schools, 67.56 percent of the eastern, but only 18.26 percent of the midwestern and 11.03 percent of the western. Finally, are there home-room devotional services in your system's schools? The East reported that schools had this in 68.39 percent of the systems; the South's figure was 60.53 percent; the Midwest's, 6.4 percent; and the West's, 2.41 percent. The Supreme Court had ''taken away'' something that less than one in twenty-five schools in the Hollywood Prayer Group's own region had and exercised!

These religious–literary, presidential–political, and educational–civil illustrations could be extended indefinitely. What is surprising is the extent to which they are based on not only generally religious but even specifically denominational histories. We have already seen how the separate denominations have, in the main, different ''turfs'' or territories. Small groups like the Reformed Church in America, the Moravians, and even the faster growing Pentecostals tend to have places apart. But it is more astonishing to see how five giants have a domain in five regions.

The map[26] that collates all the denominational experiences reveals the strength of the solid South. (Refer also to my discussion of this map at the beginning of Chapter 7.) Below the 37th parallel, except for the tips of Florida, Louisiana, and Texas, the Baptist domain is almost undisturbed. The strength of the Baptist churches and its cognates leave a stamp on the culture. Historically this may have meant that people in the culture were anti-Catholic and anti-Jewish. Few Catholics lived anywhere near the Baptist millions, so majorities could conventionally and conveniently use them as negative reference points. By attacking the Catholics, who disagreed with their view of the ''wall of separation of church and state,'' who wanted their hands in the public till for support of papist private education, and who were direct heirs of Spanish Inquisitors, Baptists could hold their own group together. Happily, that anti-Catholicism has begun to dwindle as a result of reforms among Southern Baptist educators and because of increasing urbanization and pluralism in many sectors of the South. Similarly, the language of the old Sunday school literature that saw the Jew as a ''Christ-killer'' has changed, and Baptist attitudes too are changing.[27] But there is little close-up awareness of Jews. And this Baptist culture was sorely divided along black–white racial lines, race having been an issue for centuries though it became one in northern cities only in recent decades and is still out of range in the rural North.

The Baptist South was not only anti-Catholic, anti-Jewish, and racially divided. It had other cultural marks. The rite of passage to adult faith there was the experience of being born again. What strikes Southern Baptists and their spiritual kin as something to be taken for granted as normative in Christianity is a hardly comprehensible or plausible term in the two thirds of Catholic–Orthodox Christendom and almost as rare among liturgical Protestants like Episcopalians and Lutherans. This southern faith tends to be biblicist but not historically minded. Little of significance that occurred between 70 A.D. and 1970 A.D. is supposed to inform this life. Yet several million Orthodox Christians in the northern cities, and fifty million Roman Catholics, to say nothing of many other breeds of Protestant nurtured in other regions, give much weight to postbiblical history and tradition.

The impulse to convert others is strong in the southern culture, while in Catholicism it is ordinarily weak. The southern urban newspaper will be full of advertisements of competitive churches offering their gimmicks to attract attention. A northern Catholic-dominated metropolis would see its newspapers turn bankrupt if they had to depend on such advertisements, because of the different cultural and churchly ethos. In a northern city politicians might find it advisable to run advertisements in support of a Catholic congressional candidate in diocesan newspapers. In the southern city such advertisements could kill a candidacy; what might help there is the support of some Baptist congregations. In the South evangelicals have begun to publish ''Christian Yellow Pages,'' listing conservative business people who are active in churches. In northern urban centers such a scheme produces shock—until one sees how Catholic florists and dress shops advertise *as* Catholics in bridal supplements to Catholic newspapers.

The second of the five territories that compromise pluralist America's perspectives and keep them from being a mere blur is the Methodist empire, "the North of the South and the South of the North," the legacy of the circuit rider and evangelist who crossed the Appalachians and dashed west for fifty years as far as Kansas. This belt is not solid. The middle and border states simply had too many competing voices to permit a single dominance. But Methodism, far more diffused throughout the country, still could rely on this area. In the years when Methodists were united in support of specific causes like temperance, this was a belt that could be counted on. The religious proclamation there might have been stamped as more liberal than was the Baptist version. The seminaries permitted more critical study of the Bible than did the southern Baptist counterparts. Nevertheless, Methodism created a churchly culture of significant potency in determining the mores of an area. Inhabitants there could long perpetuate "blue laws" and fail to understand what Catholic and Lutheran groups were up to when they frivolously celebrated what Methodists called the *continental Sabbath.*

By now the pattern is becoming clear. The upper Midwest is a third religious domain. There Lutherans dominate. While they are not fiercely congregational nor always insistent on local autonomy, they are not wholly united. They have separate synods, based in part on differing ethnic experiences, and these synods are often in competition. Those with Norwegian background may be pietist and protemperance in outlook, while those with German origins may be more concerned with doctrine but permissive about drink. One historian even calls the Missouri Lutherans of the upper Midwest the wettest denomination in Christendom.[28] The two groups have different musical traditions, different sets of heroes. Yet to the outsider they look similar to each other. Lutherans tend to believe that the church should not meddle in politics; they will be very patriotic and loyal but still passive as far as seeking public office and civic responsibilities are concerned. They cannot understand social gospelers, those who made religious cases out of temperance, those who believe that their efforts will "help bring in the Kingdom." Long-standing linguistic differences often kept Lutherans from being in the mainstream in their own regional culture. Very often their local newspapers were edited by ethnic and religious minorities among them. Yet their styles of churchgoing put their stamp on the whole environment.

Picture a Boston Catholic or Unitarian stepping into Chippewa County, Minnesota. There the American Lutheran Church dominates, with thirteen churches and 5262 members as of 1971. The Lutheran Church—Missouri Synod adds four more churches and 877 members, while the Lutheran Church in America has one more church, with 305 members. But there are only two Catholic churches, with 10.3 percent of the church members, while the United Church of Christ summons only 2.4 percent of the adherents.

Most intact of the empires, as I have already noted, is the Mormon kingdom in Utah. As of 1971 there was not a single county in Utah in which Mormons were outnumbered by anyone. What does it mean to be a Mormon in such a place? One may pass through life there never coming to know intimately a non-Mormon. The Church of Jesus Christ of Latter-Day Saints has been singularly successful at establishing itself as a "cognitive minority," one that offers interpretations of life that differ drastically from those of other Americans. Utah Mormons will tend to be economically and politically very conservative, clean living, clannish, and loyal. They will not understand what pluralism means, for the scout troop, the P.T.A., the public school will be infused by Mormon norms.

One can take almost any Utah county as an example. Millard County has three denominations. It is 0.6 percent Catholic, 0.4 percent Presbyterian, 98.9 percent Latter-Day Saints. What can pluralism mean in the areas of social control there, and what chance does the competition of signals on television have against such a perception and perspective? In Kane County only two churches are present. Catholics are 0.7 percent and Mormons are 99.3 percent of the churchgoing population. Even urban Salt Lake City is 86.3 percent Latter-Day Saints in nominal adherence, while none of the following, all represented, claim even 1 percent: American Baptist, American Lutheran, Disciples of Christ, Christian Reformed, Nazarene, Episcopal, Lutheran Church in America, Lutheran Church—Missouri Synod, Salvation Army, Seventh-day Adventist, Southern Baptist, Unitarian–Universalist, and United Church of Christ. Presbyterians with 1 percent and Methodists with 1 percent team up with Catholics at 7.3 percent to embody the only significant denominational pluralism on Salt Lake County's horizon, with its 365,878 total religious adherents.

Finally, there are the varied regions, almost encircling the nation, where Catholics dominate. The entire Northeast, the Great Lakes urban industrial region, the entire Southwest, including the most populous state in all its counties but two, and the three already mentioned tips of the South have more Catholics than any other denomination. But in most places Catholics share this space with black Protestants, as a result of the urban migrations of the past half century. In the larger cities myriad Jews and white Protestants are also present. Still there are vestiges of bloc voting and Catholic power, enough to make life in Philadelphia, Chicago, or Boston feel and appear different from life in a small midwestern or southern town, as far as the experience of pluralism is concerned.

Efforts have been made to map to some nondenominational features of American religion. Thus geographer

James R. Shortridge has begun to show how simple pluralism has been complicated along "liberal" and "conservative" Protestant lines.[29] Using various standards of measurement that need not concern us here, he has shown how certain types of churches will tend to be found in certain regions and areas. Thus people in one state will be very familiar with liberal, open-ended religious groups while somewhere else such liberal styles will almost never be experienced at close hand. Shortridge's map of "Liberal Protestantism, 1971" shows the entire Northeast, from Maine through Pennsylvania to West Virginia, but stopping abruptly at the Virginia line, to be familiar with liberal denominations. The liberal belt continues across Ohio, Indiana, northern Illinois, southern Iowa, Nebraska, and Kansas, into Wyoming and Colorado. The relative strength of the United Methodist Church in Nebraska and Kansas helps make it possible for these areas to be seen as liberal. It is questionable, however, given the generally conservative outlook of those states in political and cultural matters, whether Methodism there represents the same kind of liberalism it might in the Northeast.

Shortridge's "liberal" map is most useful for what it shows about where liberals are not. Once again, below the 37th parallel the entire "sunbelt" has only a couple of counties in which more than a tiny percentage of the population ever embody or come into contact with the broader mainline churches. He finds two areas outside the South where conservative churches also dominate, the Mormon territory in the intermontane West and the northern Plains and the upper Middle West of conservative Lutheran groups.

The computations of Shortridge are useful also for the ways they can show where diversity, and thus pluralism, are the most immediate realities. Where are more religious groups present than elsewhere, to jostle each other or provide alternatives? According to Shortridge, "The most diverse areas of the country are the Pacific Coast states, peninsular Florida, and a large portion of the Middle West and Central Plains." Recent and highly varied migrations account for diversity in the first two locales, while in earlier times the same factor was present in the latter two areas. "Low religious diversity characterizes the Mormon West, southern Louisiana, and much of the South, the Spanish borderlands, and the northern Plains." There one or two faiths were early entrenched, never to be successfully challenged.

It is also possible to measure an aspect of religious pluralism that is often overlooked: nonparticipation. Ever since Thomas Jefferson established the idea that our neighbors are free to have no god as long as they do not violate the terms of community life, it has been clear that Americans should have no legal grounds for ruling out the nonbeliever or the non-churchgoer. In a free society without an established church, millions of Americans have taken advantage of constitutional freedoms and historic definitions that keep them from being second-class citizens despite their nonaffiliation. After almost two centuries of almost uninterrupted growth in the percentage of churchgoing and church-joining America, the growth trend has been slightly arrested and nonchurched America is growing. However, it grows not evenly across the map but in selected areas.[30]

Mobility seems to have something to do with this aspect of pluralism as it does with many others. One pictures the far western states as being objects of the later migrations. By the time white people arrived on the coast and in Alaska and Hawaii, the power of established religions and the fires of revivalism had begun to diminish. No single group established hegemony. Rootless people kept arriving and still do. Given this pattern, it should be no surprise that seven of the least churched states are western: Hawaii, Alaska, California, Oregon, Washington, Montana, and Colorado. Utah provides the exception in the West, for the Mormon kingdom is the most churched state in the union, and its influence spills over to keep Nevada and Idaho out of the least churched ranks. West Virginia in the East is more lightly churched than most of the nation.

On the other end of the scale, the Baptist and Lutheran turfs are the territories with high indices of active church membership. The Baptist band across the South from Virginia to Texas, but excepting Florida—site of much migration and mobility—is a churchgoer's paradise. So also is the Lutheran upper Midwest from Wisconsin through the Dakotas. A wedge in the Northeast from Maine to Michigan and south into West Virginia and parts of Kentucky and Tennessee are not as strongly churched as other parts of the country, and southern Missouri and northern Arkansas are a surprising exception in the South because of their fairly low percentages of church membership.

These further elaborations of the denominational map suggest refinements of the perceptions of pluralism in America. The slugabed in Utah, Mississippi, or Minnesota is likely to look out the window on a Sabbath morn and see traffic headed for crowded church parking lots. Such a vision will have some possible impact on his or her conscience and outlook. On the other hand, the Californian or Coloradoan can be roused from slumbers to see neighbors heading for surf or ski slope. It is easier there to be casual about church participation. Similarly, in New York people are likely to be familiar with diversity. At a party one is careful not to be critical of other religious groups, because the other partner to a conversation may be a member of one, an alumnus of another, married to the member of a third. But in Georgia, in many communities, one can assume that all the people at a gathering share a Baptist or similar religious outlook. In the northern community one might speak favorably of the National or World Council of Churches because of their cosmopolitan outlook. In the southern community one might just as readily expect to see them damned for their compromises with modernism, communism, or Third World revolution.

It may be possible to speak of two basic kinds of perceptions or locations in American religion. Picture the society as a huge building, Pentagon- or Versailles-style. It will be a mazeway of corridors, full of bustling tourists, workers, custodians, guides, and functionaries whose duty it is to be familiar with many corridors and rooms. On the other hand, there are people who spend almost all their time in one or another of the rooms. They may live near the building, make their way along the same route every day, enter by the same door, steal into the same chamber, and do the same task with the same people every day.

In America the "corridor" people tend to be the migrants, the mobile people, especially the upper-middle-class movers whose jobs or retirement or taste take them from place to place, from region to region. The Iowa Methodist from a small town may retire in Orange County or Sun City, taking along elements of lifelong religious affiliation. A Methodist Church awaits this person in the new environment. But whereas once most of the people one met on the job, on the next cracker barrel, or at the Legion picnic would be another Methodist or a near miss, in the retirement community the shuffleboard partner is just as likely to have an entirely different religious outlook.

In two areas in particular, "corridor" existence has a bearing on perception. The first of these is in academia. Most analysts of American religion belong to this mobile group, working from campuses, the highest centers of religious diversity and pluralism in the culture. Most of them may have originally come from one of the "chambers" of American religion, an enclave of the like-minded. But they may be in rebellion against the closed world such existence implied, and can bask in the liberation pluralism brings. Now the new locale causes the analyst to generalize, to place a new premium on pluralist religion, to forget the traditional and familial values transmitted where everyone shares similar religious belongings and assumptions.

The other zone is that of the mass media of communications. It should be stressed that not all mass media technology is used by those with an understanding of pluralism. Radio in particular is a relatively inexpensive form of the mass media; any communicator can gain access quite easily and create a cocoon, a private world. (It should also be pointed out, however, that this communicator shares airwaves with a whole melange of competitors, and the dial twister is likely to confront the whole array of them with an intense awareness of the private visions being offered across the dial.) National magazines, national radio and television networks, and the cinema normally are dominated by people who are themselves experiencers of urban mobility, rootlessness, casual church affiliation, and diversity. This alters their perceptions and causes them to represent atypical approaches to religious reality. Few of them ever meet anyone for whom religious group loyalties are important, and they have trouble picturing the large numbers of Americans who do measure life from their local church or their membership in a denomination.

What we may conclude from these efforts at mapping American religion is that just as this is a nation of nations it is also a nation of denominations, a crazy-quilt of regionalized perceptions. "Tell me your landscape and I will tell you who you are."[31] The impact of environment and circumstance on perception and outlook remains strong for most Americans. Millions inhabit chambers or compartments where the truth of the assertion is obvious. But others forget that a corridor is *also* a place, a way of being, a life in a landscape. Tell me that you live in mobile, migrant, media-impacted America, and I can tell almost as much about you as if we both lived in a small town, shared a small church, and kept outside influences away. We may not in the corridors have a *locus standi*, a place to stand, to view the American reality. But we have a place to walk, and such a place and such a walk also have much to do with our circumstances and our sensibilities. The interplay between people who have secure places on the religious map and those where affiliations are more varied and more changeable will help determine both how tomorrow's religion will look and how it will be.

NOTES

1. A landmark in the modern discussion of pluralism was Will Herberg, *Protestant, Catholic, Jew* (Garden City, N.Y.: Doubleday, 1955); it provides an introduction to the mid-century issues.

2. The literature on "the Protestant empire" includes Robert T. Handy, *A Christian America: Protestant Hopes and Historical Realities* (New York: Oxford University Press, 1971); and Martin E. Marty, *Righteous Empire: The Protestant Experience in America* (New York: Dial, 1970).

3. Discussions of the court's attitudes appear in Arthur Frommer, ed., *The Bible and the Public Schools* (New York: Liberal Press, 1963).

4. For an historical overview, see Richard E. Morgan, *The Supreme Court and Religion* (New York: Free Press, 1972).

5. For example, see the account of the Salado and Hohokam in John Upton Terrell, *American Indian Almanac* (Cleveland: World, 1971), pp. 16ff.

6. An essay on Christian exclusivism appears in the treatment of Christianity in Walter Kaufmann, *Religions in Four Dimensions* (New York: Reader's Digest Press, 1976), pp. 108ff.

7. The entire history of Christian dissent and exile is approached in Frederick Norwood, *Strangers and Exiles* (Nashville: Abingdon, 1969, two vol.)

8. See W. H. C. Frend, *Martyrdom and Persecution in the Early Church* (Garden City, N.Y.: Doubleday, 1967).

9. The extensive literature on this subject is introduced in Martin E. Marty, *Protestantism* (New York: Holt, Rinehart and Winston, 1972), ch. 15.

10. See Henry F. May, *The Enlightenment in America* (New York: Oxford University Press, 1976); and Donald H. Meyer, *Democratic Enlightenment* (New York: Putnam's, 1975) for extensive treatment of this theme.

11. See Handy, *Christian America*, and Marty, *Righteous Empire*.

12. Herberg set out to correct this image in *Protestant, Catholic, Jew*, p. 39.

13. Essayists in Russell E. Richey and Donald G. Jones, eds., *American Civil Religion* (New York: Harper & Row, 1974) detail the civil religion themes.

14. For the literature on the ethnic revival, see Martin E. Marty, *A Nation of Behavers* (Chicago: University of Chicago Press, 1976), pp. 158ff.

15. Ernest Gellner, *Legitimation of Belief* (Cambridge: Cambridge University Press, 1974), pp. 1–9, makes these distinctions.

16. Conrad Cherry, ed., *God's New Israel: Religious Interpretations of American Destiny* (Englewood Cliffs, N.J.: Prentice-Hall, 1971) introduces this literature.

17. See Marty, *A Nation of Behavers*, 126ff., on "The New Religions."

18. Vine Deloria, Jr., *God is Red* (New York: Grosset and Dunlap, 1973) is the most extensive statement of this theme.

19. See the comments on Bellah's "Civil Religion in America" by D. W. Brogan and others in Donald Cutler, ed., *The Religious Situation 1968* (Boston, Beacon Press, 1969), pp. 356ff.

20. Thomas Luckmann, *The Invisible Religion* (New York: Macmillan, 1969).

21. John Courtney Murray, *We Hold These Truths* (New York: Sheed and Ward, 1960), p. 23.

22. William Stephenson, *The Play Theory of Mass Communications* (Chicago: University of Chicago Press, 1966) develops the concepts of convergent selectivity and social control in numerous chapters.

23. Paul Ramsey, "How Shall We Sing the Lord's Song in a Pluralistic Land?" in *Journal of Public Law*, vol. 13, no. 2 (1964), p. 401ff.

24. The testimony of the many groups is in *Hearings Before the Committee on the Judiciary House of Representatives Eighty-Eighth Congress Second Session*, "School Prayers," three vols. (Washington, D.C.: U.S. Government Printing Office, 1964). See especially II, 1541ff.

25. The complete surveys are reported in Richard B. Dierenfeld, *Religion in American Public Schools* (Washington, D.C.: Public Affairs Press, 1962).

26. The map accompanies Douglas W. Johnson, Paul R. Picard, and Bernard Quinn, *Churches and Church Membership in the United States: 1971* (Washington, D.C.: Glenmary Research Center, 1974); and Edwin Scott Gaustad, *Historical Atlas of Religion in America*, rev. ed. (New York: Harper & Row, 1976).

27. On textbooks see Bernhard E. Olson, *Faith and Prejudice: Intergroup Problems in Protestant Curricula* (New Haven, Conn.: Yale University Press, 1963).

28. Richard Jensen, *The Winning of the Midwest: Social and Political Conflict, 1888–1896* (Chicago: University of Chicago Press, 1971), pp. 83f.

29. James R. Shortridge, "Patterns of Religion in the United States" in *Geographical Review*, vol. 66 (1976), pp. 420–434.

30. A map showing nonchurched America is available from Glenmary Research Center (see footnote 26).

31. Quoted by Julián Marías, *José Ortega y Gasset: Circumstance and Vocation* (Norman: University of Oklahoma Press, 1970), p. 362.

III

Trends and Issues Shaping the Religious Future

DOUGLAS W. JOHNSON

9

Searching for Meaning and Purpose

It is . . . possible that a post-industrial society would . . . turn in the direction of many pre-industrial societies—toward the exploration of inner states of experience rather than the outer world of fact and material accomplishment. Tradition and ritual, the pillars of life in virtually all societies other than those of an industrial character, would probably once again assert their ancient claims as the guide to and solace for life. The struggle for individual achievement, especially for material ends, is likely to give way to the acceptance of communally organized and ordained roles.—*Robert L. Heilbroner*

These words of a social analyst suggest that one possible direction we might look to see what an emergent society might be like is toward a search for fundamentals of human experience. This direction is quite different from the transient packaged life envisioned by Alvin Toffler.[2] It is a "surprise free" direction, in the vernacular of Herman Kahn,[3] a futurist with the Hudson Institute, because it is a seeking for the roots of human life. The emphasis Heilbroner detects is not a "new gimmick." It is a serious pilgrimage to discover roots in a changing culture. It is the search for meaning and purpose.

This direction is grounded in religious feelings. It is the basis of life explanations that have been captured in religious communities and creeds. If this forecast is accurate, social and religious institutions need to develop the materials, propositions, and goals of a meaningful life. Heilbroner's proposal challenges such institutions, especially religious ones, to provide those raw materials of belief and supportive community that will enable people to weave a fabric of meaning for their lives. While such a task is continually being worked at by religious institutions, Heilbroner's assessment is that these raw materials will not be based on general and abstract principles derived from rational methods of research.

Meaning is based more on experience than on ration-

al processes. Religious meaning is the core of life. It contains an unexplainable dynamic, a mystery, of dependence on God. The search for meaning and purpose begins with a release and is continued by a nurturing of the religious impulse. It is assisted but not answered by teaching the rudiments of a carefully defined religion or faith.[4]

It is this search that will continue through the immediate future. This does not mean there will be a lessening of the need for religious creeds and catechism. They are a part of the religious tradition and ritual extant in our culture. The search is to find that creative force in life that results in a sensitivity to others' needs while providing a firm hold on one's own understanding of the nature of existence. This is the essence of the religious impulse. It has ". . . characteristics such as the search for wisdom, the brotherhood of all men, the meaning of being, a reverence for life. . . . We find the religious impulse among the faithful, but it is also manifest among those who do not attend church."[5]

This religious impulse is the basic ingredient in the search for meaning. It is an inner prod that compels people to discover meaning and purpose in their lives and in organizational structures. For individuals, this search ranges from involvement in the activities of institutional churches to engagement in quasi-religious secular activities. The common denominator is that the activities provide ways a person may feel a larger purpose in life. This means that people join cults, communes, groups, and churches to help in their search. It means people do things to increase self-knowledge, develop communities of caring souls, practice techniques for personal development, and engage in exercises of disciplined thinking.

The objective in this search, the joining of groups and the use of disciplined practice, is to take oneself seriously enough to want to discover how each person figures into the ultimate scheme of life. The search is a serious business now and will continue to be. It requires commitment and discipline. The search is religious even though a given group may deny any connection with religious ideas and ideals.

The current manifestations of this search are evident in four patterns. These are organizational channels for the religious impulse.

ATTITUDES TOWARD INSTITUTIONALIZED RELIGION

The first expression of the search for meaning and purpose is affiliation with organized religious institutions or the church. Attention in this discussion is on the Catholic and Protestant forms of the church. While there is a good deal of variety within both Catholicism and Protestantism, these two general groups are the basis for this examination.

People express their attitudes in behavior, which is roughly measurable when it comes to religious expression. The method used to gauge religious expression is to examine various individual attributes and relate these attributes to church membership or attendance at worship services.

Recent trends in church membership and analyses of the trends and causal factors have been presented in Part I. In this section I am taking a somewhat different perspective on the data, which is to assess attitudes toward religious expression, as manifested in church membership statistics, in order to project a future. This projection is based on people's continued use of the church as a vehicle in the search for meaning and purpose.

Church Membership

When the percentage of the population claiming affiliation with religious organizations is examined over a long term, it is apparent that religious expression has increased dramatically in our nation. There has been a continual rise in membership from the beginning years of the nation. About 4 percent of the population were church members in the very early 1700s. This rose to about one tenth of the population by 1800, a 6 percentage point increase in a century. This increase was important due perhaps in part to the First Great Awakening of the 1700s. However, it preceded the development of the more evangelical denominations that moved West with the frontier.

The percentage of church members in the population continued to rise during the 1800s. By 1850 16 percent of the population were affiliated with churches, and by the turn of the twentieth century, this figure had climbed to 36 percent. During the nineteenth century of civil strife and the rise of an industrial economy, religious affiliation had increased by one fourth. It was a period of winning the West and of the frontier preacher traveling with the migrants. People in the midst of change brought the certainty of beliefs with them. In all the change they needed those elements of hope and purpose they found in the church creeds and practices.

Since 1900 the increase has continued. By 1940 nearly half of the population claimed membership in churches, and by 1976 that had become 62 percent. In the first three quarters of this century, the percentage has risen by one fourth, with half of that increase occurring since 1940.[6] Perhaps the need for stability and purpose during this century's crises reflected itself in church membership statistics.

The long-term data show an increasingly positive disposition in the United States toward the church, although the evidence of the last quarter century examined in the first part of this book shows a downturn in the membership of some major church bodies.

The search for meaning and purpose through the church continues so long as people find churches aiding them in their search. There was rapid growth in church membership during the 1940s and 1950s, followed by a decline in the late 1960s and early 1970s. My explanation of these general trends provides the basis for expecting church membership to resume its growth.

Membership decline of certain religious bodies in the last decade represents a normal experience in the organizational life of voluntary groups. An organizational expansion in a voluntary group is followed by losses as the organization establishes an equilibrium or develops a new level of functioning. In the process of such development, a new purpose and ethos must be accepted. This will cause some defections. In this sense, declines in church membership are explainable as organizational necessities.

Contrary to the claims of Dean Hoge[7] that the United Presbyterian Church is representative of liberal Protestantism, the growth–decline–stabilization process is different within each denomination. Decline is common among liberal mainline Protestant denominations. But differences in the patterns of decline and growth are clear. For example, the American Baptist Churches do not follow the decline pattern of the United Church of Christ or the United Presbyterian Church. The American Baptist Churches reported 1,561,000 members in

1950 and 1,579,000 in 1974. The denomination declined in membership through 1970 but then made substantial membership gains.

While a theory of growth, decline, and stabilization can be applied to the American Baptists, it is modified by the nature of that denomination.[8] Congregations may leave or join the denomination without penalty, close working relations exist with some black Baptist groups, and organizational issues affect the total structure differently than some of the other denominations. In this sense, Baptists are a group of congregations which use denominational affiliation much the way individuals use membership in Episcopal or Presbyterian denominations.

The Church of Jesus Christ of Latter Day Saints (Mormon), a more structured and hierarchical denomination than the Baptists, reported 1,111,000 members in 1950 and 2,684,000 in 1974, a gain of 141 percent. Its growth was similar in pattern to the Southern Baptist Convention. In 1950 the Southern Baptists reported 7,080,000 members and in 1974, 12,513,000, a gain of 77 percent. Yet the denominations are very different.

The Mormon Church functions much like a carefully circumscribed ethnic group, although ethnicity, strictly speaking, is not a part of its heritage. The denomination has a tight, self-sufficient organization and could be classified sociologically as a cult rather than as a denomination.[9]

A part of Mormon "cultism" resides in its identification with the person and visions of Joseph Smith. In addition, the memory of persecution experienced on their forebears' journey to the Great Salt Lake is strong among Mormons, and in Salt Lake City they have erected a shrine commemorating their beginning and their leaders. The Mormon organization, built on an ideal that looks narrow to outsiders, has a place of focus and a definitive stance vis à vis society. The Mormon Church has established for its members a formula for meaning and purpose that individuals need only accept.

The Southern Baptists, by contrast, are within the traditional Christian theological spectrum. In addition, they do not practice the exclusiveness of the Mormons. The Baptist polity allows considerable freedom for local congregations, another difference from the Mormons.

Both of these groups increased significantly over the last quarter century. The key to their growth, sociologically, appeared to reside in the clear purpose and intent they provided for the lives of their adherents. In addition, neither denomination experienced major reorganization. This allowed both groups to pursue the primary objective of bringing the world their message. In presenting their interpretation of the meaning of life, they were not diverted by theological uncertainty or reorganization as was the case of denominations that grew less rapidly or showed membership losses.

The United Church of Christ, a liberal denomination, began as two separate churches. In 1950 the two groups had 1,977,000 members. The road to union was completed by a merger in 1961. In 1974, after more than a decade of being combined, the United Church of Christ reported 1,841,000 members. A membership peak had been reached in 1960, prior to the merger, which was followed by a decline. In this merger, ethnicity was a factor, as Martin Marty points out in Chapter 7. The loss of ethnic identification for those of German background in the new denomination may be a key to some losses in the merger.

The precursors of the United Methodist Church, another generally liberal denomination, reported 9,653,000 members in 1950. By 1974, there were 10,063,000 United Methodists. During the intervening quarter century the church experienced two mergers. One was the assimilation of its separate black jurisdiction, which had been the equivalent of a denomination within a denomination, during the 1960s. Then in 1968 the Evangelical United Brethren Church, a smaller group with fewer than one million members, united with the Methodist Church, a merger that included the ethnic factor. The Evangelical United Brethren Church had its origin in the United States in the late 1700s and early 1800s among German-speaking immigrants. As with the United Church of Christ merger, some E.U.B. congregations refused to join in the merger. The peak membership of the Methodist Church occurred in 1964 prior to the union with the Evangelical United Brethren. The merged denomination, the United Methodist Church, has had a decline in membership since.

The two groups that were to become a part of the United Presbyterian Church in the U.S.A. in 1950 had 2,532,000 members. In 1974, the United Presbyterians counted 2,724,000 members. The church had reached a peak of membership around 1960 shortly after the merger of the two former denominations.

The three denominations, United Church of Christ, United Presbyterian, and United Methodist, represent different types of organization. All have experienced increases and decreases over the past quarter century. They have also been involved in at least one merger. In these denominations union was followed by a decline in membership. Organizational theory indicates that such a decline is followed by stabilization, then either new growth or complete collapse.

This pattern of decline in membership following merger is evident in studies of merged congregations. Decline following merger is an *organizational* phenomenon, which affects the ability of the church to aid people in their search for meaning. The reasons for such declines revolve around group identity and loyalty. Churches are developed by committed and like-minded people who have a vision and purpose that eventually become the ethos of the organization. This ethos is communicated by the organizational style and leadership. It evidently assists those who join; they find it compatible with their search.

When this ethos is adulterated through combination with another organization that has a different ethos, the commitments of people to the old order are lost. Their belief structure, as it was based on the practices of the church or the denominational traditions, is changed. Any loyalty to the new church must be based on the past or some elements in the merged group that promise a substitute in the future.

These dynamics appear to be operative in the merger of denominations as well as of congregations. Especially important is the group identification which is lost in a denominational merger. One result has been declines in membership as the new merged denominations develop their own ethos and purposes.

Church membership statistics tell of a mood of unusual interest in or need for churches from the late 1940s through the early 1960s. After this time declines took place as some denominations particularly sought to revise their basis for being and functioning. A major part of this revision was a change from assisting individuals in their search for purpose and meaning to being an agent for social change. People were caught in a two-way squeeze. Mergers took their solid base and the new direction of program whittled away at their core of meaning, and they lost interest and faith in the institution.

Southern Baptist and Mormon data clearly show that where there is a singleness of purpose in the organization aimed at providing meaning and purpose for the individual, people joined the churches during periods when declines were plaguing merging denominations. It was not just the merging but the merging *and* change of direction that was the culprit. When the church's message is overshadowed by other concerns, such as interest in organizational matters based on merger considerations or redirection without clear purposes, and no provision is made for the development of individual commitment, members and potential members turn away.

In very simple terms, a church must function as the conveyor of faith. It must at least provide the vehicle for people as they search for meaning and purpose in their lives. If it does this well, it will increase in membership. If it decides to direct its attention to matters of internal reorganization and merger, the result will be loss of members, money, and influence.

Attendance at Worship

A second measure of the search for meaning and purpose through institutional religion is attendance at worship. The difference between Catholic and Protestant statistics is that attendance at worship over time is the primary measure for Catholics; it becomes the barometer of the Roman Catholic Church's health. The primary statistic used to measure Protestant strength has been church membership.

In 1955, 49 percent of the U.S. population reported attending church in an average week. In 1965, 44 percent and in 1975, 40 percent attended. The drop in attendance has been primarily among Catholics and not Protestants. In 1964 the Roman Catholic attendance figure was 71 percent, but ten years later it had fallen to 55 percent. Meanwhile, the attendance figure for the Protestants had fluctuated only 2 percent, between 39 and 37 percent.

When probes for possible reasons behind the decline in Catholic attendance figures are made, the cause appears to be the mood of the church brought about by revisions in doctrine and practice since Vatican II. Contrary to the explanation of Andrew Greeley cited in Part I, chapter 5, I believe that Vatican II had the same effect on organization and ethos as the mergers and organizational realignments had in Protestant denominations. The deliberations of Vatican II were disruptive to the purposes and practices of some Roman Catholic adherents. One innovation heralded as a step in modernization of the church, mass in the vernacular of the people, eliminated the common denominator of all Catholics, the Latin mass. This and other changes had the effect of devaluing for some the attraction of the church as a source of meaning.

When merger or other internal organizational adjustments take place, people's basis of meaning is disrupted. There is a loss of identity with the local church and denomination, a feeling of betrayal of a former group, an anger at being forced to change with no options. People get over such things, but this may require some years, new types of churches or quasi-religious affiliations. The religious impulse must be satisfied regardless of the organizational form.

CHARISMATICS AND EVANGELICALS

The social action of the early and mid-1960s was a religious reaction to the more complacent atmosphere of the 1950s. A catalyst in this fervor of making religion a force in a secular culture was the Supreme Court decisions on desegregation of schools, followed by federal government service programs such as VISTA, the Peace Corps, and the War on Poverty. These government programs shocked people in suburban religious institutions to an awareness that they should be concerned about racial prejudice and the poverty of cities and rural areas. Many suburbanites had felt separated from such societal ills but, because of these government programs, realized that they, too, had a stake in the social well-being of city and countryside. In what amounted to a reversal of roles, government, not religious institutions, was creating opportunities for people to find meaning and purpose in their lives through service to others.

The social action challenge of the 1960s came as many in the affluent postwar generation reached college and were seeking an avenue to express concern for the rights and freedoms they felt were denied others. They were able to act because they had the financial security and the educational background associated with affluence in this nation. They were fired by a social idealism which was part of the mood of the time.

This idealism quickly found advocates in the churches. The early negative reactions from within to church social action programs were against specific issues or incidents. In the mid-1960s, however, a more general outcry was heard. This was a warning that social activism was taking precedence over the basic tasks of the church, that the function of providing meaning and purpose was being diluted. A 1970 study of 3,000 church members in the United States and Canada found that church members were not opposed to social involvement by the church. What they opposed was a one-sided emphasis on social action to the neglect of the basic tasks of the church in providing meaning and purpose. The study results were, in effect, a request from church members for a corrective to a one-sided emphasis.[10]

By the late 1960s, various expressions of organized reaction to social activism set in. In 1967 the charismatic movement began in the Catholic Church. Characteristics of that movement include stress upon baptism of the Holy Spirit, speaking in tongues, regeneration of life, and the use of new forms of the sacraments. The aim of the movement was to reassert the personal emotional component in the church. Two years earlier, a group calling itself the Presbyterian Lay Committee had been set up as a form of reaction to the social activism advocated by some of the leaders of the United Presbyterian Church.[11] A short time later Episcopal charismatics established a fellowship with headquarters in Denver. Similarly, a conservative group, calling itself the Good News Movement, developed in the United Methodist Church as a protest to the denomination's mission activities. Subsequently it became an organization with headquarters in Wilmore, Kentucky. Similar situations prevailed in other denominations, usually revolving around some change in emphasis in the character of the denomination.

The desire of the various emerging groups seems to have been the establishment of a more personal religious form which could better provide individuals with meaning and purpose. The mood of the dissidents was to renew the church so that it could return to what they asserted were its historical purposes. The basic plea was for a religious form that the dissidents claimed would give people the opportunity to find a meaningful personal faith in a rapidly changing world. In most cases such groups functioned as pressures within their respective denominations and made no attempt to form a coalition with similar groups in other denominations.

Two things of importance should be noted about these renewal groups. First, they were emphasizing the basic elements of an "old-time" religion, which could provide the source of meaning and security some people felt were essential in the late 1960s and the 1970s. Second, these groups emerged during reorganization efforts and precisely when decline in membership was occurring in the denominations. They were theological in origin and intent.

It was no coincidence that denominational organizations faltered at this time The concept that success comes as the institution gets bigger, resulted in mergers. The concept of being "relevant" to the current mood of society resulted in social activism. Both of these new directions had come out of the social context of the 1950s, but many churchgoers felt they were at variance with the purposes of the church. Being relevant, the conservatives argued, is not a virtue of the Christian or any other faith. For them, faithfulness to historic teachings and creeds is the measure of relevance for the Christian church. The success of the church is measured not by its size, but in depth of commitment and evangelical passion. The uniqueness of the faith was being ignored.

In commenting on the importance of religious faiths as a source of meaning and purpose, Daniel Bell sums up the power of religion: "The power of religion derives from the fact that before ideologies or other modes of secular belief, it was the means of gathering together, in one overpowering vessel, the sense of the sacred—that which is set apart as the collective conscience of a people."[12]

Much of the reason for membership decline was the change in goals and in the nature of leadership in the mainline Protestant denominations during the late 1960s. In this period the national leaders of major liberal denominations were interested more in activism than in the basics of the faith. The attention of many leaders was aimed toward organizational power to reshape the social system.

The charismatic–evangelical emphasis can be seen as a reaction to what was taking place in the churches. The efforts of evangelicals were directed not so much toward overturning church organizations as toward redirecting the goals. The evangelicals brought a tradition that had been overshadowed by the social activism of the 1960s. They were attempting to reemphasize their own position within the church: ". . . evangelicals emphasized . . . the Protestant principle of the exclusive and infallible authority of the Scripture. This principle is the central feature of the evangelicalism that has survived through fundamentalism and into the twentieth century. . . ."[13]

The issue was theological. Historically, the emergence of the evangelical and charismatic movements was a predictable correction of the social activity of the 1960s. The programs of the 1960s did not provide any unique vehicle for discovering meaning and purpose in life.

The rallying cry of the evangelical movement was issued by Richard Quebedeaux, who presented in *The Young Evangelicals* a clear and forceful analysis of the ground upon which the new evangelical movement could develop.[14] It was a reaffirmation of the major theological tenets of evangelicalism:

. . . (1) the complete reliability and final authority of Scripture in matters of faith and practice; (2) the necessity of a *personal* faith in Jesus Christ as Savior from sin and consequent commitment to Him as Lord; and (3) the urgency of seeking actively the conversion of sinners to Christ (pp. 3–4).

Quebedeaux went on to describe the various types of evangelicalism as separatist, open, establishment, and new. He then added some new elements to the current evangelicalism:

. . . we might also add as important (4) the search for Christian unity without the loss of theological distinctiveness; (5) an outreach to the secular world without accommodation to its system; (6) the quest for absolutes in ethics without legalism; (7) genuine social concern; and (8) an intellectually motivated faith grounded in the deeply experiential knowledge of God as a person through Christ (pp. 68–69).

It is this desire for the establishment of a meaning system that has some consequences that is described by Roger Palms as he talks about *The Jesus Kids:* "The Jesus kids . . . feel a vital need for prayer, Bible study, and Christian fellowship—the kind that satisfies the deep spiritual and emotional needs of people . . . also the need for a place to live while they are serving the Lord and growing in their new found faith."[15]

This was the kind of evangelicalism that was promoted during the early 1970s. It was a redirection of the religious institutions to what was claimed were their historic purposes. When these evangelical voices were not heeded, the need for organization on their part was apparent. Consequently, evangelical groups within the mainline denominations developed to promote communication among the evangelicals and to bring pressure to bear on the leaders of those denominations.

While this was the Protestant process, the Roman Catholic Church in the United States was experiencing its charismatic revival. Although the revival is not strictly a Catholic phenomenon, its major adherents and supporters have been the hundreds of thousands of Catholics involved in the movement. The movement began in 1967 with what was called the Duquesne weekend named after a retreat with Duquesne Univer-

sity students. Joseph Fichter describes the charismatics as "personalized" Christians, and sees them as participants in a religious revival very much reminiscent of earlier, Protestant-dominated revivals in America.[16] He goes on to list four unexpected things that characterize the movement:

[It was unexpected] that a new and vigorous spiritual cult would: (a) be inaugurated by lay Catholics; (b) attract adherents from the more advantaged middle class; (c) stimulate a preference for the emotional rather than the intellectual experience of the faith; and (d) emerge in the midst of this scientistic, rational, American culture.[17]

Andrew Greeley makes the point that no matter how scientific or rational people or culture happen to appear, the irrational need for a purpose greater and more powerful than they are will surface.[18] There is innate in the human being a search for a larger purpose. The charismatic movement in the Catholic Church and the reemergence of the evangelical expression within some of the major Protestant denominations show the need for a religious experience that is not so much rational as emotional. It is a need to dwell on the inner being, so that external wants are not excluded but put into a longer term perspective.

A 1974 study,[19] sponsored by the Commission on Private Philanthropy and Public Needs as part of its research into philanthropy in the United States, seeking to secure information about the funds spent by churches on nonsacramental purposes found that about 16 percent of the money received in local congregations went toward nonsacramental programs. These were socially directed activities, usually in the local community, and included employment agencies, training programs for industrial jobs, recreation programs for youth in the neighborhood, and drug rehabilitation programs. The programs were wide ranging but always had the support of the local congregation.

The interesting finding in the nationwide study of congregations and synagogues was not the social dimension of their ministry but the hunger of the spirit that was communicated during the interviews. The social expression of the churches' program was taken for granted. The people providing the data were as interested in putting a foundation of faith beneath the programs as they were in the social dimension of the activities.

John E. Biersdorf, Director of the Institute for Advanced Pastoral Studies, in case histories and analysis, documents this desire by people to develop inner feelings, and the misunderstanding of the intent of the people by denominational leaders.[20] He then develops a typology that incorporates the best of Dean Kelley's thesis about the decline of liberal churches and the growth of conservative churches. His efforts summarize the fact that people in vital religious institutions had sought and found a disciplined method and group that helped to provide access to personal meaning and purpose.

NONCHURCH DIMENSIONS

To an observer of the contemporary religious situation, it is obvious that the direction of the search for meaning and purpose is not always toward the church. Some people have not been touched by it or were turned off by it earlier in their lives. They have sought other means for channeling their energies in their search. Some of these attitudes are described in case studies in a volume edited by Charles Y. Glock and Robert N. Bellah.[21] The book describes religious movements in the Oriental tradition and in the Western tradition, and quasi-religious movements. The basic intent of each group is to help the individual become a part of a group seeking meaning and purpose for life.

Data contained in this discussion of the search for a new religious consciousness indicate that the adherents are well educated, young, and from affluent backgrounds. Many had been involved in the protest movements of the 1960s and sought a religious group to help them shape a new life meaning. In nearly all cases the life being shaped is disciplined, committed to the group, and devoted to discovering a dynamic inner self. The groups also demand that some expression of the religious feelings be demonstrated or shared with society at large.

These data are supportive of the information contained in Biersdorf's book. In the description of nonchurch groups, Biersdorf concludes that discipline and commitment are key factors in the appeal to adherents.

In a week-long seminar with a futures group of Stanford Research Institute, I was exposed to the influence of the traditions and disciplines of the Eastern religions. The futures group leaders were attempting to synthesize the desire for personal fulfillment, as understood by Abraham Maslow, a humanist psychologist, with the Eastern traditions of inner consciousness. The tone was religious, but the process appeared to be developing a nontraditional vocabulary combining scientific thought and Eastern mysticism.

The human potential movement is a secularized process for aiding in the search for meaning and purpose. It has developed from humanistic psychology and has had as its focus the enhancement of personal being. It finds continuing advocates in the organization of humanistic psychologists. Gerald J. Jud and Elizabeth Jud have translated and interpreted this movement so as to make it a more religious enterprise.[22] In this fashion they have used it in churches to help people find new dimensions to their lives.

In the last decade the technique of Transactional Analysis, popularized by Thomas A. Harris's book, *I'm O.K., You're O.K.,*[23] has been applied widely to help people redirect their habits and thought patterns. The language is psychological, somewhat Freudian, and has been translated into everyday idioms. It speaks about parent, child, and adult in a manner that makes it obvious which is the most acceptable behavior. The aim is to develop a "correct" method of reacting so that one can live a more fruitful and meaningful life.

Even in these nonchurch expressions of the search for meaning and purpose, emphasis is placed on activities normally associated with the church. Discipline, commitment, witness, community, forgiveness, and confession are all vital ingredients of the processes. These are techniques that have been used successfully over the years to assist people in finding the larger purpose to which they can relate their lives. When many churches seemingly directed their activities away from the personal search for meaning and purpose, other groups arose using the techniques and activities formerly used in the churches. Perhaps this is a part of the cyclical nature of our historical development as a culture. Perhaps it is the manner in which a culture attempts to purify its institutions and redirect their efforts. Whatever the explanation, the fact is that when the churches seemed to move away from a socially important function—providing the primary avenue for individuals to search for meaning and purpose—other groups in the society stepped in to take over the function. Adherents to the new groups tend to be well educated, affluent, and young. The innate desire of people, regardless of station in life, to find meaning and purpose must be satisfied, and if one institution fails, another will arise to accommodate the need.

MULTIPLE CAREERS

A fourth variety of the search for meaning and purpose is career change. In the broadest sense it too is an effort to free the religious impulse. While changing career is not a development unique to the last twenty-five years, it is becoming more common and taking on new dimensons. Two important sources of information about how and why people change their careers are a study done at Columbia University (*Changing Careers After Thirty-Five*)[24] and a study of ministers who changed professions (*Ex-Pastors*).[25]

The Columbia study focused on people over 35 who had returned to or started at the university. Among the reasons people gave for going were that they had completed their families at a relatively young age; they had received pension rights at a young age; there was some sort of a relocation of the business or family disruption; or they had a desire to achieve a better and more satisfying life.

The author of the study, Dale L. Hiestand, talks about multiple careers as a major new social force:

Middle-aged persons now have more freedom to define new

goals. This seems to have been occurring for some time among women, although popular magazines portray the increased choices open to women in middle age as crises and dilemmas. The interesting note is that increased options at middle age also seem to be opening for men.[26]

Hiestand concludes that people return to the university as a means of pursuing new purposes or fulfilling purposes that had been delayed from earlier in their lives.

The data from *Ex-Pastors* reveal several dominant reasons why United Church of Christ ministers changed careers. These reasons included "pressures of role expectations, marital problems, frustrated leadership, health, and limited resources."[27] The authors suggest that a key factor was a changed self-concept for the ex-pastors. This is similar to the desire by college returnees to find fulfillment for their lives. In addition, any stigma for leaving the ministry had decreased from what it might have been in earlier times.

SOME IMPLICATIONS FOR THE FUTURE

In the following chapter, I set forth a variety of trends that appear likely to affect religious organizations in the future. At this point, however, I anticipate this broader list by suggesting five trends to be expected during the next decade that grow out of factors discussed in this chapter and in Part I.

1. Membership will grow as churches move into a period of stabilization. This growth will be a result of social demographics and the cyclical nature of people's interest in religion, as much as it will be a result of the church's effort to recruit members.

2. The current emphasis upon emotional, inner disciplines generated by the charismatics and the new evangelicals will continue. This emphasis in religious life is supported by a corresponding emphasis in society on technologies of self-fulfillment.

3. The underlying tension between the dual purpose of church and synagogue, prophetic social concerns and nurturing of members, will turn toward social activism before the end of the century. The cycle in this century has been in periods of between 20 and 30 years.

4. The religious impulse from secular and non-church traditions will be legitimated and incorporated into mainline religious practices. Indeed, some aspects of humanistic psychology and disciplines from Transcendental Meditation and Transactional Analysis have already been adapted for use as part of religious programs.

5. Change of careers will affect people's search for meaning and purpose. It is probable that the creeds, rituals, and traditions of church and synagogue will be more needed by some people during the next ten years.

Creeds and traditions will serve as a base of meaning upon which people, caught in rapidly changing careers, rely as they seek new avenues of fulfillment.

NOTES

1. Robert L. Heilbroner, *The Human Prospect* (New York: Norton, 1974), p. 140.
2. Alvin F. Toffler, *Future Shock* (New York: Bantam, 1972).
3. Herman L. Kahn, "Things Are Going Rather Well: A State of the World Message from Herman Kahn," *The Futurist*, vol. 9, no. 6, December 1975, pp. 290–292.
4. Irving E. Bender, "A Longitudinal Study of Church Attenders and Nonattenders," *Journal for the Scientific Study of Religion*, vol. 3, no. 2 (1968), pp. 230–237.
5. Bender, p. 237.
6. *Yearbook of American Churches* (New York: National Council of Churches, 1953), p. 282; *Yearbook of American and Canadian Churches* (Nashville: Abingdon Press, 1976), p. 229.
7. Dean R. Hoge, *Division in the Protestant House* (Philadelphia: Westminster, 1976).
8. Paul M. Harrison, *Authority and Power in the Free Church Tradition* (Princeton, N.J.: Princeton University Press, 1959).
9. Richard R. Mathison, *Faiths, Cults and Sects of America* (Indianapolis: Bobbs-Merrill, 1960).
10. Douglas W. Johnson and George W. Cornell, *Punctured Preconceptions* (New York: Friendship Press, 1972).
11. John R. Fry, *The Trivialization of the United Presbyterian Church* (New York: Harper & Row, 1975).
12. Daniel Bell, "Toward the Great Instauration: Reflections on Culture and Religion in a Post Industrial Age," *Social Research*, Autumn 1975, pp. 381–413.
13. George M. Marsdon, "From Fundamentalism to Evangelicalism: A Historical Analysis," in David F. Wells and John D. Woodbridge (eds.), *The Evangelicals: What They Believe, Who They Are, Where They Are* (Nashville: Abingdon, 1975), pp. 122–142.
14. Richard Quebedeaux, *The Young Evangelicals* (New York: Harper & Row, 1971).
15. Roger C. Palms, *The Jesus Kids* (Valley Forge, Pa.: Judson Press, 1971), p. 36.
16. Joseph H. Fichter, *The Catholic Cult of the Paraclete* (New York: Sheed and Ward, 1975).
17. Fichter, p. 140.
18. Greeley, *Unsecular Man*.
19. "A Study of Religious Receipts and Expenditures in the United States," in Research Papers sponsored by the Commission on Private Philanthropy and Public Needs, Department of the Treasury, 1977, vol. 1, pp. 365–450.
20. John E. Biersdorf, *Hungry for Experience* (New York: Seabury, 1975).
21. Charles Y. Glock and Robert N. Bellah, *The New Religious Consciousness* (Berkeley: University of California Press, 1976).
22. Gerald J. Jud and Elisabeth Jud, *Training in the Art of Loving* (Philadelphia: Pilgrim Press, 1972).
23. Thomas A. Harris, *I'm O.K., You're O.K.* (New York: Harper & Row, 1967).
24. Dale L. Hiestand, *Changing Careers After Thirty-five* (New York: Columbia University Press, 1961).
25. Gerald J. Jud, Edgar W. Mills, Jr., Genevieve Burch, *Ex-Pastors* (Philadelphia: Pilgrim Press, 1970).
26. Hiestand, p. 147.
27. Jud, Mills, and Burch, p. 51.

10

Issues in the Religious Future

The future is looked to as paradise by some people, as disaster by others, and as more of the same by still others. There is a sense in which each of these pictures is accurate. The preconceptions people hold as they walk into tomorrow will color the landscape that they see. Those who hope to make a difference in their future, the people with optimism and purpose, take seriously projections that suggest trends of significance. Their understanding of such trends will enable them to act or to react in a positive manner.

The aim of this chapter is to indicate additional trends and issues that will have an effect on religious life in the decade ahead. In selecting the trends and issues I have focused upon the aspects of the future that directly concern people rather than concentrating on technological possibilities. While the latter are important, human factors will have the most direct effect on religious expression.

The trends I highlight are based upon sources which are listed at the conclusion of this chapter. In addition, trends are included which have been discussed in the other parts of this book.

MEANING AND PURPOSE

As discussed at length in Chapter 9, a seeming eternal search by people is for meaning and purpose. Philosophers give names to the paths individuals pursue in making the search. Hedonism, asceticism, and the puritan ethic are some of the names given to the various enactments of the search. The one thing these philosophies have in common is the desire of people to find a purpose greater than themselves.

Religious institutions are the primary human institutions devoted to assisting people in this search. Elabo-

rate rituals and formal creeds are ways that answers to the search have been given formal expression over the years. These answers are not always appropriate in an age of skepticism and sophistication as indicated in Chapter 9. This search has moved beyond the churches and has included a spate of self-help and self-improvement techniques developed and utilized by psychologists. Some will be important in the future as techniques to assist in the search.

The most important fact for religious institutions is that the search will continue. People will not discover the "correct" answers once and for all either within or outside the religious framework. The search will continue, and religious groups will flourish that assist persons in finding meaningful and compelling answers to their search.

It is likely that the ups and downs of church attendance and membership will continue for some religious groups. Institutions tend to grasp answers to burning issues and hold them for a time. When those answers are inappropriate for a new era, people become disillusioned and leave the institution, and adjustments are then made in the interpretation of faith statements. Such an ebb and flow will mark the future of religious institutions as it has the past.

FAMILY

The pressures on the nuclear family that were so frequent in the late 1960s and early 1970s seem to have subsided somewhat. Alternative styles of family formation and life, such as communes and group marriage, have waned in popularity. The cycle tends to repeat some of the ideas and efforts of the community experiments in the nineteenth century when communes and free marriage were also a counterpoint to an established view of marriage and family as a sacred institution.

It is certain that the nuclear family will continue to be the norm as we move into the future. This will assist local religious congregations, which deal most directly and effectively with family units. Nevertheless, as I will note, the number of persons choosing to remain single will continue to increase. This will challenge congregations to broaden their program concerns beyond a narrow emphasis on nuclear families as they have tended to do in the past.

Three trends related to family life need to be highlighted since each will have much effect upon religion in the decade ahead. These are the birth rate which is beginning to rise, the number of single-person families, and population spread.

Birth Rate

Data for 1976 and 1977 begin to show signs of a slight increase in the birth rate. These are but two years after a series of declines beginning in 1961; yet the change is important. A change in birth rate can signal a revised appraisal of the prospect of parenthood.

Partly the increase in the birth rate is the result of the large number of persons reaching the age of marriage and family formation. There are simply more people available in the population to bear children. However, there may also be a value change in the making. The no-children and small-family emphases of the 1960s and the 1970s appear about to be tempered by a new appreciation of the family. There have been an increasing number of articles in the popular press, some reporting on research and others more speculative, indicating renewed interest in family life. Since change in the birth rate is a socially induced phenomenon, as dependent upon public attitudes toward children as on the personal desire of couples, a mood for an increase in the number of children is being created.

A recent article in *U. S. News and World Report*, (February 20, 1978) "Delayed-Baby Boom: Its Meaning," indicates the significance of the declining birth rates of the past few years as well as the potential for increases in the near future. Many married couples delayed having a baby in order to establish a home and develop financial security. These couples are now deciding it is time for children.

An increase in the birth rate will pose a new challenge for the educational programs of the churches and synagogues. Facilities built in the 1950s and 1960s to meet the educational needs of the earlier baby boom may find a renewed usage. The greatest opportunity will not, however, be in the use of facilities, but in discovering new and more meaningful ways for the religious nurture of this new generation, who will experience the world far differently than their parents did in the post-World War II years.

Religious groups, both traditional and nontraditional, that depend upon single young adults will continue to flourish, although the number of such persons will decline within the decade. Recruitment may not be so easy as now, but evidence cited in Part I and in Chapter 9 suggests that the needs of young adults will make recruitment a productive activity of religious groups that take single young adults seriously.

Single-Person Families

The highest divorce rate in American history, the desire by increasing numbers of people to postpone marriage or not to marry at all, and the willingness of more and more people to live alone are all signs of the continued growth of single-person families. The high birth rate of the 1950s and the women's movement of the late 1960s and early 1970s have combined to push the number of singles in society upward. This trend will probably continue for the next decade.

It is the young single adult with education and leisure who is a most likely candidate for nontraditional religious groups. While many such individuals are not interested in the established churches, they are interested in finding meaning and purpose in their existence. They also desire security. They seem to be attracted more than others to the new religions and to the human potential movement as a means of establishing a base for their lives. This age group, separated from family and without its support, is especially open to the popular self improvement techniques.

As I observed earlier, the mainline and established religious groups have had a difficult time relating effectively to single individuals and especially to divorced people. The program of the average local church and synagogue is aimed at the completed nuclear family, and it seems unlikely that singles will be attracted to such congregations in significant numbers in the near future unless there is a redirection or broadening of congregational programs.

Population Spread

The attention given to migration during the 1970s has focused on the number of people moving into the Sunbelt. This pattern of residential change has drained population from major metropolitan areas in the Northeast and eastern North Central states to the sunshine states of Florida, Texas, California, and Arizona. While the Sunbelt is the recipient of many migrants, other types of movement are equally important to religious groups.

Nonmetropolitan counties in many parts of the United States are showing gains in population after decades of losses. Counties with significant increases are those within easy driving distance of metropolitan centers. The migration patterns reflect people's desire to locate in smaller communities, but to remain within the trading scope of a large metropolitan center. Many such people are young adults.

Another movement is toward particular types of areas. For example, many people moving to the Sunbelt are retired people and families wanting warmer climates. Others cluster around college or university towns, recreation centers such as lakes and ski areas, and military or research facilities. None of these movements are new, but there has been an increase in the number of people involved.

Religious organizations will need to relocate their churches or synagogues or develop new ones to make services available in receiving areas. For example, Florida has become an important area for Jewish retirees, while in the recent past the main bodies of Jewish adherents have been concentrated in major urban centers in the Northeast and eastern North Central states. The Roman Catholic Church has grown rapidly in Florida, due in part to the influx of retirees.

The West remains the least churched region in the nation. It appears that many migrants lose their religious habits when they move west of the Rockies. This issue of "lost faith" faced by religious leaders in the West will continue to be a problem. It is an open question whether the relatively low participation in churches characteristic in the West is a harbinger of religious change throughout the nation in the 1980s, or whether it will continue to be a regional phenomenon.

WORK AND LEISURE

Work and leisure have a mixed history in the way they have been viewed by religion in Western society. Work has been seen both as a curse brought on by human sinfulness (Genesis 3:17–19) and as a duty owed to God (the so-called Protestant work ethic). Leisure has been viewed negatively by some ("Idle hands are the devil's workshop") and as an ideal for an elite few (in Greek philosophy). Both work and leisure experiences have undergone considerable change in recent years and will continue to do so in the future.

While automation will continue to remove some of the drudgery and routinization from work, work will not likely diminish in importance. The growing emphasis on self-development and self-fulfillment will lead many to view work as an avenue for self-expression and creativity. Types of work that make this possible, such as service occupations and various arts and crafts, will be increasingly sought after.

At the same time, leisure opportunities will also continue to expand dramatically. Both shortened work weeks and continued affluence will make this possible. As with work, and even more so, the emphasis will be on self-fulfillment. This will be particularly true for those who are not able to find work that is fulfilling.

While I say more later about work and leisure, I wish to emphasize here a basic challenge of these developments for Judaism and Christianity. The challenge is to provide a new ethic of work and leisure that is appropriate to their changing nature while giving emphasis to crucial themes of the Judeo-Christian heritage. Both religions have emphasized that self-fulfillment comes through self-giving to others. Love and service of neighbor and a concern for social justice are ways of self-giving. An ethic which stresses these themes in relation to work and leisure will be needed to counter what may be an increasingly inward and self-serving approach to fulfillment.

Employment

Increases in service and white-collar jobs and decreases in factory and blue-collar jobs have been an important trend in employment. One reason behind the trend has been a demand for technical skills essential to the communication, entertainment, and computer industries. In addition, factories are continuing to introduce automation, which reduces the number of blue-collar jobs and changes the jobs that remain.

Human relations skills are required in service and technical jobs. The appreciation of another's point of view and affirmation of the worth of people as individuals seem to be essential needs in a society that depends more and more on machines. These values and the human relations skills needed for successful careers have traditionally been a bulwark of the educational programs of religious institutions. While non-religious teaching organizations have sprung up, changes in types of employment will increase the needs of people for training in getting along with others. This aspect of the religious educational program will grow.

Some religious groups emphasize a belief system that is fatalistic and does not deal with the worth or improvement of individuals. These groups will be able to attract many adherents in a mechanized society. People who feel themselves to be cogs in the wheels of society can use this type of religion as an escape from reality.

Regardless of the type of religious expression, changes in employment patterns indicate a continued need for religion. The need for security and a faith with surety and pattern is important. Also, the need people feel to release the religious impulse will allow religious groups opportunities for encouraging the development of personal devotional disciplines.

Multiple Careers

Between 1965 and 1970, about one third of the work force in the United States changed occupations. This number will be greater when the next decennial census is taken. The reasons are multifold, but three are especially evident:

1. A change in types of industries, with increasing emphasis on people-related services and white-collar

occupations, is a major reason for career change.

2. The feeling in our society that people ought to find fulfillment in life and career.

3. The emphasis on women employees' being accorded the same opportunities for career achievement as men.

These three factors are also evident in religious circles. Many individuals who have been involved in careers in other occupations are changing to careers within religious groups. This has always been an option, but the new emphasis tends to increase the number as well as the quality of such leadership.

Increasing numbers of women are training for the ministry of Protestant churches or for other types of leadership in religious institutions. For instance, seminary enrollment shows that between 1972 and 1976 women enrollees increased from 1,077 to 3,025, an increase of 181 percent. The importance of this trend will be examined later.

Dissatisfaction with occupation, including dissatisfaction among the clergy, will be a continuing fact of life for religious groups in the future. During recent years denominational officials in charge of clergy recruitment have reported that some of the more talented beginning students later changed their minds and entered other occupations. The reason given was that the challenge and outlook for religious professionals seemed too narrow and confining. This mood will overtake others within religious institutions during the next decade.

Retirement

Three aspects of retirement will affect religious life in the next decade.

The relocation of millions of retired individuals is a fact that has been reshaping the geographical concentration of religious bodies. This relocation undoubtedly will continue, not only to warmer climates but into areas where there is less density of population and industry, such as small communities across the nation. The movement will have an initial disrupting effect on religious groups currently receiving the influx, but local congregations and synagogues which have tenacity and adaptability will have a bright future.

The upward movement of age limits for retirement will have some effect on the money flow in religious groups. Older people generally attend religious services more frequently than those of younger ages, as indicated in Part I. In addition, older people tend to support religious groups more generously until they retire. With the mandatory retirement age pushed up some years, the effective contribution level of older citizens can be maintained and support for the religious group can continue at a higher level.

The resource of talent and skills available to religious groups in the form of retired individuals will increase during the next decade or two. With a squeeze on the overall income of religious groups, the need for skilled volunteers will increase. Religious institutions will increasingly discover and utilize the time and energy of retired people. Since there is no limit to the kinds of talents religious groups can use, it is likely that a range of retired persons will be recruited for local and international activities of religious groups.

It is quite possible that the international or missionary aspect of the religious groups will be enhanced. Technicians, professionals, and others who can assist in developmental projects in other nations are in demand for religious sponsored activities. The cost to employ retired people is less than for people at the peak of their careers (since many are receiving pensions and request only expense money), and the tasks they can perform provide them with short-term work that is meaningful.

These three aspects of retirement will tend to enhance and strengthen the life of religious groups.

LEISURE AND SELF-DEVELOPMENT

One of the characteristics of society today is the significant number of people who engage in active leisure pursuits. These include forms of recreation such as swimming, camping, hunting, and the like. Between 1967 and 1972 there was an important shift in the type of recreational activities pursued. More sedentary activities, such as pleasure driving, sightseeing, picnicking, and attending outdoor sports events, declined in terms of the proportion of persons engaging in them. Increases in the proportion of people engaging in activities such as swimming, camping, nature walks, snow skiing, and hunting, occurred during the same time.

While physical activity is one means of using leisure for self-development, adult education is another form. There has been an increase in the number of people over age 30 who have enrolled in college during the past ten years. The number of women enrolled has increased dramatically as women have sought to find new careers and upgrade skills. In addition to college education, a number of communities sponsor adult schools with noncredit courses on subjects ranging from auto repair to foreign languages and modern dance. In both the college and the adult schools, participants are seeking their own self-development during leisure hours.

Religious bodies are feeling and will feel two effects of this use of leisure. Adherents to religion will be increasingly aware of their own capabilities. They will not be so accepting of the past or easy answers to complex issues. They will be more sophisticated and will require a more stimulating educational and worship experience. They will need to see the relation between their beliefs and their self-development.

Another area obviously affected by the increased number and variety of leisure time pursuits is religious activities that have typically taken place on weekends. While this trend is not new, the continued growth in leisure opportunities, primarily on weekends, will challenge religious organizations to develop alternatives to weekend worship services. Greater emphasis on the discipline of regular worship will also be needed.

Leisure Living

The retiree who lives half of the year in the family home, usually in the northern part of the nation, and spends the other half in the southern part of the country is familiar to established religious groups. These people generally are faithful in their giving and attendance when they are in the vicinity of the home church or synagogue. They also tend to worship in their new home in the south during their stay there.

Young adults who take long weekends for recreational purposes are also familiar to the established religious bodies. These individuals may go skiing, to another city for the weekend, to the beach, or to visit someone in another state. They tend not to be so faithful to established churches or synagogues and join out of a sense of duty or long-term expectation of need.

The third group with which the church is familiar has traditionally been part of the backbone of established religion. These are parents with children at home and range in age from 25 to 60. Increasing affluence has allowed many of them to purchase second homes and condominiums where they can spend weekends and vacations.

All three groups can be expected to increase in size. The incomes and the amount of money available to individuals is greater now than in any previous years. The gasoline shortage plus the desire to be active suggests an increase in the number of individuals and families who will have a home away from home, the "two-home people." If they retain a religious affiliation, it may be on a permanently split basis. Religious groups that want to keep the loyalty of two-home people must be available in two places or be willing to share the allegiance with another religious group near to the second home.

COMMUNICATIONS

Improvements in communication technology will relieve business travel, allow religious groups to hold conferences among people scattered over the country, and increase the amount of time people can give to volunteer work in religious activities.

The ability to speak long distance to several people at a time and send facsimile documents over telephone lines, compared to the high cost of small person-to-person meetings, will cut down on business travel as well as the travel of individuals involved in religious activities. While the dollar amount spent on travel will increase due to inflation and rising costs, the number of people involved in such travel will decrease. It is much more economical to have a conference call than it is to have small meetings. These innovations in the technology of communication will free the time and energy of business travelers for more frequent use in their home communities.

The same savings ought to accrue to religious groups with national and regional organizations. It ought also to facilitate more participation in such organizations' meetings by people who do not have money and time to travel. They can hear about important decisions and make their voices heard more quickly than in the past. Such use of communication ought to enhance the decision making of national and regional religious bodies.

The major result of increased use of this technology would be more time available for volunteering. Churches rely heavily on volunteers. The bonus of this "found time" is that the range of people who can participate in volunteering is broadened. This will be particularly helpful if the economic situation created by inflation and increasing costs for energy continues to have a detrimental effect on congregational expenditures.

Miniaturization

Space needs, permanent records, and easy retrieval are areas in which the process of miniaturization—the reproduction and storage of information at much-reduced size such as on microfilm or in a computer—will affect religious bodies.

Religious groups are print oriented. They have writings and scriptures that are viewed as holy. They use volumes written by scholars and leaders to interpret the scriptures. One of the most important features of a religious group is its library of commentaries and scriptures.

The space needed for these collections as well as records of meetings and official documents is not overwhelming at any time. However, the number of records and documents are increased by the number of meetings and papers required to keep the group functioning. Files begin to overflow. Archives become crowded. Space is used for "dead" purposes.

Miniaturization offers one way to cut down the cost of space used for paper storage. While religious groups will take time before putting their scriptures on film sheets, they will be able to store other writings and documents. In fact, one firm already has the Bible and related commentaries available on microfiche. Related passages of scripture are found by use of a computer. In this way the firm can respond to requests for specific topic-related scriptures. This relieves clergy of having large numbers of commentaries in their own possession. The computer saves their time by searching for the references they need quickly.

Religious bodies have records that are usually acceptable to legal entities in lieu of birth and marriage records. The need for permanence of such records is evident. The use of film makes such records available with little or no use of the original volumes. It cuts down wear and the possibility of loss.

When a copy of a record or other item is needed, the filing system is more maneuverable and the reproduction of a page or two of a document is relatively easy and inexpensive. The retrieval system obviously depends on the group, but the miniaturization process alleviates long searches through mammoth files.

The fact of miniaturization may not be understood or appreciated in the religious world for a while. It may be resisted because of the so-called impersonal nature of film as opposed to the historically acceptable print medium. In the near future, however, the use of these processes will affect the size and type of buildings religious bodies rent or build and the skills required of people who want to work with and for these bodies. The monk with a quill pen is a picture of the medieval period. A person who has the skill and knowledge in using machines will be a more typical model of current and future religious recording and writing.

Visual and Audio Aids

The preacher who utilizes television reaches audiences far greater than those imagined by the homiletics professor in most seminaries three decades ago. The movies and stage bring a religious message, albeit sometimes commercialized, to thousands who would not enter a building for religious worship. The newspaper of the air, radio and television, reports on news of religious happenings, even to the extent that some issues are created by the media.

The realm of a religious person is no longer a small room detached from the world. It is a message received and reacted to in a public setting.

The public media are only one aspect of the visualization of the religious message. Religious groups are utilizing video tapes for learning and teaching. New adherents are taught with the help of prepackaged visual aids. Religious leaders are taught organizational processes with the aid of cassettes and films. In general, the use of sophisticated visual and audio aids is increasing, at least for the religious leaders.

The use of cassettes is increasing in congregations as well. Recordings of sermons, services, and messages are made and sent or taken to people unable to attend the meetings. The opportunity of such individuals to participate is extended through the tape. While this is reserved for special groups at present, it is likely that the cassette will become a major tool in reaching those who do not come to a religious meeting. The meeting, including worship services for those with a second

home, will come to them in the form of cassettes taken by volunteers or a clergyperson.

Cable television is regarded by experts as a means through which people can respond and interact with candidates, forum leaders, and register votes for or against issues. The growth of the industry has not been as expansive as expected but it is a coming addition to public media. The use of cable television by religious groups in some communities will allow them to hold services or conferences in which people at home may participate and interact with leaders. While this may be only experimental during most of the next decade, the possibility of interaction through television could greatly enhance participation in religious services and conferences by 1990.

SOCIAL RESPONSIBILITY

During the later 1960s and the early 1970s, churches were incorporating some of their ideals into social programs. They began to work in their neighborhoods, and some congregations even hired extra staff to work specifically in the communities surrounding the church building. In the process of translating their concerns into action, congregations were exhibiting a social responsibility akin to that evident in the 1930s when social centers were established in the inner-city.

The so-called conservative swing in the late 1970s is a period of respite from social and political confrontation. It is a time when social institutions, including the church and synagogue, take stock of their habits and practices. They seek out their basic beliefs and consolidate their new learnings in terms of their heritage of faith. While this appears to be a rejection of some social responsibility, it is more of an internalization of the new and the old. The amalgamation of these two strands results in a new understanding of social responsibility.

This process of experimentation and consolidation will continue. It must if institutions are to live. Religious institutions have been able to adjust their ethical demands according to the cultures in which they exist, and it appears that the future will be no different. Given the present mood within the religious bodies, it seems that a new mood of outreach into social responsibility will be reached near the end of the decade. In the interim the gains from the push of the past decade will continue to be intertwined with the basic beliefs and traditions of the centuries.

Society at large, a reflector of values, is a guide to the extent of consolidation taking place. Concern will continue to escalate for redress of human rights and individual grievances. A balance must be established prior to another great effort for equality. This will mean that some groups in society and within religious bodies will feel that the push for equality is going backward rather than forward. This is necessary in a time of adjustment. The result will be a more clearly defined sense of social responsibility within religious groups as well as within the whole society by the turn of the century.

PLURALISM

Social institutions are adaptable creatures; they have a built-in tolerance for deviation. A rule and a law in such an institution is a norm, but this does not mean that organization practices measure up to that norm. Laws and rules are guides that are interpreted and stretched by members of the institution.

Religious institutions have been "for all persons who would believe." During the past two decades challenges to the practices in religious institutions have made people quite aware of this norm and of the distance between the practice and the norm. Indeed, much effort has been devoted to raising the standard of practice toward the norm. Especially important has been the adoption of quotas to ensure proportionate representation of ethnics, women, and youth in the boards and governing bodies of religious organizations. These quotas have been applied to organizations at the local, regional, and national levels.

The emergence of pluralism in religious circles has included the desire for strong minority-group congregations. But the practices and traditions of religious expression for minority groups generally are different from those of a white majority. The strains and misunderstandings that the theme of integration and quotas have created may result in some further fracturing of existing religious bodies. However, this will have little effect on the quality of faith or the effectiveness of the resultant bodies to inform, educate, and inspire their adherents.

Ethnicity

Ethnicity, especially relating to race, is an extension of pluralism in that it continues the development of a conscious awareness of a group's heritage. It goes beyond equality to assess the meaning of one's background and trek through social history. This has been done well for some blacks in *Roots* by Alex Haley. Two aspects of the black heritage are particularly important for the religious world.

First, black religion provides a reservoir of strength and perseverance which has not been maintained by white majority religious groups. A minority in a society uses religious forms to sustain hope as well as provide a means of acceptable social criticism. In black culture, this has been most effectively done through music and song. The sense of justice and love, expressed through song and nonviolent protests, changed the 1960s. This same mood of change and sense of purpose continues. It

will, if allowed, change the character of religious expression during the last part of the decade ahead.

Second, the emphasis upon emotion and personal relationships derived from ethnic experiences will affect the manner in which religious groups go about their business. The mood of efficiency currently in vogue in many religious groups can change to become more in tune with the societal emphasis upon the individual. A factor in this change will come from ethnic religious practices.

How effectively these two forces will influence religious life in the next decade is an open question. A part of the answer depends upon the willingness of white majority religious bodies to incorporate the quality and spirit of ethnic religious expression. This includes music, devotional life, and worship experiences. Another part of the answer lies in the willingness of religious bodies to allow their ethnic groups to establish viable and strong identities apart from dominant white traditions.

The impact of ethnic religion during the next decade will depend upon how much the ethnics are able to recover their religious heritage and how willing the white-dominated religious groups are to incorporate the quality and meaning of this religion in general practice. It appears unlikely that for the first part of the next decade much more than superficial efforts will take place. When serious attempts are made to recover and enlarge upon the themes and expressions of ethnic, especially black, religion, religious life will be much enriched.

SECULAR RELIGIONS

The development of psychologically oriented techniques for self-fulfillment, discussed in Chapter 9, has brought forth a new wave of prophets both inside and outside the religious framework. Their emphasis is upon techniques to help people feel better, do a more commendable job of relating to others, and find a philosophy that provides meaning to their lives.

The most religiously oriented of the psychological techniques is Transactional Analysis. It has been used and will be used in conjunction with religious practice and observance. It affords some individuals a framework into which they can put themselves and their lives for analysis and redirection. Many find it a more appropriate model than the conversions on the sawdust trails of the tent meetings in a former era.

Transcendental Meditation employs techniques used for centuries in religious groups. While such methods have been borrowed recently from the Eastern religions, meditation and devotional practices have a long history in Western religion.

I refer to these as secular religions because they generally adhere to beliefs that are not within the scope of one of the established religions in our society. They are secular in that they invite personal development with little emphasis, if any, on divine interference. In this sense the techniques are a product of the secular search for meaning and purpose.

It seems realistic to expect that secular religions will continue to be born and die as the needs and experiences of our culture change. The most successful will find some of their elements incorporated into the more established religions.

EVANGELICALS

Movements within several of the mainline denominations, as indicated in Chapter 9, are pressing for a more evangelical, as opposed to a social action, emphasis. The difference between these two poles of religious thought is a matter of degree. The evangelicals tend to be adamant that the emotional and devotional side of religion needs to be expressed. While the social actionists do not deny this, their emphasis is upon social equality and the righting of wrongs imposed by social attitudes and traditions.

There are no winners in a debate such as this, and there are few converts. The protagonists represent two quite different camps of thought within the religious world. One group gains superiority for a while and then the other comes to the fore. It is a constant tension that is necessary for the continued vitality of religious institutions.

The evangelical movement is strong and growing at present and will probably continue so in the near future. It is a part of the consolidation phase through which American society is and will be moving. Its legacy will be a revision of programs and emphases within religious groups. At present this is taking the form of renewed concern with outreach and nurture (evangelism and education). The process of renewal includes the opportunity to rebuild an institution to which people can give allegiance. It is an effort to provide stability to their beliefs and personal search for meaning.

The renewed emphasis upon education and evangelism will result in a much more clearly defined direction for some religious bodies. As they concentrate their energies in these areas, it is likely that they will experience growth in the next decade.

WOMEN CLERGY

The importance of the addition of significant numbers of women clergy to the religious scene cannot be overestimated. The clergy as a profession has been male for centuries, and there have long been attacks against women who have sought to exercise leadership in the church, Joan of Arc being an early example. However, the custom that only men can be ministers or priests is

no longer necessary, wise, or theologically defensible. As is clear from recent efforts to block women's ordination, the transition to accepting women clergy is not easy. There will continue to be confusion and strain. Only over time will the custom be reversed. In the meantime much heat, and possibly much wisdom also, may be generated as the pioneers develop models for future emulation.

Women clergy, as trained professionals in a male-dominated occupation, will provide role models for many other women who must function in their own occupations. The high visibility of the clergy role will help this to happen. The next decade will witness women clergy as a major asset in consolidating some of the gains won by the woman's movement.

It is likely that the resistance against women clergy will be considerably diminished within the next ten years. Their acceptance by congregations will be little different from that of their male counterparts, and they will assume important positions in established religious bodies.

ECUMENICS

Among Protestants the grand design for a unified church in the United States was initiated in the 1950s and 1960s. It had several predecessors in the tide of good feelings that followed the end of World War I. Bringing the denominations together was not visualized as a remote possibility but something to be achieved within a decade or so.

The glamor of ecumenical action has fallen by the wayside. The snarls and disagreements that erupt around even the most noncontroversial organizational issue make ecumenics an expensive endeavor that produces little of substance for the local church member. The prevailing feelings now seem to be that the theology and traditions of each religious group must be sustained. When they appear to be threatened, there is a parting of the ways, and this usually means a lack of ecumenical program or activity.

The issues of women clergy and increasing pluralism are points around which tensions are raised within various religious groups. Any ecumenical endeavor of importance may be hung up on issues involving these two aspects of religious life. This makes ecumenical debate and cooperation exceedingly slow at times.

The future of ecumenics appears to be related to practical accomplishments. When it is convenient for congregations and denominations to cooperate on issues that do not call into question their basic system of organization or theology, ecumenical action may occur. This mood, perhaps related to the trends of ethnicity and pluralism as well as the fear of institutional bigness, seems to have settled on the religious scene with little likelihood of changing during the next decade.

MANAGEMENT

One of the difficulties religious groups face is the issue of management of people and resources. Management books are written for use by organizations which have clear lines of accountability and authority. When an organization is composed of a few professionals and mostly volunteers, as are religious groups, the management is by negotiation and persuasion rather than by clear authority. This is a process not well learned in the religious world.

During the next decade, it will be imperative that models of management, including goal setting, planning, and evaluation, be developed and implemented by religious bodies. These will need to be appropriate for voluntary associations such as churches and synagogues and will need to include training for lay participants as well as clergy.

Finally, religious groups are faced with three problems that will intensify during the next decade: organizational fractures, inflation, and energy. Management skills will be required to deal with them.

Organizational Fractures

An institution that is alive will undergo strains. If this is true, the religious bodies in the United States must be vitally alive. They have undergone not only strains but fractures (such as the movements within denominations discussed in Chapter 9) and various types of splits over the past few years.

Pluralism, debates about the Bible and confessional statements, debates about women clergy, social action, and ethnic minority demands, and general dissatisfaction with programs have been causes for these problems. The accountability of leaders has been an important theme during reorganization in the national and regional levels of religious denominations. Attention to accountability, however, has not proved to be the corrective needed. Continual pressures are exerted on religious organizations by internal groups. Their criticisms often deal with theological emphases and the overall philosophy behind programs.

The near future will witness a continuation of this disorder in religious organizations, not because some people desire constant upheaval, but because it is an aspect of pluralism and regaining ethnic identity. It will result in clarity of purpose and direction for some groups by the end of the decade. It may result in the splitting of several denominations by 1990.

Inflation

Inflation has been a serious problem for religious institutions over the past decade. It has eroded reserves, cut down on the real dollars contributed by members, and made budget raising for religious groups difficult. The inflation rate of 6 percent per year means that a religious group must add to its income by at least that amount each year to remain even. While giving to religious bodies has continued to rise during the past few years, the costs for staff and programs have risen even more.

Inflation must be coupled with number of members when income is computed. During the past decade inflation has been a villain, but among mainline Protestant denominations the decline in membership has been equally devastating. While per-capita giving has increased, the number of people on which that statistic is computed has decreased.

It is likely that a turnaround has been reached in membership. Gains by some of the mainline denominations can be expected within the next few years and a mood of growth will replace apprehension about continued decline. The reasons for the likely increase are the focus upon a clear purpose for the religious body, emphasis upon evangelism and education, and changes in the population, including aging and increased birth rates.

Another aspect of inflation is the strain it places on family budgets. Increasing numbers of families have two people who work at jobs outside the home in order to provide extra income to meet obligations. One consequence for religion is a more selective use of time by people who do volunteer work for the church. These people will choose between a variety of volunteer possibilities with religion being one option among many. The attractiveness of religious activities as a means of finding personal fulfillment will directly affect the number of people who give time to religion.

This selectiveness will come at the same time that religious bodies, caught in the squeeze of inflation, must cut back on professional staff. The next decade will witness a major change in the manner in which volunteers are recruited and utilized by religious bodies.

Energy

The issue of energy is so pervasive in our society that its effects on religion may seem minor. Yet the shortage and cost of energy will force new styles in the way religious bodies conduct their business, the type of buildings they build, and the amount of budget used for energy.

It is likely that meetings, especially small gatherings, will be held in nonchurch settings. This will have two effects. The most obvious will be a reduction in the need for fuel and energy to be consumed at the church or synagogue. The second is new relationships within congregations. People meeting in each other's houses introduces a new element of intimacy and small-group development that may have been lacking in religious groups that previously met only in religious buildings.

Considerable attention to architecture will be given in new construction of religious buildings with efforts to improve energy efficiency a part of each plan. In addition, ways to conserve heat and to refit existing buildings will be developed. At present, seminars are being conducted to educate religious leaders in the various means of energy conservation. The emphasis on energy conservation will develop a consciousness of the need for new life patterns within congregations, and will affect the residences of members as well as the religious buildings. This is an area in which religious groups have an important opportunity to exert leadership in the years ahead.

SOURCES

Fry, John R., *The Trivialization of the United Presbyterian Church* (New York: Harper & Row, 1975).

Glock, Charles Y., and Robert N. Bellah, *The New Religious Consciousness* (Berkeley: University of California Press, 1976).

Handbook of Labor Statistics (Washington, D.C.: U.S. Department of Labor). Annual.

Henderson, C. William, *Awakening: Ways to Psychospiritual Growth* (Englewood Cliffs, N.J.: Prentice Hall, 1975).

Hiestand, Dale L., *Changing Careers After Thirty-five* (New York: Columbia University Press, 1961).

Johnson, Douglas W., *Managing Change in the Church* (New York: Friendship Press, 1974).

Johnson, Douglas W., and George W. Cornell, *Punctured Preconceptions* (New York: Friendship Press, 1972).

Kelley, Dean M., *Why Conservative Churches are Growing* (New York: Harper & Row, 1972).

Marty, Martin E., *A Nation of Behavers* (Chicago: University of Chicago, 1976).

Mickey, Paul A., and Robert L. Wilson, *What New Creation?* (Nashville: Abingdon, 1977).

Procter, Priscilla, and William Procter, *Women in the Pulpit* (Garden City, N.Y.: Doubleday, 1976).

Quebedeaux, Richard, *The Young Evangelicals* (New York: Harper & Row, 1974).

Series P–25 and P–60, *Current Population Reports* (Washington, D.C.: U.S. Department of Commerce, Bureau of the Census, 1977).

U.S. Department of Health, Education, and Welfare, Public Health Service, National Center for Health Statistics: Monthly and Annual Vital Statistics Report.

Washington, Joseph R., Jr., *Black Religion* (Boston: Beacon Press, 1964).

IV

Afterword: A Coming Religious Revival?

GEORGE GALLUP, Jr.

EVIDENCE is mounting that the U.S. may be in an early stage of a profound religious revival, with the evangelical movement providing a powerful thrust.

In terms of what might be described as "hard" evidence, the Gallup Poll recorded a rise in church attendance for 1976 for the first time in nearly two decades, with 42 percent of Americans attending church or synagogue in a typical week. Our 1976 surveys also showed church *membership* to be on the upswing during the year with about 7 in 10 describing themselves as church members. These figures were essentially the same in 1977 surveys. Thus, while there was not a continuation of the upward trend, neither was there a reversal of the gains of the preceding year.

Another barometer which has measured swings in religiousness—in terms of both organizational and non-organizational religion—is one which asks each person the importance of religion in his or her life. This barometer also indicated a trend upward, with about 6 in 10 saying their religious beliefs are "very important" in their lives. These gains for religion have been accompanied by considerable interest on the part of the public in what might be termed "experiential religion"— involvement in such movements as Transcendental Meditation, yoga, the charismatic movement, mysticism, and Eastern religions. A recent survey which we conducted indicates that a projected 6 million Americans are participating in, or are involved in TM, 5

million in yoga, 3 million in the charismatic movement (charismatic renewal), 3 million in mysticism, and 2 million in Eastern religions.

It is important to note that interest in these movements is not necessarily in conflict with organized religion and, in fact, is often supportive, with considerable experimentation found among church members.

The *observations* of both laity and clergy, as well as behavioral measurements, indicate an upturn in religious interest and activity.

A recent Gallup survey of U.S. adults showed that the proportion who believe religion is increasing its influence on American life is up sharply in recent months and has tripled since 1971. The observations of clergy and other religious leaders would also seem to point in this direction. I have had occasion recently to talk to religious leaders of many faiths and denominations and they are in general agreement that there is a deeper search for nonmaterial values and a renewed interest in religion.

Evangelical leaders appear to be the most convinced that there is evidence of renewed religious zeal. And, indeed, Gallup Poll findings show the evangelical movement in this nation to be an increasingly powerful one, affecting the religious character of many churches. A widely reported Gallup Poll finding in the summer of 1976 showed 1 person in 3 (34 percent) saying he or she has been "born again"—that is, has had a turning point in life of commitment to Jesus Christ. In terms of numbers, this figure represents nearly 50 million Americans, 18 and over. Among Protestants alone, nearly half

Reprinted, with changes, from *Journal of Current Social Issues*, vol. 14, no. 2, Spring 1977.

(48 percent) say they are "born again" Christians, which represents some 43 million adults. One way of defining an evangelical would be a person who (1) has had a "born again" experience, (2) holds a literal interpretation of the Bible (or accepts its absolute authority), and (3) witnesses to his or her faith. Of the total national sample, 1 in 5 meets all three tests. Among the various factors which could be pointed to as accounting for the increased activity in the religious and spiritual climate of the U.S. are the following:

- A turning inward to seek refuge from the pressures of everyday existence.
- A search for nonmaterial values in light of the disappointments of the material world and the fading of the "American dream."
- President Carter's open discussion of his own personal religious beliefs, which has focused new attention on religion in the U.S. and particularly the evangelical movement.
- A normal upswing following a decline in religious interest and activity. In broad terms, America's religious scene has historically been characterized by periods of religious zeal followed by a drift back to religious apathy. Thus there was a sharp upswing in religious interest and participation in the late 50s, a downward trend during the late 60s (primarily among Catholics), a leveling off during the first years of the 70s, and now, apparently, another upturn.
- The efforts of the nation's clergy in response to the need to make religion more appealing to young people and to satisfy their apparent spiritual hunger.

While the growth in religious interest and activity appears to be across the board in terms of population groups, it is centered largely among young adults, where the sharpest gains are recorded, not only in church attendance and membership but also in the proportion saying religion plays an important role in their lives. Thus what many religious leaders had fervently hoped would happen now may be occurring: young people, after having expressed their disenchantment in the 60s with the establishment, including organized religion, now, in the mid and late 70s, are moving back into the ranks of church members. Survey findings presented here would seem to offer solid evidence that Americans are religiously healthy. In addition, a recently completed seventy-nation survey, conducted for the Charles F. Kettering Foundation by Gallup International Research Institutes, shows the United States to be the most religious nation of the world among the advanced nations surveyed. Even in the face of these findings one must nevertheless ask: Are we really as religious as we appear? Are we perhaps only *superficially* religious? Indeed America appears to be facing a seeming paradox: *religion* is increasing its influence on society but *morality* is losing its influence. The secular world would seem to offer abundant evidence that religion is not greatly affecting our lives. The United States has one of the worst records in the world in terms of criminal victimization. We live in a "ripoff" society, and every day we read of consumer fraud, political corruption, tax cheating, bribery, payoffs and so forth.

Yet one could argue that the reports of crime and immorality in the United States would be far *worse* if religion did not in some fashion enter the lives of most of us. In fact, a study conducted for the Miami Valley Young Adult Ministry, Inc., on the "attitudes, values and lifestyles" of young adults in Greater Dayton (Ohio), suggests the strong influence religious faith can have on lives, in terms of restraint as well as in terms of guidance and inspiration.

The Dayton study, as well as numerous other studies, has clearly indicated that religiously oriented youth are happier, more confident in their futures, and less inclined to use drugs and alcohol to excess than are youth who are *not* religiously oriented.

Religious motivation also helps explain the current explosion in volunteerism in the United States. One out of every four people, 14 years of age and older, volunteers time to some nonprofit organization. Over 50 percent of this volunteer time is given to churches and synagogues.

While religion is clearly playing an important role in our lives, some religious leaders feel that much of the new interest in religion is sheer emotionalism—a temporary "high"—and question whether there is anything of substance to this religious zeal. And few religious leaders, of course, would be satisfied with evidence of merely *numerical* gains—filling up the pews. Obviously the ultimate goal for Christianity is to deepen religious faith and commitment. New survey efforts are being made to explore in greater depth the religious climate of the nation. One of the key measurements to be developed might be one to determine the level of "religious maturity." While Americans may be impressively religious in terms of outward manifestations, survey evidence indicates a wide gap between belief and practice. In addition, the prayer life of many might be considered rudimentary and underdeveloped. Surveys reveal a shocking lack of knowledge regarding certain basic facts about the doctrines and history of our own churches. Perhaps religious faith to many is merely supportive and not challenging: are our churches producing "nice" people or "new" people?

How would one describe a person who is becoming "religiously mature"? Such a person might be one who is:

- Constantly aware of the need to grow spiritually.
- Seeking to cultivate a deep inner life.
- Open to new ways of reaching God and tolerant of different ways.
- Seeking to blend a life of prayer with a life of service.
- Not afraid to take a position against society if religious convictions so dictate.

While it could be argued that many Americans are "spiritual illiterates" and far from growing into religious maturity, the new evidence of spiritual intensity and the desire for a deeper religious commitment suggests that Americans may now be entering a period of religious *adolescence*.

Time will tell whether America is on a religious "kick" or whether we are indeed becoming a more religiously committed nation. The shape of the future depends to a considerable extent on the religious beliefs, practices, and expectations of two key groups in society—the college educated, who include a high proportion of the opinion leaders among the public, and the young, who will set the tone for the church and for the nation in the years ahead.

While it is generally assumed that the more formal education one has the less religious he or she becomes, this does not appear to be the case for Americans. The seventy-nation study referred to earlier shows the United States to be unique in that we *both* have a high level of formal education and display a high level of religious belief and practice.

Youth in the United States have a far poorer church attendance record than do their elders, but they are not so antichurch nor antireligion as is sometimes believed. Nor do they raise any basic theological arguments. For them, God is very much alive.

Yet a significant number of youth fault the nation's churches and church members in one basic respect— "failing to meet the daily needs of people." What young people today are seeking, I believe, is not "social protest" (official statements from church leaders on society's ills) so much as they are seeking "social action." Youth sometimes tend to think of organized religion as a "closed club" of older, affluent people who work on committees, but don't get involved in the really tough,

unheralded but rewarding, sacrificial, person-to-person kind of work needed—helping the sick, the poor, the elderly—with their time and energy and prayers, not just their money.

Young people today have been misnamed the "self-centered generation." In fact, they have a strongly-developed sense of service to society with many hoping to enter the "helping professions," including social work. They would, therefore, likely look unfavorably upon one recent estimate that American churches spend 80 percent of their revenues for internal purposes, leaving 20 percent for the poor and the oppressed.

One of the tasks of religious leaders is to link the apparent will to believe among young people with their interest in helping others. Some might maintain that such a link would result in merely a dry "faith-in-works" kind of service rather than service energized by a living, vital, and active faith. What is needed, they would argue, are *spiritual counseling* programs—to encourage *inner* renewal for *social* renewal. In this regard, leaders of local churches should determine whether their youth ministers are merely duplicating the efforts of recreational personnel or whether they are encouraging prayer and service.

In view of the number of youth today who are caught up in the meditation movement, it clearly behooves religious leaders to provide programs for spiritual guidance. But will concentration on the inner life cause one to retreat into himself and neglect his duties to his neighbor? Many religious authorities would insist the opposite occurs—that the natural consequence of an intense inner life is an overflow of love manifested in action.

Yet one might ask: Are some people unreachable through spiritual counseling or otherwise? Are some predestined to have strong religious faith and others not? Perhaps it would seem this way, but here is what Mother Teresa of Calcutta said, as quoted in Malcolm Muggeridge's book, *Something Beautiful for God*: (New York: Harper & Row, 1971): "Love is a fruit in season at all times, and within reach of every hand. Anyone may gather it and no limit is set." But how does one attain this love? Mother Teresa says: "Everyone can reach this love through meditation, spirit of prayer and sacrifice and an intense inner life."

Table 10. Attended Church or Synagogue During Average Week°

Question: Did you happen to attend church or synagogue in the last seven days, or not?

Religion	Yes
Protestant	38%
Catholic	54
Jewish	20

°Tables 10–22 summarize information gathered by The Gallup Poll in 1975–76.

Table 11. Church / Synagogue Membership

Question: Do you happen to be a member of a church or synagogue, or not?

Religion	Yes	No
Protestant	73%	27%
Catholic	83	17
Jewish	34	66

Table 12. Importance of Religious Beliefs

Question: How important to you are your religious beliefs—very important, fairly important, not too important, or not at all important?

	Very important	Fairly important	Not too important	Not at all important	Don't know
National	56%	20%	8%	5%	1%
Sex					
Male	47	36	11	5	1
Female	66	25	5	4	°
Education					
College	49	33	11	6	1
High School	58	31	7	4	°
Grade School	70	21	3	5	1
Age					
Under 30 years	45	35	15	5	°
30–49 years	58	30	7	5	°
50 and older	63	27	5	4	1
Occupation					
White collar	54	29	9	8	°
Blue collar	47	36	13	4	°
Housewives	68	25	4	3	°
All others	56	31	6	5	2
Religion					
Protestant	68	27	4	1	°
Catholic	60	35	5	°	°
Church members	65	30	5	°	°
Nonmembers	28	32	21	19	°
Believe in God	60	31	7	2	°
God observes	66	28	5	1	°
Doesn't observe	39	37	17	7	°
Don't believe in God	11	20	17	52	°
Believe in immortality	69	26	4	1	°
Don't believe	27	39	17	17	°
Very happy	62	27	7	4	°
Fairly happy	52	34	9	4	1
Not too happy	56	24	8	11	1

°Less than 1 percent.

Table 13. Influence of Religion

Question: At the present time, do you think religion as a whole is increasing its influence on American life or losing its influence?

	Increasing	Losing	Same	Don't know
National	39%	51%	7%	3%
Sex				
Male	35	55	8	2
Female	44	48	6	2
Education				
College	37	53	9	1
High School	41	51	6	2
Grade School	36	49	8	7
Region				
East	32	59	7	2
Midwest	38	54	7	1
South	43	46	7	4
West	47	44	8	1
Age				
Total under 30	44	51	4	1
18–24 years	44	50	5	1
25–29 years	44	54	2	°
30–49 years	35	55	7	3
50 and older	40	48	9	3
Income				
$20,000 and over	32	56	11	1
$15,000–$19,999	38	56	4	2
$10,000–$14,999	39	54	6	1
$ 7,000–$ 9,999	42	49	3	6
$ 5,000–$ 6,999	52	37	8	3
$ 3,000–$ 4,999	39	50	9	2
Under $3,000	38	45	10	7
Politics				
Republican	39	49	10	2
Democrat	43	49	6	2
So. Democrat	49	41	6	4
Other Democrat	40	53	6	1
Independent	35	58	5	2
Religion				
Protestant	42	48	7	3
Catholic	38	53	8	1
Occupation				
Professional and Business	34	55	8	3
Clerical and Sales	39	56	5	°
Manual Workers	42	50	6	2
Non-Labor Force	40	46	10	4
Church goers	47	45	6	2
Non-Church goers	34	56	7	3

°Less than 1 percent.

Table 14. Involvement in Experiential Religion

Question: Which, if any, of these are you involved in or do you practice—yoga, TM, Eastern religions, the charismatic movement, faith healing, and mysticism?

Faith healing	—7 percent, 10 million
Transcendental meditation	—4 percent, 6 million
Yoga	—3 percent, 5 million
The charismatic movement (charismatic renewal)	—2 percent, 3 million
Mysticism	—2 percent, 3 million
Eastern religions	—1 percent, 2 million

Table 15. Have Had a "Born Again" Experience

Question: Would you say that you have been "born again" or have had a "born again" experience—that is, a turning point in your life when you committed yourself to Christ?

Nationwide	34%
Protestants	48
Catholics	18
Men	28
Women	39
College	27
High School	36
Grade School	42
18–29 years	29
30–49 years	33
50 and over	39
East	23
Midwest	34
South	55
West	20

Table 16. Belief in God

Questions: Do you believe in God or a universal spirit? Do you believe that this God or universal spirit observes your actions and rewards and punishes you for them?

	Believe in God	God observes	Doesn't observe	Don't know	Don't believe in God	Don't know
National	94%	68%	19%	7%	3%	3%
Sex						
Male	92	65	19	8	5	3
Female	96	72	19	5	2	2
Education						
College	91	56	27	8	6	3
High School	96	76	14	6	2	2
Grade School	96	79	11	6	3	1
Age						
Under 30 years	92	67	19	6	5	3
30–49	94	69	18	7	4	2
50 and older	96	70	18	8	2	2
Occupation						
White collar	92	64	20	8	5	3
Blue collar	94	69	20	5	4	2
Housewives	97	75	17	5	2	1
All others	90	66	16	8	5	5
Religion						
Protestants	98	77	15	6	1	1
Catholics	98	76	15	7	1	1
Beliefs very important	99	80	13	6	1	°
Fairly important	96	64	22	10	2	2
Not too important	83	38	38	7	7	10
Not at all important	45	15	28	2	38	17
Believe in immortality	99	78	15	6	1	°
Don't believe	80	47	30	3	15	5
Church members	98	75	15	8	1	1
Nonmembers	81	45	30	6	11	8
Very happy	95	71	16	8	3	2
Fairly happy	94	68	19	7	3	3
Not too happy	88	57	24	7	8	4

°Less than 1 percent.

Table 17. Immortality

Question: Do you believe in life after death?

	Yes	No	Undecided
National	69%	20%	11%
Sex			
Male	65	25	10
Female	73	16	11
Education			
College	66	23	11
High School	70	19	11
Grade School	75	16	9
Age			
Under 30 years	64	25	11
30–49 years	72	17	11
50 and older	71	19	10
Occupation			
White collar	77	14	9
Blue collar	64	28	8
Housewives	74	15	11
All others	69	18	13
Religion			
Protestants	80	12	8
Catholics	74	18	8
Church members	77	15	8
Nonmembers	44	41	15
Believe in God	73	18	9
God observes	79	14	7
Doesn't observe	56	33	11
Don't believe in God	14	86	°
Beliefs very important	84	10	6
Fairly important	59	27	14
Not too important	36	43	21
Not at all important	19	72	9
Very happy	72	19	9
Fairly happy	69	20	11
Not too happy	59	28	13

°Less than 1 percent.

Table 18. Confidence in Organized Religion

Question: How much confidence do you, yourself, have in the church or organized religion—a great deal, quite a lot, some, or very little?

	Great deal	Quite a lot	Some	Very little	None	Don't know
National	44%	24%	20%	9%	1%	2%
Sex						
Male	41	26	21	10	1	1
Female	47	23	19	7	1	3
Education						
College	36	25	24	12	2	1
High School	45	24	21	8	°	2
Grade School	53	23	12	6	2	4
Region						
East	38	29	20	10	1	2
Midwest	41	26	24	7	°	2
South	58	19	14	6	1	2
West	37	24	21	13	2	3
Age						
Total Under 30	35	23	28	12	1	1
18–24 years	36	21	29	11	2	1
25–29 years	34	27	25	14	°	°
30–49 years	45	25	20	7	1	2
50 and older	50	25	14	7	1	3
Income						
$20,000 & over	37	29	22	11	°	1
$15,000–$19,999	45	24	24	6	1	°
$10,000–$14,999	42	25	20	8	1	4
$ 7,000–$ 9,999	44	20	19	16	°	1
$ 5,000–$ 6,999	49	18	22	7	1	3
$ 3,000–$ 4,999	44	28	19	4	2	3
Under $3,000	54	22	11	8	2	3
Politics						
Republican	50	27	14	6	1	2
Democrat	47	23	20	8	°	2
So. Democrat	62	17	14	5	°	2
Other Democrat	40	26	23	9	°	2
Independent	38	24	24	10	1	3
Religion						
Protestant	48	24	19	6	1	2
Catholic	45	28	19	6	°	2
Occupation						
Professional and Business	37	29	23	8	2	1
Clerical and Sales	41	21	24	13	°	1
Manual Workers	44	22	21	10	1	2
Non-Labor Force	48	25	15	6	1	5

°Less than 1 percent.

Table 19. Confidence in Key Institutions in the United States

	Great deal	Quite a lot	Some	Very little	None	No opinion
The church or organized religion	44%	24%	20%	9%	1%	2%
The military	27	31	25	11	1	5
Public schools	22	34	25	15	1	3
The presidency	23	29	29	14	2	3
The Supreme Court	22	27	28	16	1	6
Congress	14	26	38	18	1	3
Big business	10	24	36	23	2	5
Labor unions	12	21	32	25	2	8

Table 20. Religious Preferences in the U.S.

Question: What is your religious preference—Protestant, Roman Catholic, Jewish, or what?

	Protestant	Roman Catholic	Jewish	All others	No religious preference
Latest	61%	27%	2%	4%	6%
1974	60	27	2	5	6
1971	65	26	3	2	4
1966	68	25	3	2	2

Table 21. Interpretation of the Bible

Question: Which *one* of these statements comes closest to describing your feelings about the Bible—actual word of God; inspired word of God; book written by men; none of these; can't say?

	Actual Word of God	Inspired Word of God	Ancient Book Written by Man	None of these	Can't say
Nationwide	38%	45%	13%	1%	3%
Protestants	46	42	8	°	4
Catholics	31	55	10	1	3
Men	33	45	16	2	4
Women	47	46	9	1	3
College	17	58	22	°	3
High School	42	45	9	1	3
Grade School	60	23	7	·3	7
18–28 years	32	45	17	2	4
30–49 years	34	50	13	°	3
50 and over	45	41	9	1	4
East	27	52	15	1	5
Midwest	42	43	9	1	5
South	49	39	9	°	3
West	30	48	20	1	1

°Less than 1 percent

Table 22. Have "Witnessed"

Question: Have you ever tried to encourage someone to believe in Jesus Christ or to accept Him as his or her Savior?

Nationwide	47%
Protestants	58
Catholics	38
Men	40
Women	54
College	37
High School	47
Grade School	65
18–29 years	41
30–49 years	44
50 and over	54
East	38
Midwest	48
South	63
West	35

Index

Abington School District v. Schempp, 85
Academia, religion of, 89
Activism, social, in churches, 40–42, 96–97, 98, 106–107, 113
Advent Christian Church, 74
Adventists
   geographical distribution, 63, 74
   history in U.S., 63, 74
   membership statistics, 14–15
Advertising Council of America, 18
Age, influence on religious practice, 37–39
American Baptist Churches, 53
   membership statistics, 12–14, 94–95
American Institute of Public Opinion (AIPO), 5, 18
American Way of Life, religion of, 81
Amish, 74
Anglican church, history of, 68
Anglican Church of North America, 69
Anomie, 8
Argyle, Michael, 25
Assemblies of God, membership statistics, 12–15, 76
Association of Evangelical Lutheran Churches, 70
Astrology, percent believing in, 25–26
Attendance, church, 18–22, 96, 111, 114
   by age, 21, 113
   by educational level, 21–22
   of nonwhites, 22
   by region, 21–22, 88
   by sex, 21
"Audiences," church, 44

Baptists
   church attendance, 19–20
   geographic distribution, 52, 53–55, 86
   history in U.S., 53–55
   political participation of, 10
Beachy Amish Mennonite Churches, 75
Beit-Hallahmi, Benjamin, 25
Belief in God. *See* God, belief in
Beliefs, religious
   scarceness of data on, 28
   trends in, 28–45
   validity of data on, 28–29
Bell, Daniel, 97
Bellah, Robert N., 81, 99
Bibby, Reginald W., 16
Bible, belief in, percent, 24, 116
Bible readers, percent, 24
Biersdorf, John E., 98, 99
Biofeedback, 7
Birth rate, effect on churches, 102
"Birth-type converts" of evangelicals, 16
Black (ethnic) religion, future of, 107

Black Manifesto of 1969, 6
Boehler, Peter, 75
Bohemian Brethren, 75
"Born again" experiences, having, 86, 111–112, 113
"Boundaryless" church, 44
Bright, Bill, 11
Brinkerhoff, Merlin B., 16
Building of churches, trends, 41
Business, confidence in, percent, 116

Cable television, use by churches, 106
Campbell, Alexander, 54
Campbell, Thomas, 54
Campus Crusade, 11, 26
Careers, change of, 99–100, 103–104
Cassettes, use by churches, 106
Catholic Church. *See* Roman Catholic Church
Catholic Digest surveys
   of belief in God, 29–30
   of belief in Jesus Christ, 32–33
   of belief in life after death, 31–32
   of belief in Pope's authority, 33
   of Bible reading, 24
   of concept of God, 29–30
   of prayer, 24–25
Catholics. *See* Roman Catholics
Changing Careers After Thirty-Five, 99
Charismatic movement, 96–99, 111
Charles F. Kettering Foundation, 112
Children of God movement, 26
Christian Church (Disciples of Christ), 54
Christian Churches and Churches of Christ, 54
Christian Embassy, 11
Christian Reformed Church, 76
Christian Scientists, 78
Christian World Liberation Front, 25
"The Christian Yellow Pages," 11, 86
Church attendance. *See* Attendance, church
Church, confidence in, percent, 116
Church membership. *See* Membership, church
Church of God (Anderson, Indiana), financial contributions to, 23–24
Church of God (Cleveland, Tennessee), membership statistics, 76
Church of God in Christ, 76
Church of God in Christ (Mennonite), 75
Church of Jesus Christ of Latter Day Saints (Mormon)
   history in U.S., 95
   membership statistics, 95
Church of the Nazarene
   financial contributions to, 23–24
   membership statistics, 12–15
Church school membership, relation to church membership, 16
Churches and Church Membership in the United States 1971, 50, 52

Churches of Christ, 54
Circuit riders, 70, 80
"Cognitive minority" (Mormons), 87
Columbia University, 99
Columbian Exposition, Chicago (1893), 82
Commission on Private Philanthropy and Public Needs, 22
Communications, improvements in, effect on churches, 105
Community change, effect on churches, 43–44
Computers, use by churches, 105–106
Concept of God. See God, concept of
Conference of the Evangelical Mennonite Church, 75
Confidence in, percent
    business, 116
    church, 116
    Congress, 116
    labor unions, 116
    military, 116
    presidency, 116
    schools, 116
    Supreme Court, 116
Congregational Christian Churches, 13, 73
Congregationalists and Plan of Union, 71, 73
Congress, confidence in, percent, 116
Conservative Mennonite Conference, 75
Conservatives (Protestant), 34
"Constantinianism," 79
Consultation on Church Union (COCU), 6
Continental Sabbath, 87
Contributions, financial. See Financial contributions to church
Convergent selectivity of media, 84
Converting, percent practicing, 116
Cuius regio eius religio, 51, 79
Cumberland Presbyterian Church, 71
"Custodianship of the culture," 11

Davis, Angela, 41
Dawson, Christopher, 81
Dayton study of youth, 112
Delta Ministry, 40
Demerath, N.J., III, 30, 32
Denominational statistics, validity of, 4–5
Denominations, religious, by county, 49–77
Detroit area studies
    belief in God, 29–30
    belief in life after death, 31
Devotional literature, analysis of, 32
Dierenfeld, Richard, 86
Disciples of Christ
    geographic distribution, 54, 56, 68
    history in U.S., 54, 56, 68
    political participation of, 10
Dornbusch, Sanford, 32
Duquesne weekend, 98
Durkheim, Emile, 8

Eastern religions, in U.S.
    growth of, 25–26, 82, 111
    members of, 99
Ecumenism, Christian
    beginning of, 81
    future of, 108
Eliot, T. S., 81
Emerson, Ralph Waldo, 82
Employment, effect on religion, 103
Energy, effect on churches, 109–110
Engel v. Vitale, 85
England
    church attendance in, 25
    percent who pray in, 25
Episcopal Church
    financial contributions to, 22–24
    geographic distribution, 57, 68–69
    history in U.S., 57, 68–69
    membership statistics, 12–15, 38

Episcopalians
    church attendance, 19
    geographic distribution, 57, 68–69
    history in U.S., 57, 68–69
    political participation of, 10–11
Errand of Mercy, 71
est, 7, 25, 26
Eternal life. See Life after death
Ethnic community changes, effect on churches, 43
Ethnic religion
    beginning of, 83
    future of, 107
Europe, western, percent believing in God, 30
Evangelical and Reformed Church, 13, 73, 76
Evangelical Mennonite Brethren, 75
Evangelical movements, 96–99
    future of, 108, 111
    membership growth of, 16, 111
Evangelical United Brethren Church, 95
Evangelicals
    defined, 112
    political participation of, 11
Exclusivism of religion, 79
Ex-Pastors, 99
Experiential religion, 111, 114. See also Secular religions; Charismatic movement; Non-Western religious movements
Exurb growth, effect on churches, 43–44

Family, future of the, 101–103
Family life cycle, influence on religious practice, 37–39
Federal Council of Churches, 71
Fichter, Joseph, 98
Films, use by churches, 106
Financial contributions to church, 22–24
    Church of God, 23–24
    Church of the Nazarene, 23–24
    Episcopal, 23–24
    Lutheran Church in America, 23
    Lutheran Church—Missouri Synod, 23
    reasons for, 22
    related to membership, 24
    Southern Baptist, 23
    United Church of Christ, 23
    United Methodist, 23
    United Presbyterian Church of the U.S.A., 23–24
Financial contributions to nonprofit organizations, 23
First Great Awakening, 53, 73, 77, 80, 94
France, percent believing in God, 30
Franklin, Benjamin, 80, 81
Freylinghuysen, Theodore Jacobus, 77
Fundamentalists (Protestant), 34

The Gallup Opinion Index, 5
Gallup polls
    belief in astrology, 25–26
    belief in Bible, 116
    belief in God, 29–30, 115
    belief in life after death, 31–32, 115
    of Bible reading, 24
    "born again" experience, having, 115
    church attendance, 18–22, 111, 114
    church membership, 111, 114
    confidence in church, 116
    confidence in key institutions, 116
    experiential religion involvement, 114
    importance of religion, 114
    influence of religion, 33–34, 111, 114
    religious preference, 9, 25, 116
    witnessing, practicing, 116
Gaustad, Edwin Scott, 9, 52
Gellner, Ernest, 81
General Conference Mennonite Church, 75
General Convention Special Program (Episcopal), 40, 41
German Reformed Church, 76
Glazer, Nathan, 8, 21

Glenn, Norval D., 11–12, 22
Glock, Charles Y., 4, 18, 28, 34, 99
God, belief in, 29–30, 115
  by age, 30, 115
  by country, 30
  by education level, 115
  by occupation, 115
  by religion, 115
  by sex, 115
God, concept of, 29–30
  by age, 30
God's Word, belief in Bible as, percent, 24
Good News Movement, 97
Gotard, Erin, 11–12, 22
Graham, Billy, 6
Great Britain, percent believing in God, 30
Greeley, Andrew, 6, 7, 8, 20, 25, 28, 42, 96, 98
Greenblum, Joseph, 8, 19, 37

Haley, Alex, 107
Harris, Thomas A., 99
Hartman, Warren, 44
Heaven, belief in, 31
Heilbroner, Robert, 93
Hell, belief in, 31
Herberg, Will, 8, 9, 81
Hiestand, Dale L., 99–100
Historical Atlas of Religion in America, 52
Hoge, Dean R., 24–25, 39, 94
"Homogeneous unit principle," 44
Honest to God, 29
Hope, Bob, 22
Hudson, Winthrop, 5
Human potential movement, 99
Humanae Vitae, 16, 42
Hutterian Brethren, 72

Identification, religious, 8–17
I'm O.K., You're O.K., 99
Importance of personal religion, 114
India, percent believing in God, 30
indifferentism, 81
Inflation, effect on churches, 109
Influence of religion, 33–34, 114
  by age, 33
"Inner worldly ascetic" orientation, 11
Institute of Church Growth, 44
Institutions, key, confidence in, percent, 116
Interreligious Foundation for Community Organization (IFCO), 40
Interview questions, problems with in polls, 5
Invisible religion, 83

Japan, percent believing in God, 30
Jefferson, Thomas, 80, 81, 86
Jehovah's Witnesses, 78
Jesus Christ, belief in, 32–33
The Jesus Kids, 98
Jesus movement, 7, 25
Jews
  believing in Bible, percent, 24
  believing in God, percent, 30
  believing in life after death, percent, 31
  Bible readers, percent, 24
  political participation of, 10–11
  who pray, percent, 24–25
  synagogue attendance, 19, 20–21, 114
John XXIII, Pope, 6
Johnson, Douglas W., 50, 52
Jud, Elizabeth, 99
Jud, Gerald J., 99
Judaism
  membership statistics, 12–13, 114
  "this-worldly" orientation in, 11

Kahn, Herman, 93

Kelley, Dean, 16, 34, 98
Krishna Consciousness Movement, 26

Labor unions, confidence in, percent, 116
Land-use changes, effect on churches, 43
Latter-Day Saints (Mormons)
  geographic distribution, 52, 87
  political participation of, 10
Leisure time, effect on churches, 103, 104–105
"Liberal Protestantism, 1971," 88
Liberals (Protestant), 34
Liebman, Joshua, 6
Life after death, belief in, 30–32, 114
  by age, 32, 115
  by education level, 115
  by occupation, 115
  by religion, 115
  by sex, 115
Literature, devotional, analysis of, 32
Littell, Franklin, 9
Luckmann, Thomas, 83
Lutheran Church in America
  financial contributions to, 23
  membership statistics, 12–16
Lutheran Church—Missouri Synod
  financial contributions to, 23
  membership statistics, 12–16
  schism in, 59, 60
Lutheranism, "mystic component" in, 11
Lutherans
  church attendance, 19
  geographic distribution, 52, 58, 69–70, 87
  history in U.S., 58, 69–70
  political participation of, 10–11

McCarthy, Joseph, 6
McCourt, Kathleen, 20, 25
McCready, William, 7, 20, 25
Madison, James, 80, 81
Management techniques, use by churches, 109–110
Marty, Martin, 11, 28, 34, 44
Maslow, Abraham, 99
Maturity, religious, 112–113
Mead, Margaret, 39, 83
Mead, Sidney E., 81
Meaning, search for, 93–100, 101
Media
  effect on pluralism, 89
  use by churches, 106
Melting pot, 81
Membership, church, 12–17, 24, 94–96, 111, 114
  validity of statistics on, 4–5
Mennonite Church, 72
Mennonites
  geographic distribution, 64, 74–75
  history in U.S., 64, 74–75
Methodist Church of the North, 71
Methodists
  church attendance, 19
  geographic distribution, 52, 59, 70–71, 86–87
  history in U.S., 59, 70–71
  political participation of, 10–11
Miami Valley Young Adult Ministry, Inc., 112
Microfiche, use by churches, 105–106
Military, confidence in, percent, 116
Miller, William, 74
Millerites, 74
Miniaturization, effect on churches, 105–106
Ministers, women, 104, 108
Mobility, effect on religion, 88–89, 102–103
Moderates (Protestant), 34
Moon, Sun Myung, 7
Morality, influence on society, 112
Moravian Church in America, Northern Province, 75
Moravian Church in American, Southern Province, 75

Moravian Travel Guide, 75
Moravians
    geographic distribution, 65, 75–76
    history in U.S., 65, 75–76
Mormons. *See* Latter-Day Saints (Mormons)
Muggeridge, Malcolm, 113
Muhlenberg, Henry Melchior, 69
Murray, John Courtney, 83
"Mystic component" in Lutheranism, 11
Mysticism, 25, 111

Nash, Dennison, 38
National Council of the Churches of Christ (NCC), 40
National Opinion Research Center (NORC), 5
"New Morality Index," 40
Nichol, John Thomas, 76
1950s
    general trends, 6
    religious trends, 6, 82
1970s
    general trends, 7
    religious trends, 7, 98, 112
1960s
    general trends, 6, 96–97
    religious trends, 6–7, 82, 96–97
"no-growth theology," 42
Nonparticipation, religious, 88
Nonprofit organizations, contributions to, 23
Non-Western religious movements
    growth of, 25–26, 82, 111
    members of, 99

Old Order Amish Mennonite Church, 75
Old Order Mennonite Church, 75
"Old-time" religion, 97
"One-audience" church, 44
Orientation, religious, and political participation, 11
Ozman, Agnes, 76

Palms, Roger, 98
Parent-Teacher Association (P.T.A.) membership, relation to church
    membership, 38
Parochial school membership. *See* Church school membership
Paul VI, Pope 42
Peale, Norman Vincent, 6
Penn, William, 80
Pentecostalists
    geographical distribution, 66, 76
    history in U.S., 66, 76
The Pentecostals, 76
"Personalized" Christians, 98
Picard, Paul R., 50, 52
Plan of Union (Presbyterians and Congregationalists), 71, 73
Pluralism, religious
    defined, 51, 78
    development of, 78–84
    in Europe, 79–80
    in future, 107
    prehistoric, 79
    in the U.S., 79–84, 107
Political office holding, 9–11
    by Baptists, 10
    cultural influences, 11
    by Disciples of Christ, 10
    by Episcopalians, 10–11
    by evangelicals, 11
    geographical influences, 11
    by Jews, 10–11
    by Latter-Day Saints (Mormons), 10
    by Lutherans, 10–11
    by Methodists, 10–11
    by Presbyterians, 10–11
    by Protestants, 9–11
    by Roman Catholics, 10–11
    by social class, 11

    by Unitarian-Universalists, 10
Polls, validity of, 5–6, 9, 28–29
Pope, belief in authority of, 33
Population changes, effect on churches, 43, 102–103
Practices, religious, trends in, 18–27
Prayer
    by age, 25
    by Jews, 24–25
    by Protestants, 24–25
    by Roman Catholics, 24–25
Preference, religious, 3, 9–12, 116
Premillennialism, 74
Presbyterian Church in America, 71
Presbyterian Church in the United States, 71
    membership statistics, 12–16
Presbyterian Lay Committee, 97
Presbyterians
    church attendance, 19
    geographic distribution, 60, 71–72
    history in U.S., 60, 71–72
    political participation of, 10–11
Presidency, confidence in, percent, 116
Private Protestantism, 28
"Proselyte-type conversion" of evangelicals, 16
"Protean" church, 44
Protestant, Catholic, Jew, 81
Protestant churches, membership statistics, 12–17, 114
Protestantism, two-party system of, 28, 34
Protestants
    believing in Bible, percent, 24, 116
    believing in God, percent, 115
    believing in Jesus Christ, percent, 33
    believing in life after death, percent, 31, 115
    Bible readers, percent, 24
    church attendance, 19–20, 96, 114
    confidence in church, percent, 116
    decline of, 9–10
    on influence of religion, 33
    in politics, 9–11
    who pray, percent, 24–25
Psychosynthesis, 7
Public Protestantism, 28

Quasi-religious movements
    growth of, 25–26, 82
    members of, 99
Quebedeaux, Richard, 98
Quinn, Bernard, 50, 52

Ramsey, Paul, 85
"Reaffiliation" of evangelicals, 16
Reformed Church in America, membership statistics, 43, 76
Reformed churches
    geographical distribution, 67, 76–77
    history in U.S., 67, 76–77
Reformed Mennonite Church, 75
Regionalism in religion, 84–88
"Relevance" in religion, 97
Religion
    as community, 8
    confidence in, percent, 116
    importance of, 114
    influence on society, 112
Religion in American Life Campaign, 18
Religiosity, dimensions of, 4
Religious maturity, 112–113
Resurrection of the dead. *See* Life after death
Retirement, effect on churches, 104
Robinson, John A.T., 29
Roman Catholic Church
    definition of membership, 4–5
    membership statistics, 12–16, 114
    "siege mentality" of, 6
Roman Catholics
    attending charismatic meetings, percent, 25

attending confession, percent, 25
attending retreats, percent, 25
believing in Bible, percent, 24, 116
believing in God, percent, 30, 115
believing in Jesus Christ, percent, 33
believing in life after death, percent, 31, 115
believing in Pope's authority, percent, 33
Bible readers, percent, 24
church attendance, 20, 25, 96, 114
confidence in church, percent, 116
geographic distribution, 52, 61, 72–73, 87
history in U.S., 61, 72–73
on influence of religion, 33
making Day of Recollection, percent, 25
making a mission, percent, 25
political participation of, 10–11
who pray, percent, 24–25
reasons for decline in, 42
Roncalli, Angelo Giuseppe (John XXIII, Pope), 6
Roots, 107
Rutgers University, 77

Scandinavia, percent believing in God, 30
Schneider, Louis, 32
Schools, public, confidence in, percent, 116
Schroeder, Widick, 37–38
Scientology, 26
Scott, Walter, 55
Second Great Awakening, 53, 61, 73
Second Vatican Council (1962–1965), 6, 16, 24, 25, 33, 42, 73, 96
Secular religions, future of, 107–108
Secularization of society, 28
Seventh-day Adventists. *See* Adventists
Sheen, Fulton J., 6
Shortridge, James R., 87–88
Single persons, challenge for churches, 102
Sklare, Marshall, 8, 19, 37
Smith, Joseph, 95
Social controls, effect on pluralism, 84
Society for the Propagation of the Gospel, 68
Something Beautiful for God, 113
Southern Baptist Convention
    definition of membership, 4
    financial contributions to, 23
    membership statistics, 12–15, 25, 53
Spangenberg, Augustus, Bishop, 75
Spending by churches, 98
Spengler, Joseph J., 39
Stark, Rodney, 4, 18, 28, 34
Statistics, denominational, validity of, 4–5
Stephenson, William, 84
Stiles, Ezra, 73
Stone, Barton, 54
Suburb growth, effect on churches, 43–44
Sunday School membership, relation to church membership, 38
Supreme Court, confidence in, percent, 116
Survey Research Center (University of Michigan), 5
Surveys. *See Catholic Digest* surveys; Dayton Study of youth; Detroit area studies; Gallup polls
Syllabus of Errors, 72
Synagogue attendance, 19, 20–21, 114
Synanon, 25

"Technologies of the spirit," 4, 7
Television, cable, use by churches, 106
Teresa, Mother, of Calcutta, 113
Theosophy, 82
"This-worldly" orientation, in Judaism, 11
Tocqueville, Alexis de, 3
Toffler, Alvin, 93
Tolerance, religious, history of, 79–84
Transactional Analysis, 99, 107
Transcendental Meditation, 7, 25, 26, 107, 111
Trend data, definition of, 4

Unification Church, 7
Unions, confidence in, percent, 116
Unitarian-Universalists, political participation of, 10
United Church of Christ
    financial contributions to, 23
    geographical distribution, 62, 73–74
    history in U.S., 62, 73–74, 76
    membership statistics, 12–15, 95
United Methodist Church
    definition of membership, 16
    financial contributions to, 23
    membership statistics, 4, 12–17, 25, 38, 95
United Presbyterian Church in the United States of America
    financial contributions to, 23–24
    membership statistics, 12–16, 71, 95
Urban migration, effect on churches, 43
U.S. News and World Report, 102

Values, general, and religious practice, 39–40
Vatican II. *See* Second Vatican Council (1962–1965)
Videotapes, use by churches, 106
Volunteers in religion, 105, 109, 112
von Zinzendorf, Ludwig, Count, 75
Voting and religious affinity, 85

Wagner, C. Peter, 114
Walrath, Douglas A., 43
Weber, Max, 11
White, Ellen G., 74
Whitefield, George, 75
Why Conservative Churches are Growing, 16, 34
Williams, J. Paul, 81
Williams, Robin, 81
Williams, Roger, 53
Witnessing, percent practicing, 116
Women as clergy, 104, 108
Word of God, belief in Bible as, percent, 24
Work, ethic of, challenge for churches, 103
World's Parliament of Religions, 82
Wuthnow, Robert, 25

Yankelovich, Daniel, 40
Yearbook of American and Canadian Churches, 4, 22, 50
Yearbook of American Churches, 5
Yoga, 25, 26, 109
The Young Evangelicals, 98
Young people and religion, 25–26, 33–34, 36, 37–40, 112, 113

Zangwill, Israel, 81
Zen, 26